Chasing the *Bounty*

ALSO BY DONALD A. MAXTON

The Mutiny on H.M.S. Bounty: A Guide to Nonfiction, Fiction, Poetry, Films, Articles, and Music (McFarland, 2008)

EDITED BY DONALD A. MAXTON AND ROLF E. DU RIETZ. BY PETER HEYWOOD AND NESSY HEYWOOD

Innocent on the Bounty: The Court-Martial and Pardon of Midshipman Peter Heywood, in Letters (McFarland, 2013)

Chasing the *Bounty*
The Voyages of the Pandora *and* Matavy

Edited by DONALD A. MAXTON

McFarland & Company, Inc., Publishers
Jefferson, North Carolina

As Told Through the Narratives of
Edward Edwards, Captain, H.M.S. *Pandora*
George Hamilton, Surgeon, H.M.S. *Pandora*
Peter Heywood, Midshipman, H.M.S. *Bounty*, Prisoner
James Morrison, Boatswain's Mate, H.M.S. *Bounty*, Prisoner
David Thomas Renouard, Midshipman, H.M.S. *Pandora* and *Matavy*

LIBRARY OF CONGRESS CATALOGUING-IN-PUBLICATION DATA

Names: Maxton, Donald A., 1951– editor.
Title: Chasing the Bounty : The Voyages of the Pandora and Matavy / edited by Donald A. Maxton.
Description: Jefferson, North Carolina : McFarland & Company, Inc., Publishers, 2020 | Includes bibliographical references and index.
Identifiers: LCCN 2020002676 | ISBN 9781476679389 (paperback : acid free paper) ∞
ISBN 9781476639741 (ebook)
Subjects: LCSH: Bounty Mutiny, 1789—History—Sources. | Pandora (Frigate)—History—Sources. | Matavy (Schooner)—History—Sources. | Sailors—Great Britain—Correspondence. | Sailors' writings, English. | Voyages and travels.
Classification: LCC DU20 .C43 2020 | DDC 996.18—dc23
LC record available at https://lccn.loc.gov/2020002676

BRITISH LIBRARY CATALOGUING DATA ARE AVAILABLE

ISBN (print) 978-1-4766-7938-9
ISBN (ebook) 978-1-4766-3974-1

© 2020 Donald A. Maxton. All rights reserved

No part of this book may be reproduced or transmitted in any form or by any means, electronic or mechanical, including photocopying or recording, or by any information storage and retrieval system, without permission in writing from the publisher.

Front cover: "The Long Arm"—H.M.S. *Pandora* Leaving Portsmouth—August, 1790 (Paul Garnett, Paul Garnett Studio, www.paulgarnett.com)

Printed in the United States of America

McFarland & Company, Inc., Publishers
Box 611, Jefferson, North Carolina 28640
www.mcfarlandpub.com

To the memory of my dear friend,
Lee Shepard

Table of Contents

Acknowledgments	ix
Introduction	1
A Note on the Text	9
Part One. The *Bounty* Mutineers in Tahiti	13
Part Two. Outward Bound on H.M.S. *Pandora*	25
Part Three. Capturing the Mutineers	40
Part Four. Searching for Fletcher Christian	64
Part Five. Shipwreck in Torres Strait	96
Part Six. Sailing to the Dutch East Indies	108
Part Seven. Passage to Batavia and England	121
Part Eight. The Unforeseen Voyage of *Matavy*	143
Appendix 1	157
Appendix 2	165
Appendix 3	171
Glossary	175
Notes	181
Bibliography	183
Index	187

Acknowledgments

This book would not have been possible without the generous assistance, expertise and enthusiasm of the late E. Lee Shepard, vice president for collections and Sallie and William B. Thalhimer III senior archivist, Virginia Museum of History & Culture/Virginia Historical Society, Richmond, Virginia. Lee clarified numerous pages of archaic handwriting. I miss our discussions and camaraderie.

Special thanks to my wife, Marie Moss Maxton, for managing to find time from her busy schedule to patiently read, re-read, and proofread the manuscript.

Many thanks to Rolf E. Du Rietz for his interest, encouragement, comments and suggestions.

I thank the following institutions and people for their assistance: Alexander Library, Rutgers University, New Brunswick, New Jersey; Inger Sheil, Project Officer, Australian National Maritime Museum, Sydney; Georgia Stratton, Cambridge University Press; Jesse Mann, Drew University Library, Madison, New Jersey; Scott Ellwood, Grolier Club Library, New York; Michele Ryan, Museum of Tropical Queensland, Townsville; Kevin Chambers, National Archives Record Copying, Kew, Richmond; Sigourney Jacks, National Gallery of Victoria, Melbourne; Gina Martin, National Geographic; Susie Riggs, National Geographic Magazine; Deanna Cronk and Emily Witt, Document Supply Services, National Library of Australia, Canberra; John Powell and Lisa Schoblasky, Newberry Library, Special Collections Services, Chicago; The Old Book Shop, Morristown, New Jersey; Herbert Ford and Katharine Van Arsdale, Pitcairn Islands Study Center, Pacific Union College, Angwin, California; Oliver Pollak; Shane Appleby, Queensland Museum; Philippa Sandall and Ad Long; Bronwyn Searles; Dr. Martin Bellamy, Society for Nautical Research, *The Mariner's Mirror*, Glasgow; Anne Drayton and Rosie Olk, State Library of New South Wales, Sydney; Walsh Library, Seton Hall University, South Orange, New Jersey; Yale Center for British Art, New Haven, Connecticut. I thank my good feline buddy, Jake, for his steadfast companionship.

Acknowledgments

Peter Heywood's correspondence is published courtesy of McFarland & Company, Inc.

Selections from James Morrison's *Journal* are published courtesy of the Mitchell Library, State Library of New South Wales.

David Thomas Renouard's narrative of *Matavy*'s voyage and Captain Edwards' sailing orders are reproduced by kind permission of the Society for Nautical Research from, respectively, H. E. Maude, "The Voyage of the *Pandora*'s Tender," *The Mariner's Mirror* 50, no. 3 [August 1964]: 217–235; and D. Bonner Smith, "Some Remarks about the Mutiny of the Bounty," *The Mariner's Mirror* 22 [April 1936]: 200–237.

"Verses on the Loss of His Majesty's Bounty and Pandora" is published courtesy of the State Library of New South Wales.

Introduction

Fascination with the mutiny that occurred on H.M.S. *Bounty* on April 28, 1789, remains undiminished after nearly 250 years. The *Bounty*'s mission to gather breadfruit plants in Tahiti as a cheap food source for the slaves of English planters in the West Indies was disrupted when Fletcher Christian and a group of mutineers set Lieutenant William Bligh and 18 loyal members of his crew adrift in the ship's 23-foot launch. After an astonishing journey of nearly 4,000 miles to Timor in the Dutch East Indies, Bligh sailed for home on the Dutch East Indiaman *Vlydt*, returning to England in March 1790. A year later, he was granted a second opportunity to transport breadfruit plants from Tahiti to Jamaica, which he successfully completed in February 1793.

The mutiny was of minor historical significance, but it has captured the imagination of historians, writers, artists, and filmmakers for more than two centuries. Innumerable non-fiction books; articles; novels; poems; short stories; radio broadcasts; stage plays; television programs, and films have made the mutiny and the conflict between Bligh and Christian an enduring part of our culture. The historical novels co-authored by Charles Nordhoff and James Norman Hall and published in the 1930s—*Mutiny on the Bounty, Men Against the Sea,* and *Pitcairn's Island*—remain in print, and contemporary authors continue to be intrigued and inspired by the *Bounty* story. Millions of people discovered this great seafaring saga through major films released in 1935, 1962 and 1984, which are frequently repeated on television, attracting new audiences.

Surprisingly, an epic voyage and human drama inextricably linked with the *Bounty* mutiny is unfamiliar to the public, with the exception of *Bounty* history enthusiasts and scholars. Eight months after Bligh's return from Timor, the British Admiralty dispatched Captain Edward Edwards and a crew of 132 men in the 24-gun frigate H.M.S. *Pandora* to capture the mutineers and return them to England for court-martial. In many ways, this voyage is as compelling as the *Bounty* mutiny itself.

The story of *Pandora* encompasses a number of gripping episodes: A journey to the remote and fabled South Sea island of Tahiti; capturing and

This wood engraving portrays William Bligh and members of his loyal crew boarding the *Bounty*'s 23-foot launch. It appeared in the May 26, 1838, issue of *Chronicles of the Sea*, a weekly issued in 100+ installments, 1838–1840.

Seizure of Lieutenant Bligh.

A small engraving that illustrates the mutiny. It shows that some crew members were not involved in the rebellion. In a letter to his mother, Peter Heywood described himself as "A silent Spectator of what was going on." This illustration is from *Aleck; The Last of the Mutineers; Or The History of Pitcairn's Island*, published 1848 (courtesy Pitcairn Islands Study Center).

imprisoning 14 *Bounty* crew members who chose to remain on Tahiti rather than follow Christian, a group that included mutineers as well as loyalists who wished to continue their naval careers; the prisoners' suffering in "Pandora's Box," an appalling prison constructed on the ship's quarter deck; a fruitless search through the South Seas for Christian and his companions, who had sailed into the unknown from Tahiti on September 23, 1789, eventually settling on Pitcairn Island; shipwreck near Torres Strait[1] with the loss of 31 crew and four prisoners; a torturous open boat voyage to the Dutch East Indies and the deadly, fever-ridden city of Batavia; and the remarkable voyage of *Matavy*, a schooner built by *Bounty* crew members on Tahiti (named by them *Resolution*) that Captain Edwards commandeered to serve as *Pandora*'s tender, renaming it after Tahiti's Matavai Bay. The *Matavy* lost sight of *Pandora* near the Samoan island of Tutuila during a storm at sea and for three months its crew fought to survive on painfully meager provisions among islands largely populated by hostile natives. Purely by chance, they made a major mark on Pacific history when they became the first Europeans to make contact with the people of Fiji.[2]

Even so, maritime archaeologist Peter Gesner, who has directed numerous expeditions to the *Pandora* wreck since its discovery in 1977, writes that *Pandora*'s voyage has "…languished in almost total obscurity…This state of historical obscurity is remarkable because the *Pandora* was linked to all the notoriety surrounding the mutiny on the *Bounty*."[3] This may be due to the fact that the three major "Bounty" films either ignored *Pandora*'s role completely or treated it briefly and inaccurately.[4]

This probably would not be the case if director David Lean, who recognized *Pandora*'s historical significance and its potential appeal to moviegoers, had been able to complete two projected films in the late 1970s: *The Lawbreakers*, dramatizing the *Bounty* mutiny, and *The Long Arm*, devoted to *Pandora*'s voyage. They never came to fruition, largely due to Lean's creative differences with screenwriter Robert Bolt, the latter's illness, and a lack of financial backing.[5]

A motion picture devoted to *Pandora* may eventually be made, but in the meantime we fortunately possess five unique narratives composed by eyewitnesses: Captain Edward Edwards; Surgeon George Hamilton; Boatswain's Mate James Morrison and Midshipman Peter Heywood (both of the *Bounty*); and Midshipman David Thomas Renouard, one of nine *Pandora* seamen and officers ordered to sail *Matavy*. Perhaps their accounts may inspire other directors or screenwriters.

Just as there has been a seemingly endless debate about the conflict between Fletcher Christian and William Bligh—and *why* the *Bounty* mutiny happened in the first place—the *Pandora* voyage has generated a great deal of discussion about Captain Edwards' handling of his mission, especially his treatment of the captured mutineers. The British Admiralty ordered Edwards to "…keep the Mutineers as closely confined as may preclude all possibility of their escaping, having however, proper regard to the preservation of their Lives, that they may be brought Home to undergo the Punishment due to their Demerits."[6]

Criticism of Edwards began soon after his return to England. Commodore Thomas Pasley, Peter Heywood's uncle, interviewed Edwards and several members of the *Bounty*'s crew. He then wrote in a letter to Nessy Heywood (Peter's sister):

> I have no doubt of the Truth of your Brother's Narrative—the Master, Boatswain, Gunner, and Carpenter, late of the *Bounty*, I have seen, and have the Pleasure to assure you that they are all favorable and corroborate what he says. That *Fellow*, Captain Edwards, whose inhuman rigor of Confinement I shall never forget, I have likewise seen. He cannot deny that Peter avowed himself late of the *Bounty* when he came on board—this is a favorable circumstance.[7]

Following the execution of three convicted *Bounty* mutineers on October 29, 1792, the *London Chronicle* reported, "The sufferings of the unhappy mutineers of the Bounty were greater than it could be imagined human nature is capable of bearing. They have been upwards of nineteen months in irons, fastened to a bar, five months of which time both legs and hands were secured, when they were entirely without clothing …"[8]

In *The Eventful History of the Mutiny and Piratical Seizure of H.M.S. Bounty: Its Cause and Consequences*, Sir John Barrow, a senior Admiralty official, wrote, "From this total indifference towards these unfortunate men, and their almost unparalleled sufferings, Captain Edwards must be set down as a man whose only feeling was to stick to the letter of his instructions, and rigidly to adhere to what he considered the strict line of his duty; that he was a man of a cold phlegmatic disposition, whom no distress could move, and whose feelings were not easily disturbed by the sufferings of his fellow-creatures."[9]

Barrow's book (early editions were published anonymously) was the first to present the *Bounty* mutiny, Bligh's open boat voyage, the *Pandora* voyage, *Bounty* court-martial, and the mutineers' settlement on Pitcairn Island in one volume. It has frequently been reprinted, and Barrow's opinion of Edwards continues to influence *Bounty* and *Pandora* studies.

The United Service Journal published two (anonymous) articles by Rear-Admiral William Henry Smyth that offer a more thorough, evenhanded assessment of Edwards' behavior. In "The Bounty Again!" (1831) Smyth quoted from Barrow's book, passing even harsher judgment upon Edwards, but he moderated his views 12 years later in "The Pandora Again." During the interval he had obtained access to several important documents, including Edwards' personal papers.

Smyth learned that in 1782 Edwards was serving as Commander of

H.M.S. *Narcissus* when "A desperate fellow, of the name of Wood, and fifty others, had agreed to rise in the night, murder all the officers, and to carry the ship into a port belonging to the Americans."[10] The mutiny was thwarted, but Edwards would never forget this harrowing experience. A court-martial condemned six of Edwards' crew to death and 14 others to severe flogging. Smyth conjectured that "Now, the recollection of this event ... may have influenced the professional views of Capt. Edwards, and induced him to stick to what he considered the letter of his instructions, thereby keeping his prisoners in safe custody."[11]

Contemporary historians tend to agree with Smyth. Sven Wahlroos, a professional psychologist and keen *Bounty* scholar, wrote, in *Mutiny and Romance in the South Seas*, "Edwards of course never forgot this event and the memory of it undoubtedly contributed to the extraordinary harshness and cruelty with which he treated the *Bounty* men he captured and the almost paranoid fear he had of their inciting his own crew to mutiny."[12] Smyth also pointed out that while anchored at Tahiti, Edwards heard rumors of a native conspiracy to cut *Pandora*'s cables and run the ship aground, which forced him to limit the prisoners' contact with their Tahitian friends, wives, and six children. They also were forbidden to converse in the Tahitian language.[13]

Confining the prisoners in "Pandora's Box" successfully addressed the Admiralty's orders to prevent a possible escape, but the conditions in this makeshift prison were atrocious. The alternative would have been detaining the prisoners below deck, where the tropical heat and lack of fresh air may have been even more intolerable. In either circumstance, Edwards could have mitigated the prisoners' suffering by allowing them, properly guarded, to occasionally walk on deck for exercise, and to use the ship's head instead of the buckets placed in Pandora's Box. His fear, even obsession, of the prisoners influencing the crew precluded more humane options.

To his credit, Edwards provided the prisoners full rations instead of the two-thirds allowance dictated by the Royal Navy. The *Pandora* crew respected and admired him, perhaps because he ordered far less punishment during the voyage than most commanders. When the shipwreck survivors reached Batavia, one of them even commemorated their open boat voyage and survival by composing a long poem praising Edwards.[14] (See Appendix 1).

Edwards also has been accused of being a poor navigator, whose incompetence led to the loss of *Pandora*. Bligh himself doubted that Edwards would complete the voyage. A notation in the Rev. James Bligh's copy of Bligh's *A Voyage to the South Sea*, states, "Captain Bligh told me repeatedly that Captain Edwards would never return, as he did not know the navigation of Endeavour Straits."[15] In an early draft of his journal, James Morrison writes, suggestively, "On the evening of the 29th Augt. the Pandora went on a Reef, I might say how, but it would be to no purpose."[16]

Smyth disputes these contentions in "The Pandora Again" by printing Edwards' statement on the loss of *Pandora* and commenting, "It really gives us pleasure to place this seaman-like document before our readers, since though we are well aware, from various circumstances, that there are always more who attend to a charge than to its refutation, we think it a full and conclusive reply to all the *brutum fulmen* which has been discharged upon the last days of the Pandora."[17] Nevertheless, Smyth strongly condemned Edwards' indifference to the plight of the *Bounty* prisoners: "Here it must be distinctly remembered, that our approbation bears upon the professional talents of Edwards in the conduct of his ship: the awful silence of the above document as to the poor mutineers, leaves unimpeached the details we have already given. We are, therefore, here treating with the Captain as a seaman and a navigator."[18]

We may concede that Edwards was at least a competent navigator, and that he was justified in keeping the prisoners isolated, but his callousness while *Pandora* was sinking and subsequent behavior during the open-boat voyage to Timor are much more difficult to defend. The prisoners knew that the ship could disappear beneath the waves at any moment and some of them managed to break free from their iron shackles. Edwards ordered that they not only be chained again but also shot if they made another attempt. He ordered their release just seconds before *Pandora* sank, and this delay resulted in the deaths of Henry Hillbrant, Richard Skinner, George Stewart, and John Sumner, who died with manacles still on their wrists. When the survivors gathered on a nearby, barren key, Edwards denied the 10 surviving prisoners shelter from the scorching sun while his crew was protected by makeshift tents.

Edwards' behavior grew increasingly harsh during the open boat voyage to Timor. His treatment of James Morrison and Thomas Ellison, who Edwards had shackled to the floor of his boat, seems totally unwarranted. In *What Happened on the 'Bounty,'* South Seas adventurer and historian Bengt Danielsson wrote, "When the four ship's boats finally set off for Timor, Morrison had the misfortune to be assigned to the captain's boat, and from his reports of Edwards' treatment of him and the other prisoners in it during the course of his journey, one is forced to conclude that the captain of the *Pandora* was a sadist."[19] Danielsson may or may not be correct in his "diagnosis" of Edwards, but it is likely that at least one sadist was on board the *Pandora*: 1st Lieutenant John Larkan, who apparently took pleasure in making the prisoners as uncomfortable as possible, even as they suffered the horrors of Pandora's Box.

Morrison's comments when he was on the Dutch ship *Rembang*, bound for Batavia, may throw some light on both Edwards' and Larkan's behavior toward the prisoners:

> The ship was very leaky and we were ordered out of Irons two at a time, for two hours in the fore noon, & two hours in the afternoon with Centinals over us to work the Pumps—this new liberty, as we thought it, we gladly embraced, but soon found our strength unequal to the Task—and I one day told Mr. Larkan that I was not able to stand to the pump at Spell & Spell (the ship requiring the pump continually at work) to which he replyd Tauntingly, 'You dam'd Villain, you have brought it on yourself and I'll make you stand it; if it was not for you we should not have been here nor have met with this trouble,' to which I replied 'trouble often comes unsought' and he then ordered me to be silent.[20]

Morrison and the other prisoners endured this harsh treatment until they boarded the British ship *Gorgon* at the Cape of Good Hope, on which they returned to England.

Can any aspect of the *Pandora* voyage be considered successful or was it, like the *Bounty* mission, a tragic failure? On the plus side, Edwards added to contemporary knowledge of the South Pacific by discovering five islands during his search: Tureia, Nukunonu, Rotuma, Fataka, and Anuta.[21] He safely conveyed ten of the prisoners to England for court-martial, although that number might have been higher if he had not callously ignored their desperate predicament as *Pandora* was sinking. Earlier in the voyage, five men on board the ship's yawl were lost during a storm, and, in Torres Strait, Edwards lost the ship and 31 members of his crew.

Pandora's primary mission was to find Fletcher Christian, all of the mutineers and the *Bounty* itself. Edwards failed to accomplish these tasks, but neither the prisoners nor any of the South Seas natives had any idea where Fletcher Christian sailed after *Bounty* left Tahiti for the last time. The Admiralty thought it likely that he would choose to settle on Whytootackee (Aitutaki, discovered by Bligh and now one of the Cook Islands) or a neighboring island, and ordered Edwards to proceed westward in that direction—more than 2,000 miles from Pitcairn Island, where Christian landed in January 1790, burned the *Bounty*, and started a new settlement.

Sir John Barrow's assessment of the *Pandora* voyage, published nearly 200 years ago, remains both fair and accurate:

> This voyage was in the sequel almost as disastrous as that of the Bounty, but from a different cause. The waste of human life was much greater, occasioned by the wreck of the ship, and the distress experienced by the crew not much less, owing to the famine and thirst they had to suffer in a navigation of eleven hundred miles in open boats; but the Captain succeeded in fulfilling a part of his instructions, by taking fourteen of the mutineers, of whom ten were brought safe to England, the other four being drowned when the ship was wrecked.[22]

In his dispatch to the Admiralty, Edwards acknowledged his failures, writing "That that [*sic*] of my Orders which I have been able to fulfill, with the discoveries that have been made will be some compensation for the disappointment & misfortunes that have attended us and should their Lordships upon the whole think that the Voyage will be profitable to our Country it will be a great consolation to Sir Your most obed^t. & humble Servant, Edwd. Edwards."[23]

On September 10, 1792, Edwards faced the Royal Navy's mandatory court-martial for the loss of a ship, and was honorably acquitted, cleared of any carelessness or wrongdoing:

> The Court is of opinion that the loss of His Majesty's Ship Pandora was occasioned by her striking upon a Reef near the Entrance of Endeavour Straits and soon afterwards sinking and that her loss was not in any respect owing to mismanagement or a want of proper attention to her safety of the said Captain Edward Edwards his Officers and Company but that the said Captain Edward Edwards his Officers and Ships Company did every thing that was possible to be done for the preservation of His Majesty's said Ship Pandora and for the good of His Majesty's Service and the said Captain Edward Edwards and the other Officers and Company of His Majesty's said Ship Pandora are hereby honorably acquitted.[24]

Owen Rutter, whose Golden Cockerel Press published many primary *Bounty*-related documents in the 1930s, considered this decision—which fails to mention the loss of crew members and prisoners—to be a "whitewashing."[25]

Edwards' greatest failure was disregarding the Admiralty's order to have "Proper regard to the preservation of their [the prisoners'] Lives" as *Pandora* sank. It is heartening to learn in James Morrison's *Journal*, that moments before *Pandora* foundered, two members of Edwards' crew acted bravely and selflessly in the face of imminent disaster: Armourer's Mate Joseph Hodges, who managed to unshackle two prisoners as the ship was sinking, and Boatswain's Mate William Moulter, who opened the hatch of "Pandora's Box," enabling ten prisoners to survive.

We are fortunate that these five eyewitness accounts have survived the passage of nearly 250 years. All of them should be considered to attain a balanced view of a voyage that not only fell short of achieving its mission but also brought about great suffering and loss of life. Ironically, much of this might have been avoided if Edwards had taken a slightly different route on the voyage from England to Tahiti: "On March 16, Captain Edwards discovered Ducie Island and, had he continued on the same parallel, he would have seen Pitcairn and probably captured Christian and his men."[26]

A Note on the Text

My intention in this volume is to present the voyages of H.M.S. *Pandora* and *Matavy* through texts that are faithful to the originals by Edward Edwards, George Hamilton, Peter Heywood, James Morrison, David Thomas Renouard, and one anonymous poet. Consequently, I have made few changes or corrections in spelling, punctuation, grammar or syntax. I hope that encountering the distinct "voices" of these people draws readers closer to their extraordinary experiences.

Most of Edwards' *Pandora*-related reports and letters to the Lords Commissioners of the Admiralty were published for the first time in 1915 in *Voyage of H.M.S. "Pandora" Despatched to Arrest the Mutineers of the "Bounty" in the South Seas, 1790–91*, edited by Basil Thomson. Unfortunately, the editor made a number of errors and unnecessary changes in Edwards' official dispatch to the Admiralty and several other documents. I have corrected or deleted these by comparing Thomson's text to "Captain Edwards' Reports to the Lords Commissioners of the Admiralty from November 1790 to July 1792," held at the National Archives, Kew. This appears to be the document that Thomson used.

Edwards' official dispatch is now part of a bound volume, and some words and letters were drawn into the gutter during the binding process. In cases where a word cannot be deciphered, I have made what I think is the most logical choice, based on the context. What appears to be a draft of the dispatch can be found in the "Personal Papers of Admiral E. Edwards, Commanding the Pandora, Concerning the Mutiny on the Bounty and the Voyage of the Pandora," which came to light in 1965.

Two important documents were not included in *Voyage of H.M.S. 'Pandora'*: "The Admiralty's Sailing Orders," and "Statement by Capt[n] Edwards as to the Loss of Ship Pandora." These were first published in *The United Service Journal* (1843). The "Sailing Orders" also appeared in *The Mariner's Mirror* (April 1936). I have compared these transcripts to the originals in "Personal Papers of Admiral E. Edwards," making what I believe are appropriate edits. Three brief manuscripts were not available for comparison, so I am presenting them here as printed in *Voyage of H.M.S. 'Pandora'*: "Pandora at Rio Janeiro, the 6th January, 1791"; "A list of convicts, deserters from Port Jackson"; and "A List of one Petty Officer and four Seamen lost in a cutter."

The editor of *Voyage of H.M.S. 'Pandora'* made a significant contribution to *Bounty* literature by incorporating George Hamilton's rare *A Voyage Round the World in His Majesty's Frigate Pandora* into the volume. It remains a lucid, entertaining work that I am presenting here in full, transcribed directly from the text of the first edition. Hamilton's language poses few difficulties for the reader, although he occasionally uses foreign words, phrases, and mythological references. I have incorporated most of these in a Glossary that also includes nautical terms.

Peter Heywood's long letter to his mother and a short letter to his sister, Nessy, were transcribed from "Correspondence of Miss Nessy Heywood during 1790–92, relating to the imprisonment, as a mutineer on the *Bounty*, conviction and pardon of her brother Peter." This bound collection, held at the Newberry Library, Chicago, is one of five surviving copies of the Heywood correspondence made for circulation among family and friends. It was published in *Innocent on the Bounty: The Court-Martial and Pardon of Midshipman Peter Heywood, in Letters* (McFarland, 2013).

The selections from James Morrison's *Journal* have been transcribed from an online edition provided by the Mitchell Library, State Library of New South Wales, which I have checked against the first printed edition, titled *The Journal of James Morrison, Boatswain's Mate of the Bounty, Describing the Mutiny & Subsequent Misfortunes of the Mutineers, Together With an Account of the Island of Tahiti* and published by The Golden Cockerel Press in 1935. It was the only complete edition of the Morrison manuscript available until the publication of *After the Bounty: A Sailor's Account of the Mutiny and Life in the South Seas* (Potomac Books, 2010), which modernized the text; and *Mutiny and Aftermath: James Morrison's Account of the Mutiny on the* Bounty *and the Island of Tahiti* (University of Hawai'i Press, 2013), which preserves Morrison's idiosyncratic spelling and punctuation but modernizes Polynesian names and words. In my Introduction, I also have quoted from *Memorandum and Particulars Respecting the Bounty and her Crew*, a manuscript that is essentially a first draft of Morrison's *Journal*, dated October 10, 1792. Breaks or deletions in the text of James Morrison's *Journal* and Peter Heywood's letters are indicated by ellipses.

An abbreviated and apparently edited version of David Thomas Renouard's personal account of the *Matavy* voyage appeared in William Henry Smyth's "The Last of the Pandoras" (1842). A longer and presumably complete account, published by H. E. Maude in "The Voyage of the *Pandora*'s Tender" (1964), is reproduced here. Maude faithfully transcribed it from a copy made by Alfred Purshouse Driver that came to light in 1961. Renouard's original manuscript and the *Matavy*'s logbook are presumably lost.

I have transcribed "Verses on the Loss of his Majesty's Ships, Bounty and Pandora" from the only surviving manuscript of this anonymous poem. This undated copy was presented to the State Library of New South Wales in 1902 by William Bligh's grandson, William Russell Bligh, but the copy is not in Bligh's hand. The original is presumably lost.

Part One

The *Bounty* Mutineers in Tahiti

When the survivors of the *Pandora* wreck reached Timor in the ship's four small boats, H.M.S. *Bounty* midshipman and prisoner Peter Heywood—along with *Pandora*'s crew and his fellow prisoners—embarked on the Dutch East Indiaman *Rembang*, bound for Batavia. From there Heywood wrote a long letter to his mother recounting his distressing experiences on the *Bounty* and *Pandora*. Fearing she was aware that William Bligh had accused him of being one of the mutineers, he explained in detail why he had remained on board the *Bounty* instead of joining Bligh's party of loyalists in the ship's launch. He also provided a succinct account of Christian's failed attempt to establish a refuge from British law on the island of Tubuai (referred to here as Toobouai) and how Christian and his followers sailed into the unknown after landing Heywood and 15 other men on Tahiti to await the inevitable arrival of an English ship searching for the mutineers.

Boatswain's Mate James Morrison of H.M.S. *Bounty* was one of the 16 men, including Heywood, who chose to remain on Tahiti rather than follow Fletcher Christian. Most of them settled down to enjoy the charms of that island paradise, but Morrison had no intention of becoming a beachcomber. Rather than wait for the arrival of an English ship, he decided to build a schooner, sail it to Batavia, board a ship for England and resume his naval career.

With the help of several other *Bounty* crew members and native friends, Morrison built a 30-ton vessel using native woods, a handful of tools and a great deal of ingenuity. Named *Resolution*, this seaworthy craft was destined to play a major role during *Pandora*'s voyage and, fortuitously, in the history of South Pacific exploration. Morrison provides a detailed description of its construction in a long narrative written during and after the *Bounty* court-martial. Published in 1935 as *The Journal of James Morrison, Boatswain's Mate of the Bounty*, it provides a full account of the eighteen eventful months that passed in Tahiti before *Pandora* anchored in Matavai Bay on March 23, 1791.

Above and Opposite: The first two pages of a lengthy letter written by Peter Heywood to his mother, explaining his conduct during the *Bounty* Mutiny and its aftermath. The letter is from "Correspondence of Miss Nessy Heywood during 1790–92, relating to the imprisonment, as a mutineer on the *Bounty*, conviction and pardon of her brother Peter." This volume is one of several copies that the Heywood family transcribed from a large collection of correspondence (courtesy The Newberry Library, Chicago).

Mr. Peter Heywood to Mrs. [Elizabeth] Heywood.

Batavia, November 20th, 1791.

My ever honored and dearest Mother,

At length the time has arrived when you are once more to hear from your ill-fated Son, whose Conduct, at the Capture of that Ship in which it was my Fortune to embark, has, I fear (from what has since happened to me), been grossly misrepresented to you by Lieutenant Bligh, who, by not knowing the real Cause of my remaining on board, naturally suspected me (unhappy for me) to be a Coadjutor in the Mutiny.... How I came to remain on board was thus. The Morning the Ship was taken (it being my Watch below), happening to awake just after Daylight and looking out of my Hammock, I saw a Man sitting upon the Arms Chest in the Main Hatchway with a drawn Cutlass in his Hand, which I could not divine the Reason of, so I got out of Bed, and having asked him the Reason, he told me, that Mr. Christian (assisted by some of the Ship's company) had taken and put the Captain in Confinement, and had taken the Command of the Ship upon himself, and was going to take him Home a Prisoner, to have him tried by a Court Martial for his long tyrannical and oppressive Behaviour to his People! I was quite thunderstruck, and turning into my Birth again, told one of my Messmates who was asleep of what had happened; then, dressing myself, went up the fore Hatch and saw what he had told me to be but too true, and again I asked some of the People who were under Arms what was going to be done with the Captain (who was then on the larboard Side of the quarter Deck, with his Hands tied behind his Back and Mr. Christian along-side him, with a Pistol and drawn Bayonet), most of whom told me quite a different Story, from what I had heard below, which was that he was to be sent ashore to Tofoa[27] in the Launch, and those who would not join Mr. Christian might either accompany him, or be taken in Irons as Prisoners to 'Taheite and be left there. The Relation of two so different Stories made me unable to judge which could be the true one, but seeing them hoisting the Boats off, it seemed to prove the Latter. In this trying Situation, young and inexperienced as *I was*, and without an Adviser (every Person being, as it were, infatuated, and not knowing what to do), I remained for a while a silent Spectator of what was going on; and after revolving the Matter clearly within my Mind, I was determined to chuse the lesser of two evils, because I knew that those who went on Shore would in all probability be put to death by the savage Natives, whereas the 'Taheiteans, being a humane and generous Race, one might have some Hopes of being kindly received and remaining there till the Arrival of another Ship, which seemed to silly me the most consistent with Reason and Rectitude. While this Resolution possessed my Mind, at the same time lending my Assistance to hoist out the Boats, the Hurry and Confusion Affairs were in, and thinking my Intention just, I never thought of going to Mr. Bligh for Advice, besides, what confirmed me in it was, my seeing two experienced Officers, when ordered into the Boat by Mr. Christian, desire his Permission to remain in the Ship, one of whom my own Messmate, Mr. Hayward, and I being assisting to clear the Launch of Yams, he (Mr. Hayward) asked me what I intended to do. I told him to remain in the Ship. Now this Answer I imagine he has told Mr. Bligh I made to him, from which, together with my not speaking to him that Morning, his Suspicions of me have arose, construing my Conduct into what is foreign to my Nature. Thus, my dearest Mother, 'twas all owing *to my Youth and unadvised Inexperience*, but has been interpreted into Villainy and disregard to my Country's Laws, the ill Effects of which I at present and still am to labour under for some Months longer. And now, after what I have asserted, I may still once more retrieve my injured Reputation, be again reinstated in the Affection and Favor of the most tender of Mothers, and be still considered as her ever dutiful Son. How it grieves me to think I must be so explicit when I have got such a Burden to unfold, but Necessity obliges me! However, I must continue my Relation. I was not undeceived in my erroneous Intention till too late, which was after the Captain was in the Launch, for whilst I was talking to the Master at Arms (one of the Ringleaders of the Affair) upon the Starboard Boom aft, my other Messmate whom I had left in his Hammock in the Birth, came up to me and asked me if I was not going in the Launch? I told him No! upon which he told me not to think of such a thing as staying behind, but take his Advice and go down below with him and get a few necessary Things and make Haste to go with him into the Launch, and said that by remaining in the Ship I should incur an equal Share of Guilt with the Malcontents themselves, upon which he and the Master at

Arms had some Altercation about my Messmate's Intention of going in the Boat. I reluctantly took his Advice—*reluctantly* I say, because I knew no better and was foolish, and the Boat swimming very deep in the Water, the Land being far distant, the Thoughts of being sacrificed by the Natives on (or soon after) landing, and the self-consciousness of my own Intention being just—all these Considerations, corroborating each other, almost staggered my Resolution. Yet I preferred his Judgment before my own, and we both jumped down the main Hatchway for that Purpose; but as soon as we were in the Birth, the Master at Arms ordered the Centry (who I before mentioned) to keep us both in the Birth, till he should receive Orders for our Releasement and would not suffer my Messmate to go out, though he made an Attempt, so that he then desired the Master at Arms to acquaint Mr. Bligh of our Detention, which I fear he omitted, and we ourselves did not come upon Deck till the Launch was a long Way astern. I now saw my Error in Belief.

At the latter End of May we got to an Island to the Southward of 'Taheite called Toobouai, where they intended to make a Settlement, but finding no Stock there of any kind, they agreed to go to 'Taheite, and after procuring Hogs, Fowls, etc., to return there and remain. So on June 6th we arrived at 'Taheite, where I was in Hopes I might find an Opportunity of running away and remaining on Shore; but I could not effect it, as there was always too good a look-out kept to prevent any such Steps being taken; and besides they had all sworn, that should any one make his Escape, they would force the Natives to restore him and would then Shoot him as an Example to the Rest; well knowing that anyone by remaining there might (should a Ship arrive) be the Means of discovering the Place of their Abode. Therefore, finding it impracticable, I saw no other Alternative but to rest as content as possible and return to Toobouai and there wait till the Masts should be taken out, and then take the Boat, which might carry me to 'Taheite, and disable those remaining from Pursuit. But Providence so ordered it, that we had no Occasion to try our Fortune at such a Hazard, for after returning there and remaining till the latter End of August, in which Time a Fort was almost built, but nothing could be effected, as the Natives could not be brought to friendly Terms and with whom we had many Skirmishes and narrow Escapes from being cut off by them, and, what was still worse, internal broils and discontent. This determined part of the People to leave the Island and go to 'Taheite, which was carried by a Majority of Votes, and being put in Execution and on the 22d of September having anchored, the next Morning my Messmate and I went on Shore to the House of an old landed Man our former Friend, and being now freed from a L[awles]s C[re]w, determined to remain as much so as possible, and wait patiently for the Arrival of a Ship. Fourteen more of the People came likewise on Shore (two of whom, the Master at Arms and Centry I before mentioned have been killed by the Natives), and Mr. Christian and eight Men went away in the Ship, but God knows whither.

Whilst we remained there, we were used by our Friends (the Natives) with a Friendship, Generosity, and Humanity almost unparalleled, being such as never was equalled by the people of any civilized Nations, to the Disgrace of all Christians. We had some few Battles with the Enemies of the People we resided amongst, but I was always protected by a never-failing Providence. To be brief—living there till the latter End of March 1791, on the 26th, H.M.S. *Pandora* arrived... [The correct date of *Pandora*'s arrival is March 23, 1791.]

From The Journal of James Morrison, Boatswain's Mate of the Bounty

November 1789. Finding ourselves Settled I began to think it would be possible to build a small Vessel In which I had hopes of reaching Batavia & from thence to England. I comunicated this to McIntosh and Millward, and the Matter was agreed on; but we resolved to keep the real motive a Secret, and to Say that she was only for the purpose of Pleasuring about the Island; and for this purpose, I having observed that Mathw. Thompson had got a Quadrant (formerly Mr. Hallets) and some of Mr. Haywards books, tho He could neither read nor write, I was determined if Possible to get posession of them, and with a little perswasion I got the Quadrant for Six small trade Adzes (Calld here loeys) & a Gallon of Wine but when I wanted the Books he began to have some suspicion, and was sorry that He had let me have the Quadrant, which I told him was only for Amusement. He said He had No Cartridge paper and the books would answer that purpose, I told him that I would give him paper in lieu which would answer that purpose better, but this only served to Confirm his Oppinion; however as I had a Seamans Daily Assistant[28] I took no further Notice, and affected to be easy about them tho I was sorry that I could not get them.

Norman & Heildbrandt having agreed to be of our party, McIntosh and them removed to Maatavye on the 1st of November bringing their Effects with them and having got Houses prepared on a Square piece of Ground raised above the level where we fixd a Flag staff to Hoist the Collours on Sundays; we were also Joind here by Burkett (who returned on the Second, & brought Brown[29] with Him) Sumner, Ellison, Churchill & Byrn, and having appointed Divine Service to be read on Sundays evry thing at present seemd right. I now made a publick proposal to build a small Vessel to Cruize about the Island in which was agreed to, as McIntosh said it was possible to put one together and He had no objection, Norman & the Cooper being both Workmen, and the rest of us Could Chop off the rough parts ready for their Use.

Having agreed on this Head, I informd Poeno [a local chief] that we intended to build a little Ship, as we did not understand the Method of Handling Canoes, and in which I told Him that we could carry Him & Matte [a Tahitian chief] with some of our Friends to the Neighbouring Islands, he was well pleased, and told us to Cut down what timber we pleased, as there was plenty in Maatavye. ...

On the 11th we began to Cut down Trees for our Intended Vessel, and having Cleard a place near the Square under the Shade of some trees, we laid the Blocks, and on the 12th laid the Keel which was 30 feet.

The Plan being drawn to the Following dimentions,—Length of the Keel 30 feet, Length on Deck 35 feet, Length of the Stern post 6 f. 6 in., Stem 7 f. 2

in., Breadth 9 f. 6 in. on the Midship frame; dept[h] of the Hold 5 feet; breadth of the Floors & Timbers 4 inches to 3½ thickness 3¼ to 2½; Keel Stem & Stern post 8 inches by 4 Saturday the 14th Employd trimming Stuff for Molds & Cuting trees down for Planks.

16th. Having got some Molds made, I took part of them and got some of the Natives to assist me when I procured three or four floors & some timbers. Churchill also took some & went to Oparre & Tettahah on the Same Errand, and returned on the 20th with Some Pieces of Poorou but only one answer'd to the present Molds—in the mean time McIntosh Superintend[ed] the Cutting down trees and Splitting them for Plank, and I had Collected several more pieces of Poorou which was the Best to answer the purpose of Timbering, and the Bread fruit for Plank.

20th. Having Colleted Several More Floors, we set about triming them for Use, in Which I assisted, by doing part of the rough Work, while McIntosh & Norman fitted them; in the Mean time the rest were busy in Cutting down Trees, and Splitting them For Plank, which were laid up to Season but at this the progress was but Slow, it being as Much as we Could do to trim one plank of 30 feet long in two days; and what work We had now Cut out lasted us all the Week.

Monday 30th. This day we erected a Shed to work under, to keep off the heat of the Sun, which we found very intense, and to prevent us from being interrupted by the rain which we now began to expect from the appearance of the Weather.

December 1st. this day we received a Present of Hogs and Provisions from Poeno by order of Matte and this day according to our expectation the rain began, and lasted with some few intermissions for near three weeks, during which time no work was done out of the Shed. Mean time and we fitted what Floors & Timbers we had trimd, the Stem & Stern post, & Plank of 2½ inch for the Stern.

21st. The Weather being Fair, we set to search for more Timbers, and set up the Stem & Stern posts. It must here be observed, that as we had but few Molds, we were under the necessity of altering them to evry Frame, and the timbers being Scarce in the low lands, we were only able to procure one & some Knees, nor was this the only difficulty that we labour'd under, for We found that Several of those which were already trim'd & fitted, had started, & became Straight, so as to alter their form some inches, to remedy which we found it answer'd our purpose best, only to Side them for the present, and let them dry before we took in hand to finish them, or put them in their places. The removing of those timbers which had started, & siding the Others kept McIntosh & Myself Employd till Christmas, while Norman and the rest were making Plank.

We kept the Hollidays in the best manner that we could, killing a Hog for Christmas Dinner, and reading Prayers which we never Omitted on Sundays, and having wet weather we were not able to do any thing out of doors for the remainder of the Year.

We informd the Natives of the reason of our Observing these Hollidays, and especially Christmas Day; all of which seemd to regard with attention, and readily believed all that we could inform them of, never doubting that the Son of God was born of a Woman, and they always behooved with much decency when present at our worship; tho they Could not understand one word; yet several were desirous to have it explaind to them, and some of them wishd to learn our prayers which they all allowed to be better then their own; those who were constantly about us knew when our Sunday came, and were always prepared accordingly. Seeing that we rested on that day they did so likewise and never made any diversions on it. One of them was always ready to hoist the Ensign on Sunday Morning, and if a stranger happened to pass, and enquire the meaning, they were told that it was Mahana ' Atooa (Gods Day) and tho they were intent on their Journey, would stop to see our manner of keeping it, and would proceed next day, well pleased with their Information.

January 1790. On the 4th the Weather being fair, I set out to the Hills accompanied by some of Poenos Men, & one who lived with myself Constantly, in quest of timbers, and returned with several, the Poorow being plenty in the Mountains; but Mostly at a Good distance as they always take the first at hand for their own Use—these We sided as usual and laid them to dry, the Natives Frequently assembled about us to see our work, and seemd much surprized at our method of building, and always assisted willingly to haul the Trees to hand, & hew off the rough; they are very dexterous at Spliting, but as they have no Idea of working by rule, they could be of no use in triming the Plank.

Amongst our visitors Came a Blind Man, who they led to the place, and he examined the work by feeling evry part and asking the use and intention; and seemd amazed at the Construction of the Vessel of which he Seemd to have a good Idea and said to His Country Men 'our Canoes are foolish things compared to this one.' He askd us many questions, and received answers, with which he went away well satisfied.

7th. This day we got more timbers and trimmd them as before, Norman and the Others Still making plank, and as we wanted Iron nails the Cooper (Heildbrandt) was set to work to Cut Amai, for that purpose, this being the best wood which we could find for that use.

11th. Went in search of More timbers, & had tolerable Sucess. The business of searching for timber always took up a whole day, having Several Miles to go before any Could be found to answer our purpose, and when we found them we frequently had the misfortune to break them by tumbling them down the precipices, which we could not avoid, it being impossible to Carry them along the Steep Clifts, and what we Cut in one day would keep McIntosh

& Myself employd for three or four, having as before Observed the Molds to alter for each frame.—Nor was the making of Plank less troublesome, having no Saws (except handsaws) the largest tree would afford no more then two thicknesses of Plank, Some of the trees Cut for that purpose measuring six feet round which took a deal of Labour to reduce into plank of Inch & a quarter with axes & adzes; and as we had but two Adzes we were forced to make the Small trade hatchets (such as are sold in London at 9d. each) answer that purpose, by lashing them to handles after the manner of the Natives which answered our purpose very well.

And here I may also observe that a deal of Labour might have been saved by workmen, who understood their business, by trimming the Timber in the Mountains, which would have made a Considerable Odds in the Weight, but of this I was not a sufficient Judge, and was therefore obliged to bring it home in the rough, and Trim it afterwards, however this appeard but trifling in point of difficulty and was not Sufficient to make us abandon our project.

18th. Brought home some more timber; and having got several dry enough to Work, we Cut up a plank for Ribbands and set up several frames to guide us in our work, and as we had but little Iron Work, we made shift with Ironnails, putting a Spike in evry other Floor, and Irennails [*sic*] in the rest. This kept McIntosh & myself employd till the 30th as Norman could not be spared from making Plank it being necessary to keep one workman in each branch of the Business....

Monday the 15th. The Frame being now Compleat, we began to trim the Timbers fair for Planking, and Coleman being quite recovered, we proposed to Him to make the Iron Work for the rudder Bowsprit &c.—to which he agreed on Condition that a pair of Bellows could be made and Coals procured to get sufficient heat, having no objection to assist himself in making the Bellows, & getting the Forge in order.—We immediately fixd on a plan for making the Bellows and Heildbrandt was set to work to assist Coleman; the Breadfruit planks made a tolerable set of Boards. Canvas supplyd the place of Leather, and the Iron handle of a Sauspan made the Nozzel, a Frame of Plank filld with Clay was made for the Forge, and Coleman Cut a hole through a stone to point the Nozzel of the Bellows through, the Pig of Ballast made a good anvil & the Carpenters maul answerd the purpose of a Sledge.—in the meantime we got Charcoal Burnt, and the Forge was got to work, but we found it necessary to keep the Canvas constantly wet to make it keep in the wind, which answered the purpose very well and Coleman having Heildbrandt to assist him soon Got some part of the Ironwork into form, Making eye Bolts instead of Braces for the Rudder with a Bolt to go through the Whole...

April 1st. Burkett, Sumner & Churchill set out for Papaara, and Byrn & Ellison went to live at Oparre, and our number being reduced, we devided ourselves thus—Norman & Millward to make Plank, McIntosh & Myself to put them on, & Coleman & Heildbrandt to make the Ironwork.—and by Easter Sunday we compleated Six Streaks on the Starboard side, our Manner of Proceeding was this, after McIntosh had fitted one Plank, and placed it, he left me to bore it off, and prepared another, when it was bored off he secured it by driving one Nail, and one Irennail in each timber, and three Nails in each butt,—....

As we were like to be Soon out of Plank it being now a whole weeks work to make one of 30 feet, we therefore set about the Beams and Knees till there should be some more plank ready, having now Compleated 8 Streaks on each Side. For the Knees I was forced to go to the Mountains while McIntosh fitted the Beams....

The work had gone on very well during my absence and by the 30th both sides were plankd up, the Ceiling in & the Beams Secured. but now Norman and Heildbrandt left off Work and did not return to it till the Middle of May, however as the heavy Iron work was done and Coleman was now able to proceed by him Self with making nails & small work, and we set about Collecting Bread fruit Gum, Which we Boild into a very good Substitute for Pitch and with What rope had been brought (by ourselves and the Natives) from the Ship, we Musterd Oakum Sufficient to Caulk the Vessel all over....

As we found it a tedious Jobb to gather the Gum or pitch, we Employd a Number of Natives. Dressing a Large Hog we made a feast for a Number of the poorer Sort and desired evry one that partook, to bring in his proportion of Gum, which they did not fail to perform according to the quantity of Pork they had received, as we found this answerd our purpose we repeated it till we had sufficient for our Purpose. We found that by Boiling it down it made Good Pitch and Hogs lard being Mixd with it made it answer the purpose of Tar.

Tho the Method of Procuring this gum was dear yet the Hogs Cost us Nothing, and the people were not over paid for their Labour, and a Hog of 200 lbs weight would not bring 50 lbs of Pitch. Their Method of Procuring it is this—they take a peg made of Toa which with a Stone they drive through the bark in several places and having served a Number of Trees in this manner they let it stay till next morning, when the Gum is run out and hardend. This they scrape off with a shell, and make it up in a Ball; but a Man can hardly get a pound of it by himself in two days.—no other tree affords this Pitch but the Breadfruit and when it first runs is as white as Milk and as thin but it soon hardens and looks like white wax and when Boild becomes black and is in all respects like pitch extracted from pine, tho' this Comes from the Bark only and not from the Tree.

17th. Norman & Heildbrandt having returned to work, we got about laying the deck, which was finishd by the 1st of June, and in the Mean time Heildbrandt set about making Casks out of a White Wood Calld by the Natives

Fwhyfwhye, the grain of which resembles White Oak; the Young Chesnut trees which grow in abundance in the Hills making Hoops.—we also Cut Masts Boom Bow Sprit & Gaffs intending to rigg her Schooner fashion and made a Kellick with Toa and Weighted it with lead.

4th. This day We fired a Volly & Drank a Keg of Cyder which had been prepared from the Apples Calld Vee on purpose for the Occasion. We were also visited by Byrn & Ellison who had come to Point Venus in their way to Tettooroa. We now Set about Caulking, Making rope, Blocks &c. The Poorow answerd for the Shells of the Blocks, and the Toa for Shievs & Pins. The Bark of the Poorow being Cleand made very good rope, & a sheet of Copper made a Barrel for a Pump, with Colemans Assistance.—in Caulking the Vessel we observed that an insect Calld here Hoohoo had eaten into a part of the Stem Which We found it Necessary to shift & put a new piece in its place. The Rudder being fixd, & the Vessel Caulkd all over, We paid Her with pitch, and by the 1st of July She was ready for Launching with Masts Boom Bowsprit & Gaffs Compleat.

We had frequent Visitors while She was building Who examined her inside and out and viewd each part with surprize wondering how it was possible to make such a Vessel, and what seemd to draw their attention most was the Method we used of twisting the Plank which sometimes proved an over match for us, and we broke several, after expending a whole weeks labour on them, and being Assisted by Fire, Water and a good workman who understood his business—notwithstanding which, and all the Schemes which Necessity could invent we were frequently forced to throw the Planks away which with Iron work would have been of Use.—We lost only one pair of Compasses during the time She was in hand and them we supposed to have been lost in the rubbish, and now put up our Tools and prepared for setting her afloat.

July 1790. With what rope we Could Muster we slung the Masts on the Sides making a kind of Cradle under Her Bottom and having done with Most of the augur Shanks we made use of them as Bolts & Clenchd them through the Keel & Kelson to strengthen that Department.

And being all ready on the 5th We applied to Poeno Who told me that the Priest must perform His prayers over Her, and then He would have her Carried to the Sea.—the Priest being sent for and a Young Pig & a Plantain given Him When he began Walking round and round the Vessel, stopping at the Stem & Stern, and Muttering short sentences in an unknown dialect; and having a Bundle of Young Plantain trees brought to Him by Poenos Order, he now and then tossd one in on Her deck. He kept at this all day and night and was hardly finishd by sunrise on the 6th. When Poeno & Tew, Matte's father, Came with Three or four Hundred Men, and having each made a long Oration, their Men were devided in two partys, and the Servants of Tew having received a Hog & Some Cloth which was provided by Poeno for the Occasion, one of the Priests went on board and Several plantain trees was tossd to him from both sides. He then ran fore & aft, and exorted them to exert themselves, and on a Signal being given they Closed in, and those who Could not reach by hand got long Poles, A Song being given they all Joind in Chorus & She soon began to Move and in Half an hour She reachd the Beach, where She was launchd & Calld the Resolution.

PART TWO

Outward Bound on H.M.S. *Pandora*

Captain Edward Edwards composed his official dispatch on H.M.S. *Pandora*'s voyage to the Admiralty (titled here *Captain Edwards' Report*) in the form of a 32-page letter, written in an appropriately straightforward style that differs considerably from Ship's Surgeon George Hamilton's colorful, vibrant language in *A Voyage Round the World in His Majesty's Frigate Pandora*. Here is an example of Edwards' matter-of-fact prose followed by Hamilton's description of the same incident:

> EDWARDS: "We saw a burying place and several Wolves near the watering place but we saw no natives."[30]
>
> HAMILTON: "The morning was ushered in with the howling of wolves, who had smelt us in the night, when prowling for food. Lieut. Corner and a party were sent at day-light, to search again for water; and, as we approached, the wild beasts retired, and filled the woods with their hideous growling."[31]

Of course, Edwards was writing for a specific audience, concentrating on information that would interest the Admiralty. His language becomes more compelling when *Pandora* arrives in Tahiti and the hunt for the *Bounty* mutineers begins. Hamilton's book, which was written and published for a much wider audience, is filled with vivid descriptions of Tahiti and other landfalls, including Santa Cruz, Rio de Janeiro, Coupang, and Batavia.

Not surprisingly, the content of Edwards and Hamilton's narratives stands in sharp contrast to that of Peter Heywood and James Morrison's, who were cruelly confined in Pandora's Box for more than four months.

The Admiralty's Sailing Orders

> By the Commissioners for executing the Office of Lord High Admiral of Great Britain & Ireland etc.
>
> Whereas, by an order from the late Board of Admiralty, dated the 16th of August 1787, Lieutenant William Bligh was appointed to command His Majesty's Armed ves-

> By the Commissioners for executing the Office of Lord High Admiral of Great Britain & Ireland &c.
>
> Whereas, by an order from the late Board of Admiralty, dated the 16th of August 1787, Lieutenant William Bligh was appointed to command His Majesty's Armed vessel the Bounty, and by Instructions from the said Board, dated the 20th of November following, was directed to proceed in that vessel to the Society Islands in the South Seas, in order to procure and transport from thence to some of the British Possessions in the West Indies, Bread Fruit Trees and other useful Plants the product of the said Islands.
>
> And Whereas the said Lieutenant Bligh sailed from Spithead, on the 23d of December following, in prosecution of his destined Voyage, and by Letter to our Secretary dated at Coupang (a Dutch Settlement in the Island of Timor) on the 10th of August 1789, acquainted us that the

The first manuscript page of the Admiralty's sailing orders to Captain Edward Edwards, which delineate the steps to be taken during his search for H.M.S. *Bounty* and the mutineers who seized the ship from Captain William Bligh (courtesy National Library of Australia).

sel the Bounty, and by Instructions from the said Board, dated the 20th of November following, was directed to proceed in that vessel to the Society Islands in the South Seas, in order to procure and transport from thence to some of the British Possessions in the West Indies, Bread Fruit Trees and other useful Plants the product of the said Islands.

And whereas the said Lieutenant Bligh sailed from Spithead, on the 23^d of December following, in prosecution of his destined Voyage, and, by Letter to our Secretary dated at Coupang (a Dutch Settlement in the Island of Timor) on the 18th of August 1789, acquainted us that the said vessel, on her return from Otaheite with a large Cargo of those Plants in a very flourishing state, had been violently & forcibly taken from him, on the 28th of April preceding, by Fletcher Christian, who was Mate of her and Officer of the watch, assisted by others of the inferior Officers and Men, armed with Musquets and Bayonets; and that he (the said Lieutenant Bligh) together with the Master, Boatswain, Gunner, Carpenter, Acting Surgeon and others of her Crew (being nineteen in number, including himself) were forced into the Launch and cast adrift ten Leagues to the South West of Tofoa, the Northwesternmost of the Friendly Islands, without Fire Arms and with a very small quantity of Provisions and Water; and that having landed at Tofoa, and been beat off by the Natives with the loss of one of his Party, he bore away for New Holland and Timor, and, on the 15th of June following, arrived at Coupang abovementioned, distant twelve Hundred Leagues from the place where the vessel was seized as aforesaid; from whence he and those who survived are now returned to England.

And whereas the Ship you command has been fitted out for the express purpose of proceeding to the South Seas, in order to endeavor to recover the abovementioned Armed vessel, and to bring, in Confinement, to England the abovementioned Fletcher Christian and his Associates (a list of whose names you will receive herewith) or as many of them as have survived and you may be able to apprehend, in order that they may be brought to condign Punishment; You are hereby required and directed to put to Sea, with the very first opportunity of Wind and weather, and make the best of your way to Teneriffe, where you are to take in, with the utmost dispatch, such wine and necessaries as you shall judge proper for the use of the Ship's Company, and then proceed, as expeditiously as possible, to the Southward, and shape your Course round Cape Horn; and, having weathered that Cape, make the most direct course to get within the limits of the Tradewind, and steer for, Matavai Bay or Oparré Harbour on the north side of Otaheite (one of the Society Islands) which is in Latitude 17° 29' South and about the Longitude of 149° 35' West.

On your arrival at Otaheite, and not finding the abovementioned armed vessel there, you are to endeavor to get the best Information possible respecting her; carefully observing yourself, and strictly charging your Officers and Crew, to avoid saying anything in regard to the cause of the Enquiry, until you shall have discovered whether the Inhabitants of the said Island have a knowledge of Lieutenant Bligh's having been dispossessed of her, as, abovementioned; where she is, and whether any of the Mutineers are on that Island.

If you shall find that the Mutineers, or any of them, are on the Island of Otaheite, you are, the first moment it shall be in your power, to detain such of the Chiefs as you may be able to get hold of, and then, declaring the object of your voyage and immediately appointing a strong Party, well armed, to go in quest of the Mutineers, require assistance, and guides to direct the said Party where to find them.

In case you shall not be able to gain any Information of the Mutineers at Otaheite, you are to proceed to the Island Whytootackee, in Latitude 18° 52' South and longitude 159° 41' west; calling, in your way, at Huaheine and Uliatea, where you need not anchor, as numbers of the natives may be expected to come off to you, of whom you may probably get the necessary Information, observing, however, that it will be always in your power to judge of their Reports, by sailing round the Islands and looking into the Bays and Harbours, to discover if the abovementioned Armed vessel be in any of them.

Should the Mutineers not be at Whytootackee, which there is reason to think is the place of their resort, you are (before you get farther to the westward) to make a Circuit of the neighbouring Islands, in search of them.

Having so done, and not finding them at any of the abovementioned Islands, you are to proceed to Anamoka Road in the Friendly Islands (touching at Palmerstone's and the other Islands in the way) and pursue the like means for finding them; And having succeeded, or failed, in your endeavors for that purpose, proceed on your return to England, through Endeavor's Straits which seperate New Guinea from New Holland; passing to the Southward of Java, unto Princes Island in the Straits of Sunda; and, as in this route, the prevailing winds are to be attended to, it is necessary that you should remember that the Changes of the Monsoons, amongst the Islands to the Eastward of Java and about Endeavor Straits, are about May and November; there being no Dependence (of which we have any certain knowledge) of passing the Straits after the month of September or beginning of October, altho' it may perhaps be accomplished in the month of November.

From Princes Island you are to make the best of your way, by the Cape of Good Hope, to England; repairing to Spithead, from whence you are to send to our Secretary an account of your arrival and Proceedings; and where you are to remain until you receive further order.

In case you are so fortunate as to fall in with the abovementioned Armed vessel and Mutineers, or any of them, you are to put on board her such of your Officers, Petty Officers and Foremastmen as you can best spare, & you shall judge best qualified and most to be depended upon, to navigate her to England, furnishing her with such Stores & Provisions, from the Ship you command, as maybe necessary for that purpose; And you are to keep the Mutineers as closely confined as may preclude all possibility of their escaping, having, however, proper regard to the preservation of their Lives, that they may be brought Home to undergo the Punishment due to their Demerits.

During your passage Out and Home, you are to take every advantage of the Rains to keep up your Stock of water, and if you find it necessary to stop for a supply on your way out, you will observe that Rio Janeiro, and new year's Harbour in Staten Island, are the most eligible places for that purpose.

Given under our hands the 25th October 1790.
Edward Edwards Esqr.   Arden
Captain of His Majesty's Ship   Hood
Pandora at Spithead   A. Gardner
By Command of their Lordships.
Ph. Stephens.

From Captain Edwards' Report

Sir

Be pleased to acquaint my Lords Commissioners of the Admiralty that I sailed again from Jack in the Basket[32] with His Majesty's Ship Pandora under my command on the 7th of November and Anchored in Sta. Cruiz bay Teneriff on the 22^d. That nothing particular occurred in my Passage to this Place except that of my falling in with His Majesty's Sloop Shark on the 17th. of Nov^r: in Lat. 32°. 33' Long. 13° 40' W^t: bound to Madeira with Dispatches for Rear Admiral Cornish, and my learning from them that the Matters in dispute with Spain were amicably settled, of which circumstance I was unacquainted when I left England. I am now compleating my Water, and have taken on board full three Months Wine for my complement with some fruit and Vegetables; and purpose and flatter my self that I shall be able to sail from hence this Evening. Inclosed I send the state and condition of His Majesty's Ship Pandora for their Lordships information and I have the honor to be Sir,

Your most obed. & very humble Servant—
Edwd. Edwards Phillip Stephens, Esqr:

Pandora at Rio Janeiro,
the 6th January 1791.
[Received 29th June and read.]

Sir

Be pleased to acquaint my Lords Commissioners of the Admiralty that I sailed from Teneriff with His Majesty's Ship Pandora on the afternoon of the 25th November, agreeable to my intentions signified to their Lordships by letter from that Island, and anchored off the city Rio Janeiro on the evening of the 31st of December with a view to compleat my water and to get refreshments for the ship's company and from my being persuaded that very long runs, particularly with new ships' companies, are prejudicial to health, and as my men are of that description, and have also suffered in their health from a fever which has prevailed amongst them in a greater or less degree every since they left England, were other inducements for my touching at this port. I shall stay here no longer than is absolutely necessary to procure these articles, and which I expect to be able to accomplish by the seventh of this month, and I shall then proceed on my voyage as soon as wind and weather will permit.

Herewith I send the state and condition of His Majesty's Ship Pandora, and I have the honour to be, Sir,

Your most obed.^{t} and humb.^{le} servant,
Edw. Edwards

Batavia the 25th of November 1791
29 May 1792.
from Amsterdam

Sir

In a Letter dated the 6th of Jany. 1791 which I did myself the honor to address to you from Rio Janeiro I gave an account of my proceedings up to that time and inclosed the State and Condition of His Majesty's Ship Pandora under my Command, and having completed the water and procured such Articles of Provision &c. for the use of the Ships Company as they were in want of, and I thought necessary for the Voyage; I sailed from that Port on the 8th Jany. 1791 Run a long the coast of America, Terre Del Fuego & Staten Land round Cape Horn, and proceeded directly to Otaheite, and arrived at Matavy Bay in that Island on the 23^d of March without having touched at any other Place in my Passage Thither—

It was my intention to have put in to New Years Harbour or some other Port in its neighbourhood to complete our Water and to refresh my people, could I have effected that business within the Month of January; but as I arrived too late on that Coast to fullfil my Intentions within the time, it determined me to push forward without delay, by which means I flattered my self I might avoid that extreme bad Weather & all the evil consequences that is usually experienced in doubling Cape Horn in a more advanced Season of the Year, and I had the good fortune not to be disappointed in my expectation.

After doubling the Cape, and advancing to the Northward into Warmer Weather the Fever which had prevailed onboard gradually declined, and the diseases usually succeeding such Fevers prevented by a liberal use of the antiscrobutics and other norishing and useful articles, with which we were so amply supplied, and the Ships Company arrived at Otaheite in perfect Health except a few whose debilitated Constitutions no Climate, Provision or Medicine could much improve.

In our Run to Otaheite we discovered three Islands. The first which I called Ducie's Island lies in the Lat. 24°. 40'. 30" S°. & Long. 124°. 36'. 30" W^r. from Greenwich it is between 2 & 3 miles long. The second I called Lord Hoods Island it lies in the Lat. 21°. 31' S°._ & Long. 135°. 32'. 30" W^r. is about 8 miles long.

The third I called Carysforts Island it lies in Lat. 20°. 49' S°. and Long. 138°. 33' W^r.—and it is four miles long. They are all three, low Lagoon Islands, covered with Wood, but we saw no Inhabitants on either of them. Before we Anchored in Mativy Bay…

From George Hamilton, A Voyage Round the World in His Majesty's Frigate Pandora

Government having resolved to bring to punishment the mutineers of His Majesty's late ship Bounty, and to survey the Straits of Endeavour, to facilitate a passage to Botany Bay, on the 10th of August 1790, appointed Captain Edward Edwards to put in commission at Chatham, and take command of the Pandora Frigate of twenty-four guns, and a hundred and sixty men.

A great naval armament then equipping retarded our progress, and prevented that particular attention to the choice of men which their Lordships so much wished; as contagion here crept amongst us from infected clothing, the fatal effects of which we discovered, and severely experienced, in the commencement of the voyage.

Every thing necessary being completed, and an additional complement

Part Two. Outward Bound on H.M.S. Pandora

A
VOYAGE
ROUND THE
WORLD,
IN
HIS MAJESTY's FRIGATE
PANDORA.

Performed under the Direction of
CAPTAIN EDWARDS
In the Years 1790, 1791, and 1792.

With the DISCOVERIES made in the South-Sea; and the many Diftreffes experienced by the Crew from Shipwreck and Famine, in a Voyage of Eleven Hundred Miles in open Boats, between Endeavour Straits and the Ifland of Timor.

By Mr GEORGE HAMILTON,
LATE SURGEON OF THE PANDORA.

BERWICK:
PRINTED BY AND FOR W. PHORSON; B. LAW AND SON,
AVE-MARIA-LANE, LONDON.

M DCC XCIII.

The title page of the first edition of George Hamilton's *A Voyage Round the World in His Majesty's Frigate Pandora*, published 1793.

of naval stores, received for the refitment of the Bounty; dropped down to Sheerness, saluted Admiral Dalrymple, payed the same compliment to Sir Richard King, in passing the Downs, arrived at Portsmouth, and found there Lord Howe with the Union Flag at the main, and the proudest navy that ever graced the British seas under his command.

Here the officers and men received six months pay in advance, and after receiving their final orders, got the time-keeper on board, weighed anchor, and proceeded to sea.

As the white clifts of Albion receded from our view, alternate hopes and fears took possession of our minds, wafting the last kind adieu to our native soil.

We pursued our voyage with a favourable breeze; but Pandora now seemed inclined to shed her baneful influence among us, and a malignant fever threatened much havoc, as in a few days thirty-five men were confined to their beds, and unfortunately Mr Innes, the Surgeon's only mate, was among the first taken ill; what rendered our situation still more distressing, was the crowded state of the ship being filled to the hatchways with stores and provisions, for, like Weevils, we had to eat a hole in our bread, before we had a place to lay down in; every Officer's cabin, the Captain's not excepted, being filled with provisions and stores. Our sufferings were much encreased, for want of room to accommodate our sick, notwithstanding every effort of the Captain that humanity could suggest.

In this sickly lumbered state, near the latitude of Madeira, we observed a sail bearing down upon us: from her appearance and manœuvres, we had every reason to believe she was a ship of war; and a rumour of a Spanish war prevailing when we left England, rendered it necessary to clear ship for

A view of Santa Cruz, Tenerife, where Captain Edward Edwards was directed to take on wine and other articles at the start of his mission to capture the *Bounty* mutineers. H.M.S. *Pandora* Ship's Surgeon George Hamilton described the city as "Beautifully picturesque.... It stands in the centre of a spacious bay, on a gentle acclivity surrounded with retiring hills." By John Webber, 1776 (courtesy Yale Center for British Art, Paul Mellon Collection).

action; as soon as our guns were run out, and all hands at quarters, got along side of her, when she proved His Majesty's Ship, Shark, sent out with orders of recall to Admiral Cornish, who had sailed for the West Indies a few days before we left Spithead.

This little disaster deranged us much, having at the same time bad weather, attended with heavy thunder squals. The Peek of Teneriff now began to shew his venerable crest, towering above the clouds; and in two days more came to an anchor in the road of Santa Cruz, but did not salute, as the Commandant had not authority to return it.

Immediately on our arrival we were boarded by the Port-master, by whom we learnt they had been in much apprehension of a disagreeable visit from the English, but were happy to hear that matters were amicably settled between the Courts of Madrid and St James's.

With respect to site nothing can be more beautifully picturesque than the town of Santa Cruz. It stands in the centre of a spacious bay, on a gentle acclivity surrounded with retiring hills, and the noble promontory of the Peek rising majestically behind it, dignifies the scene beyond description, being continually diversified with every vicissitude of the surrounding atmosphere, emerging and retiring thro' the fleecy clouds, from the bottom of the mountain to its summit.

All the circumjacent hills on the margin of the beach are tufted with little forts, and barbett batteries, forming an Eoplanade [sic] round the bay, affords a most agreeable landscape. The houses being all painted white, pretty regularly built, and standing on a rising ground, raises one street above another, and heightens the scene from the water; to which the Governor's garden contributes much to beautify the town.

In the centre of the principal square, is a well built fountain, continually playing, which, in a warm climate, has a desirable cooling effect. There is but one church, which contains a few indifferent paintings.

The inhabitants are civil, but reserve, and the inquisition being on the island, spreads a gloomy distrust on the countenance of the people.

The troops are miserably cloathed, and poverty and superstition lords it wide. The wines of this place, from a late improvement in the vines, are equal to the second kind of Madeira, and I cannot pass over this subject without making honourable mention of the candour of Mr Rooney our wine merchant.

Here we completed our water from an acqueduct admirably constructed for the convenience of the shipping, and after receiving on board lemons, oranges, pomegranates, and bananas, with every variety of fruits and other refreshments with which this island most plentifully abounds, proceeded again on our voyage.

The fever that prevailed on our leaving England became now pretty general, and almost every man had it in turn, and as we approached the line many of the convalescents had a relapse, but the Lords of the Admirality, previous to our sailing, had supplied us with such unbounded liberality in every thing necessary for the preservation of the seamens health, that I may venture to say many lives were saved from their bounty, and I should be wanting in my duty to their Lordships, as well as the community, was I to pass over in silence the uncommon good effects we experienced from supplying the sick and convalescent with tea and sugar; this being the first time it has ever been introduced into his Majesty's service; but it is an article in life that has crept into such universal use, in all orders of society, that it needs no comment of mine to recommend it. It may, however, be easily conceived that it will be sought with more avidity by those whose aliment consists chiefly in animal food, and that always salt, and often of the worst kind. Their bread too is generally mixed with oatmeal, and of a hot drying nature. Scarcity of water is a calamity to which seafaring people are always subject; and it is an established fact, that a pint of tea will satiate thirst more than a quart of water. But when sickness takes place, a loathing of all animal food follows; then tea becomes their sole existence, and that which can be conveyed to them as natural food will be taken with pleasure, when any flip flop, given as drink, will be rejected with disgust. Suffice it to say, that Quarter-masters, and real good Seamen has ever been observed to be regular in cooking their little pot of tea or coffee, and in America seamen going long voyages, always make it an article in their agreement to be supplied with tea and sugar.

The air now becoming intolerably hot, and to evacuate the foul air from below where the people slept, had recourse to Mr White's new ventilator, but found little benefit from it; not from any fault in the machine, but from the crowded state of the ship, it was impossible to throw a current of air into those places where it was most wanted, but by the addition of a flexible leather tube, like a water engine, it might be rendered of the utmost importance to the service, as in Tenders press-holds, and in line of battle ships at sea, when the lower deck ports cannot be opened; where often the jail fever, and all the calamities that attend human nature, in crowded situations, are engendered, that might be entirely obviated by Mr White's ingenious machine. I should beg to recommend wheels to be substituted for legs to it, for its easier conveyance from one part of the ship to the other, and that he would sacrifice beauty to strength, as a slight mahogany jim crack is not well calculated to the severity of heat we are exposed to, in climates where it is most wanted.

There were now many water spouts about the ship, at which we fired several guns: the Thermometer fluctuated between seventy-nine and eighty, and without any thing worthy of remark, in the common occurrence of things at sea, on the twenty-eight of December saw the land of the Brazils, and in two

Part Two. Outward Bound on H.M.S. Pandora

days saluted the Fort at Rio Janiero with fifteen guns, which was immediately returned.

On our coming to an anchor, an officer came to acquaint the Captain, that a party of soldiers should be sent on board of us, agreeable to their custom, which was most peremptorily denied as inadmissible with the dignity of the British flag, nor would Captain Edwards go on shore to pay his respects to the Vice Roy, till that etiquete was settled, that his boat should not be boarded.

After the usual compliments were paid the Vice Roy, his suit of carriages were ordered to attend the British officers, and Monsieur le Font, the Surgeon General, who spoke English with ease and fluency, shewed us every mark of politeness and attention on the occasion, in carrying us through the principal streets, then visited the public gardens, built by the late Vice Roy, and laid out with much taste and expence. All the extremity of the garden is a fine Terrace which commands a view of the water, and is frequented by people of fashion, as their Grand Mall: at each end of the Terrace there is an octag-

The Duff anchored at Rio Janiero (Rio De Janeiro). This print of the harbor appeared in *A Missionary Voyage to the Southern Pacific Ocean, Performed in the Years 1796, 1797, 1798, in the Ship* Duff, published 1799.

onal built room, superbly furnished, where Merendas are sometimes given. On the pannels are painted the various productions and commerce of South America, representing the diamond fishery, the process of the indigo trade. The rice grounds and harvest, sugar plantation, South Sea whale fishery, &c. these were interspersed with views of the country, and the Quadrupedes that inhabit those parts. The ceilings contained all the variety, the one of the fish, the other of the fowl of that continent. The co[m]partments of the ceiling of the one room was enriched in shell work, with all the variegated shells of that country, and in the copartments are delineated all the variety of fish that the coast of South America produces. The other copartment is enriched with feathers and so inimitably blended as to produce the happiest effect. In this ceiling is painted all the birds and fowls of the country, in all their splendid elegance of plumage. The sofas and furniture are rich in the extreme: and in this elegant recess, an idle traveller may have an agreeable lounge, and at one view comprehend the whole natural history of this vast continent. In the centre of the terrace there is a Jet d'eau, in the form of a large palm-tree, made of copper, which at pleasure may be made to spout water from the extremity of all the leaves. This tree stands on a well disposed grotto, which rises from the gravel walk below, to the level of the terrace, and terminates the view of the principal walk. Near the foot of the grotto two large aligators, made of copper, are continually discharging water into a handsome bason of white marble, filled with gold and silver fishes.

There are fine orangeries, and lofty covered arbours, in different parts of the garden, capable of containing a thousand people. Here the cyprian nymphs hold their nocturnal revels; but intrigue is attended with great danger, as the stilletto is in general use, and assassination frequent, the men being of a jealous sanguinary turn, and the women fond of gallantry, who never appear in public unveiled. When Bouganvile,[33] the French circumnavigator called here, his chaplain was assassinated in an affray of that kind; but since that accident, orders were given that a commissioned officer should attend all foreign officers, and a soldier the privates; and all strangers, on landing, are conducted to the main guard for their escort. This answers a double purpose, as they are much afraid of strangers smugling or carrying money out of the country, under the mask of personal protection, every motion is watched and scrutinized, nor can you purchase any thing of a merchant, till he has settled with the officer of the police how much he shall exact for his goods; so you have always the satisfaction of being rob'd as the act directs.

The trade of this country is much cramped by the improper policy of the mother country; for although it abounds with every thing that the earth produces, wealth is far from being diffusive, and a spirit for revolt seems to prevail amongst them; but they were rather premature in the business, a conspiracy being detected whilst we were there, many of the first people in the country thrown into dungeons, a strong guard put over them, and all intercourse denied them. But in order to check that spirit of rebellion among the colonists, a regiment of black slaves is now embodied, who will be very ready to bear arms against their oppressive masters; but should a revolution in South America take place, which sooner or later must eventually happen, some of our South Sea discoveries would then prove an advantageous situation for a little British colony.

All public works are done here by slaves in chains, who perform a kind of plaintive melancholy dirge in recitative, to sooth their unavailing toil, which, with the accompanyment of the clanking of their irons, is the real voice of wo, and attunes the soul to sympathy and compassion, more than the most elaborate piece of music.

The troops are remarkably well cloathed, and in fine order, both infantry and cavalry; the horses are small, but spirited, and tournaments frequently performed as the favourite amusement of the inhabitants, as which the cavaliers display a wonderful share of address.

The town is large, built of stone, and the streets very regular; there are several handsome churches, monasteries, and nunneries, and contains about forty thousand inhabitants; but, like the old town of Edinburgh, each floor contains a distinct family, and of course liable to the same inconveniencies, cleanliness being none of its most shining virtues.

The officers of the army shewed us uncommon kindness, and made us some presents of red bird skins for the savages we were going amongst.

I cannot, in words, bestow sufficient panegyric on the laudable exertions of my worthy messmates, Lieutenants Corner and Hayward, for their unremitting zeal in procuring and nursing such plants as might be useful at Otaheitee or the islands we might discover.

We now took leave of our friends here, and it was with some regret, as it was bidding adieu to civilized life, for a very undetermined space of time. Lieutenant Hayward having finished his astronomical observations on shore, came on board with the time-keeper and instruments, and again proceeded on our voyage, on the morning of January 8, 1791. In running down the coast of the Brazils, saw several spermacæti whales, and vessels employed on that fishery, could it have been accomplished in the month of January, it was intended to take in a supply of water at New-Year's harbour, but the season was too far advanced. The weather now became cold, and the health of the people mended apace, passed by the straits of Magellan, and on the 31st of January saw Cape St Juan, Staten Island, and New Year's Island. The Thermometer was at 48 degrees. We were fortunate enough to weather the tempestuous regions of Cape Horn, without any thing remarkable happening, although late in the season.

The weather, as we advanced, became now exceedingly pleasant, and the many good things with which we were supplied, began to have a wonderful good effect on the health and strength of our convalescents. I here beg the reader's indulgence for a small digression on the health of the seamen, as it is a subject of much national importance, and those voyages the only test of what is found to succeed best, my duty leads me to the attempt, however unequal to the task:

It may be remarked, the sour Crout kept during the voyage, in the highest perfection, and was often eat as a sallad with vinegar, in preference to recent, cut vegetables from the shore. A cask of this grand antiscorbutic was kept open for the crew to eat as much of as they pleased; and I will venture to affirm, that it will answer every purpose that can be expected from the vegetable kingdom.

The Essence of Malt afforded a most delightful beverage, and, with the addition of a little hops, in the warmest climates, made as good strong beer as we could in England. We were likewise supplied with malt in grain, but should prefer the essence, as it is less liable to decay, and stows in much less room, which is a very valuable consideration in long voyages.

Cocoa we found great benefit from; it is much relished by the men, stows in little room, and affords great nourishment. At the close of the war in 1783, in the West Indies, men that had been the whole war on salt provisions, from a liberal use of the cocoa, got fat and strong, and in the Agamemnon we had five hundred men who had served most of the war on salt provisions; but after the cocoa was introduced, we had not a sick man on board till the day she was paid off. Indeed it is the only article of nourishment in sea victualling; for what can in reason be expected from beef or pork after it has been salted a year or two?

Wheat we found answer extremely well, rough ground it in a mill occasionally as we wanted it, and with the addition of a little brown sugar, it made a pleasant nourishing diet, of which the men were extremely fond. Another great advantage attending it, that it does not require half the quantity of water that pease do.

Soft bread was found extremely beneficial to the sick and convalescent, and we availed ourselves of every opportunity of baking for half the complement at a time. As the flour keeps so much longer sound than biscuit, it may be needless to remark its superior advantages; besides, it is not liable to be damaged by water or otherwise, so much as bread, as a crust forms outside, which protects the rest. In point of stowage it likewise is preferable.

As the fate of every expedition of this kind depends much on the exertion of the subordinate departments of office, the thanks of every individual in the Pandora is due to Mr Cherry, for his uncommon attention to the victualling.

The dividing the people into three watches had a double good effect, as it gave them longer time to sleep, and dry themselves before they turned in; and

Part Two. Outward Bound on H.M.S. Pandora

as most of our crew consisted of landsmen, the fewer people being on deck at a time, rendered it necessary to exert themselves more in learning their duty.

The air became now temperate, mild, and agreeable; but unfortunately we sprung a leak in the after part of the ship, which reached the bread room, and damaged much of it, as one thousand five hundred and fifteen pounds were thrown over-board, and a great deal much injured, that we kept for feeding the cattle. Many blue Peterals were seen flying about, and on the 4th of March saw Easter Island. We now set the forge to work, and the armourers were busily employed in making knives and iron work to trade with the savages. On the 16th we discovered a Lagoon Island of about three or four miles extent; it was well wooded, but had no inhabitants, and was named Ducie's Island in honour of Lord Ducie.

On the 17th we discovered another Island, about five or six miles long, with a great many trees on it, but was not inhabited: this was called Lord Hood's Island.

On the 19th we discovered an Island of the same description as the former, which was named Carrisfort Island, in honour of Lord Carrisfort.

On the 22d passed Maitea, and on the morning of the 23d of March anchored in Matavy bay, in the Island of Otaheety....

Part Three

Capturing the Mutineers

From Captain Edwards' Report

Before we Anchored in Mativy Bay Jos^h. Coleman Armourer of the Bounty and several of the Natives came onboard, from whom I learnt that Christian the Pirate had Landed and left sixteen of his Men on the Island, some of whom were then at Matavy and some had Sailed from thence the Morning before our arrival (in a Schooner they had built) for Papara a distant part of the Island; to join other of the Pirates that were settled at that Place, and that Churchill Master at Arms had been Murdered by Math^w. Thompson and that Mathw Thompson was killed by the Natives and offered as a sacrifice on their Alters for the Murder of Churchill whom they had made a Cheif.

Geo. Stewart & Peter Heywood Mids^n. of the Bounty came on board the Pandora soon after she came to an Anchor, and I had also information that Rich^d. Skinner was at Matavy. I desired Poen an Inferior Cheif (who in the absence of the Otoo was the Principal Person in the district) to bring him onboard. The Chief went onshore for the purpose and soon after he returned again, and informed me that Skinner was coming onboard, before Night he did come onboard but whether it was in consequence of the Chiefs directions or of his own accord I am at a loss to say.

As soon as the Ship was Moored the Pinnace & Launch were got ready & sent under the direction of Lieuts. Corner & Hayward in pursuit of the Pirates & Schooner in hopes of getting hold of them before they could get information of our arrival, and Ordiddee a Native of Bolabola and who had been with Capt. Cook, &c.—went with them as a guide.

The Boats were discovered by the Pirates before they had arrived at the place where those People had Landed, & they immediately embarked in their Schooner & put to Sea, and she was Chased the remainder of the day by our Boats, but it blowing fresh she out Sailed them and the Boats returned to the Ship.

Jno. Brown the Person left at Otaheite by Mr. Cox of the Mercury and from whom their Lordships supposed I might get some useful information, had been under the Necessity for his own safety to associate with the Pirates but he took the opportunity to leave them when they were about to embark in the Schooner & put to Sea[. H]e informed me that they had very little Water or Provisions onboard or Vessels to hold any, & of Course could not keep the Sea long. I entered Brown [on] the Ships Books as part of the Complement & found him very intelligent & useful in the different capacities of a guide a Soldier & a Seaman. I employ'd different people to look out for & to give me information on their Landing either on this or the Neighbouring Islands.

On the 26th in the Evening sent the Pinnace to Edee by desire of the Old Otoo or King to bring him onboard the Pandora. Early on the Morning of the 27th had information that the Pirates were return'd with the Schooner to Papara & that they were Landed & retired to the Mountains to endeavour to conceal & defend themselves. I immediately sent Lieut. Corner with 26 Men in the Launch to Papara to Pursue them. At Night the Otoo his two Queens & suit came onboard in the Pinnace and slept onboard the Pandora and which they afterwards frequently did. The next Morning Lieut. Hayward was sent with a party in the Pinnace to join the party in the Launch at Papara.

I found the Otoo ready to furnish me with guides and to give me any other Assistance in his power but he had very little authority or influence in that part of the Island where the Pirates had taken refuge & even his right to the Sovereignty of the Eastern part of the Island had been recently disputed by Tamarie one of the Royal family. Under these circumstances I conceived the taking [of] Otoo and the other Cheifs attached to his interest into custody would alarm the faithful part of his subjects and oporate to our disadvantage. I therefore satisfied my self with the Assistance he offered and had in his power to give me and I found means at different times to convey presents to Tamarie (and invited him to come on board which he promised to do but never fulfilled his promise) and convinced him I had it in my power to lay his Country waste which I Imagined would be sufficient at least to make him withhold that support he hitherto through policy had occasionally given to the Pirates in order to draw them to his interest & strengthen his own party against the Otoo.

I probably might have had it in my power to have taken and secured the Person of Tamarie but I was apprehensive that such an attempt might irritate the Natives Attached to his interest and induce them to act hostilely against our party at a time the Ship was at too great a distance to afford them timely & necessary assistance in case of such an event, and I adopted the milder method for that reason, and from a perswasion that our business would be brought to a conclusion at less risque and in less time by that means.

The Yawl was sent to Papara with spare hands to bring back the Launch which was wanted to Water the Ship and on the 29th. the Launch returned to the Ship with James Morrison, Charles Norman, & Thos. Ellison, belonging to the Bounty & who had been made prisoners at Papara. On the 1st. of April the Pinnace returned with the detachment from Papara and brought with them the Pirate Schooner which they had taken there. The Natives had deserted the place & I had information that the six remaining Pirates had fled to the Mountains.

On the 5th I sent Lieut. Hayard [sic] with 25 men in the Schooner & Yawl to Papara. The Old Otoo and several of the Chiefs &c. went with him[.] On the 7th. in the Morning Lieut. Corner was Landed with 16 Men at Point Venus in order to March round to the back of the Mountains in which the Pirates had retreated to coopporate with the Party sent to Papara. Oripia the Otoo's Brother and a party of Natives went with him as guides & to carry the Provisions &c. On the 9th Lieut. Hayward returned with the Schooner & Yawl & brought with him Henry Hillbrant, Thos. M'Intosh, Thos. Burkitt, Jnº. Millward, Jnº. Sumner and Wm. Muspratt—the six remaining Pirates belonging to the Bounty. They had quitted the Mountains and had got down near the Sea Shore when they were discovered by our party on the opposite side of a River. They submitted on being summoned to lay down their Arms. Lieut. Corner with his party Marched across the Mountains to Papara and a Boat was sent for them there & they returned onboard again on the 13th in the Afternoon. I put the Pirates into a Round house which I built on the after part of the Quarter Deck for their more effectual security airy and healthy situation & to separate them from & to prevent their having communication with or to croud & incommode the Ships Company.

Contrary to my expectation the Water we got at the usual place at Point Venus turned out very bad & on searching for better most Excellent Water was found issuing out of a Rock in a little bay to the Southward of one Tree Hill; I mention this circumstance because it may be of importance to be known to other Ships that may hereafter touch at that Island.

The Natives had in their Possession a Bower Anchor belonging to the Bounty which that ship had left in the Bay and I took it onboard the Pandora and made them a Handsome present by way of Salvage & as a reward for their ingenuity in Weighing it with materials so ill calculated for the purpose.

I learnt from different people and from Journals kept onboard the Bounty which were found in the Chests of the Pirates at Otaheite, that after Lieut. Bligh and the people with him were turned a drift in the Launch the Pirates proceeded with the Ship to the Island of Toobouai in Lat. 20°. 13' S°. and Long. 149°. 35' W^r. where they Anchored on the 25th of May 1789.[34] Before their arrival there they threw the greatest part of the Bread fruit Plants over board and the Property of the Officers & people that were turned out of the Ship was divided amongst those who remained onboard her; and the

Royals & some other small Sails were cut up and disposed of in the same manner.

Notwithstanding they met with some opposition from the Natives they intended to settle at this Island but after some time they perceived they were in want of several things Necessary for a settlement & which was the cause of disagreements & quarrels amongst themselves. At last they came to a resolution to go to Otaheite to get such of the Things wanted as could be procured there and in consequence of that resolution they sailed from Toobouai on the latter end of the Month and arrived at Otaheite on the sixth of June. The Otoo & other Natives were very inquisitive & desirous to know what was become of Lieut. Bligh and the other absentees and the Bread fruit Plants &c. They deceived them by saying that they had fallen in with Captain Cook at an Island he had lately discovered called Whytootackee and where he intended to settle and that the Plants were Landed & planted there, and that Lt. Bligh & the other absentees were detained to assist Capt. Cook in the business he had in hand & that he had appointed Christian Captain of the Bounty & order'd him to go to Otaheite for an additional supply of Hogs, Goats, fowls Bread fruit Plants &c. These humane Islanders were imposed upon by this Artful Story and they were so rejoiced to hear that their Old Friend Capt. Cook was alive and so near them, that they used every means in their power to procure the things that were wanted, that in the course of a few days the Bounty took onboard 312 Hogs, 38 Goats, 8 doz. of fowls, a Bull & a cow and a quantity of bread fruit plants &c. They also took with them 9 Women 8 Men & 7 boys with these supplies they Sailed from Otaheite on the 19th June and arrived again at Toobouai on the 26th. They landed the live stock on the Keys that were near the Harbour Lighten'd the Ship and wharped her up the Harbour into 2½ fath^{ms}. water opposite [the] place where they intended to build a Fort. On this Occasion their spare Masts Yards & Booms were got out & Moored but they afterward broke adrift and were lost. On the 9th July they began to build the fort, its dimensions 50 Yards Square. These Villains had frequent quarrels amongst themselves which at last carried to such a length that no order was observed amongst them and by the 30th of August the Work at the fort was discontinued. They had also almost continual disputes and skirmishes with the Natives which were generally brought on by their own Violence and depredations.

Christian perceiving that he had lost his authority & that nothing more could be done desired them to consult together and consider what step would be the most advisable to take and that he would put into Execution the Opinion that was supported by the most Votes. After long consultations it was at last determined that the Scheme of settling at Toobouai should be given up, and that the Ship should be taken to Otaheite where those who chose to go onshore should be at liberty to do so, and that those who remained by the

Ship take her away to whatever place they should think fit. In consequence of this final determination preparations were made for the purpose & they Sailed from Toobouai on the 15th and arrived at Matavy Bay Otaheite, on the 20th Sept. 1789.

The Bull which they took from Otaheite died on its Passage to Toobouai, & they killed the cow before they left that Island, yet notwithstanding this and the depredations they committed there, the Natives will derive considerable advantage from their Visits as Several Hogs, Goats, fowls, & other Things of their introduction were left behind.

These 16 men mentioned before were Landed at Otaheite Viz^t. Jos^h. Coleman, Peter Heywood, Geo. Stewart, Rich^d. Skinner, Mich^l. Burn, Jas. Morrison, Chas. Norman, Thos. Ellison, Hen^y. Hilbrant, Jno. Sumner, Thos. M'Intosh, Wm. Muspratt, Thos. Burket, & Jno. Wilward. [Millward]. These 14 were made Prisoners by my people & Chas. Churchill & Matth^w. Thompson were Murdered at that Island. Previous to these peoples being put on shore the small arms, powder, Canvas, & the small stores belonging to the Ship were equally divided amongst the whole Crew[.] After building the Schooner six of those people actually sailed in her for the East Indies but meeting with bad Weather (& suspecting the abilities of Morrison whom they had chosen to be their Captain) to Navigate her there, they returned again to Otaheite. The Bounty Saild from Otaheite on the Night between the 21st & 22nd of Sept 1789 and was seen in the Morning to the NW of Point Venus.

Fletcher Christian, Edwd. Young, Math^w. Quintall, Wm: McKoy, Alex^r. Smith, Jno. Williams, Isaac Martin, Wm. Brown & Jno. Mills went away in the Ship & they also took with them several Natives of these Islands both Men & Women, but I could not exactly learn their numbers only that they had onboard a few more Women than white Men, a deficiency of whom had formerly been one of their grievances and a principal cause of their quarrels.

From George Hamilton, A Voyage Round the World in His Majesty's Frigate Pandora

In the dawn of the morning, a native immediately, on seing us, paddled off in his canoe, and came on board, who shewed expressions of joy to a degree of madness, on embracing and saluting us, by whom we learnt that several of the mutineers were on the island; but that Mr. Christian and nine men had left Otaheitee long since, in the Bounty, and amused the natives, by telling them Captain Bligh had gone to settle at Whytutakee, and that Captain Cook was living there. Language cannot express his surprise on Lieutenant Hayward's being introduced to him, who had been purposely concealed.

At eleven in the forenoon the Launch and Pinnance was dispatched with

Lieutenants Corner and Hayward, and twenty-six men, to the north west part of the island, in quest of the mutineers. Immediately on our arrival Joseph Coleman, the armourer of the Bounty, came on board, and a little after the two midshipmen belonging to the Bounty; at three Richard Skinner came off, and on the 25th the boats returned, after chasing the mutineers on shore, and taking possession of their boat. As they had taken to the heights, and claimed the protection of Tamatrah, a great chief in Papara, who was the proper king of Otaheitee, the present family of Ottoo being usurpers, and who intended, had we not arrived with the assistance of the Bounty's people, to have disputed the point with Ottoo.

On the twenty-seventh we sent the Pinnance with a present of a bottle of rum to king Ottoo, who was with his two queens at Tiaraboo, requesting the honour of his company, but the bottle of rum removed all scruples, and next day the royal family paid us a visit, and in his suit came Oedidy, a chief particularly noticed by Captain Cook.

On the first visit they make it a point of honour of accepting of no present; but they make sufficient amends for that, by introducing a numerous train of dependents afterwards, to obtain presents.

The King is a tall handsome looking man, about six feet three inches high, good natured, and affable in his manners. His principal queen, Edea, is a robust looking course woman, about thirty, and was extremely solicitous in learning and adopting our customs, and on hearing our English ladies drank tea, became very fond of it. The other queen, or concubine, named Alredy, is a pretty young creature, about sixteen years of age: they all three sleep together, and live in the most perfect harmony.

A detachment of men were immediately ordered, under the command of Lieutenant Corner, to march across the country, and if possible to get between the mountains and the mutineers; this gentleman was extremely well calculated for an expedition of this kind, having, in the early part of his life, bore a commission in the land service, and next morning they landed on Point Venus, attended by the principal chiefs as conductors, and a number of the common people to assist in carrying the amunition over the heights: what rendered their assistance more necessary, was their having to cross a rapid cataract, or river, which came down from the mountains, and formed so many curves. They had to ford it sixteen times in the course of their journey, which gave evident proofs of the superior strength of the natives over the English seamen. The former went over with ease, where the sailors could not stem the rapidity of the torrent without their help. They were, however, forced to send to the ship for ropes and tackles to gain some heights which were otherwise inaccessable.

On the party coming to a rest, the Lieutenant expressed a wish to one of the natives for something to eat, who told him he might be supplied with plenty of victuals ready dressed; he immediately ran to a temple, or place of worship, where meat was regularly served to their god, and came running with a roasted pig, that had been presented that day. This striking instance of impiety rather startled the Lieutenant, which the other easily got over, by saying there was more left than the god could eat.

It was with much difficulty they could restrain the natives from committing depradations on the Cava grounds of the upper districts, as they were on the eve of a war with them respecting the hereditary right of the crown.{.}

The party now arrived at the residence of a great chief, who received them with much hospitality and kindness; and after refreshing them with plenty of meat and drink, carried the officer to visit the Morai of the dead chief, his father. Mr Corner judging it necessary, by every mark of attention, to gain the good graces of this great man, ordered his party to draw up, and fire three vollies over the deceased, who was brought out in his best new cloaths, on the occasion; but the burning cartridge from one of the muskets, unfortunately set fire to the paper cloaths of the dead chief. This unlucky disaster threw the son into the greatest perplexity, as agreeable to their laws, should the corpse of his father be stolen away, or otherwise destroyed, he forfeits his title and estate, and it descends to the next heir.

There was at the same time a party embarked by water, under the command of Lieutenant Hayward, who took with him some of the principal chiefs, amongst whom was Oedidy, before mentioned by Captain Cook, who went a voyage with him, but fell into disrepute amongst them, from affirming he had seen water in a solid form; alluding to the ice. He also took with him one Brown, an Englishman, that had been left on shore by an American vessel that had called there, for being troublesome on board: but otherwise a keen, penetrating, active fellow, who rendered many eminent services, both in this expedition and the subsequent part of the voyage. He had lived upwards of twelve months amongst the natives, adopted perfectly their manners and customs, even to the eating of raw fish, and dipping his roast pork into a cocoanut shell of salt water, according to their manner, as substitute for salt. He likewise avoided all intercourse and communication with the Bounty's people, by which means necessity forced him to gain a pretty competent knowledge of their language; and from natural complexion was much darker than any of the natives.

Captain Edwards had taken every possible means of gaining the friendship of Tamarrah, the great prince of the upper district, by sending him very liberal presents, which effectually brought him over to our interest. The mutineers were now cut off from every hope of resource, the natives were harrassing them behind, and Mr Hayward and his party advancing in front; under cover of night they had taken shelter in a hut in the woods, but were discovered by Brown, who creeping up to the place where they were asleep, distinguished them from the natives by feeling their toes; as people unaccustomed to wear shoes are easily discovered from the spread of their toes. Next day Mr Hayward attacked them, but they grounded their arms without opposition; their hands were bound behind their back and sent down to the boat under a strong guard.

During the whole business there was only two natives killed, one was shot in the dusk of the evening, two nights before the people surrendered, by one of the centinels, who had his musket twice beat out of his hand, from the natives pelting our party with large stones; but the instant he was shot, some of his friends rushed in and carried off the corpse.

The other native was shot by the mutineers, when attacked by the natives they took to a river; a stone being thrown by one of the natives at the wife, or woman, of one of the mutineers, enraged him so much, that he immediately shot the offender.

A prison was built, for their accommodation, on the quarter deck, that they might be secure, and apart from our ship's company; and that it might have every advantage of a free circulation of air, which rendered it the most desirable place in the ship. Orders were likewise given that they should be victualled, in every respect, in the same as the ship's company, both in meat, liquor, and all the extra indulgencies, with which we were so liberally supplied, notwithstanding the established laws of the service, which restricts prisoners to two thirds allowance: but Captain Edwards very humanely commisserated with their unhappy and inevitable length of confinement. Oripai, the king's brother, a discerning, sensible, and intelligent chief, discovered a conspiracy amongst the natives on shore to cut our cables should it come to blow hard from the sea. This was more to be dreaded, as many of the prisoners were married to the most respectable chiefs daughters in the district opposite to where we lay at anchor; in particular one, who took the name of Stewart, a man of great possession in landed property, near Matavy Bay: a gentleman of that name belonging to the Bounty, having married his daughter, and he, as his friend and father-in-law, agreeable to their custom, took his name.

Ottoo the king, his two brothers, and all the principal chiefs, appeared extremely anxious for our safety; and after the prisoners were on board, kept watch during the night; were always keeping a sharp look out upon our cables, and continually spurring the centinels to be careful in their duty. The prisoners wives visited the ship daily, and brought their children, who were permitted to be carried to their unhappy fathers. To see the poor captives in irons, weeping over their tender offspring, was too moving a scene for any feeling heart. Their wives bought them ample supplies of every delicacy that the country afforded while we lay there, and behaved with the greatest fidelity and affection to them.

Mr. Peter Heywood to Mrs. [Elizabeth] Heywood.

Batavia, November 20th, 1791.

To be brief—living there till the latter End of March 1791, on the 26th, H.M.S. *Pandora* arrived, and scarce came to an Anchor when my Messmate and I went aboard and made ourselves and the Manner of our being on the Island known to Captain Edwards, the Commander; and knowing from one of the Natives, who had been off in a Canoe, that our former Messmate Mr. Hayward (now promoted to the Rank of Lieutenant) was aboard, we asked for him, supposing he might prove our Assertions; but he, like all other worldlings when raised a little in Life, received us very coolly and pretended Ignorance of our Affairs; yet formerly he and I were bound in brotherly Friendship—But! So that Appearances being so much against us, we were ordered in Irons and looked upon—infernal words!—as piratical Villains and treated in the most indignant Manner. Such a severe Rebuff as this, to a Person unused to Troubles, would perhaps have been insupportable; but by me, who had now been long inured to the Frowns of Fortune, and being supported by an inward Consciousness of not deserving it, it was received with the greatest Composure, and a full Determination to bear it with Patience; ascribing it to the corrective Hand of an allgracious Providence, and fully convinced that Adversity is the Lot of Man, sent to wean him from these transient Scenes here below, and fix his Hopes on Joys more permanent, lest by a too long and uninterrupted round at Good Fortune he should forget the frailty of his Nature, and almost doubt the Existence of a supreme and omnipotent Being. Had my Confinement alone been my only Misfortune, I could patiently have resigned myself to it, but one Evil seldom comes unaccompanied. Alas! I was informed of the greatest Misfortune that could have befallen me, which was the Death of the most indulgent of Fathers, which I naturally supposed to have been hastened by Mr. Bligh's ungenerous Account of my Conduct. This Thought made me truly wretched. I had certainly been overpowered by my Grief, had not Mr. Hayward again assured me that he had paid the Debt of Nature before the Arrival of the *Bounty*'s Fate in England, and that he had the News by Letter from my ever dearest and much beloved Sister Nessy, which made me somewhat easier; so I endeavoured to bear it, as a Man ought so heavy a Misfortune. Yet I have still my Fears on my dear Mother's Account lest such an Account of me, when added to the recent Affliction you must then labour under for so severe a Loss, might (should you be so credulous enough to believe so hardly of me) overpower your Spirits and Constitution, and make your Grief too poignant and burdensome for Life. But may God of his infinite Mercy have ordered otherwise! and that this may find you and all my Brothers and Sisters as well as I could wish, and have the desired Effect of rooting in you and all a Belief of my injured Innocence, and eradicate your Displeasure (if it ever subsisted) at my suspected Behaviour, the Thoughts of which make me most unhappy!

What I have suffered I have not Power to describe, but, though they are great, yet I thank God for enabling me to bear them without repining! I endeavour to qualify my Affliction with these three Considerations: first my Innocence, not deserving them, second, that they cannot last long, and third, that the Change may be for the better. The first improves my Hopes, the second my Patience, and the third my Courage, and makes me thankful to God for them. I am young in Years, but old in what the World calls Adversity, and it has had such an Effect upon me as to make me consider it as the most beneficial Incident that could have occurred to me at my Years. It has made me acquainted with three Things, which are little known, and as little believed by any but those who have felt their Effects—first, the Villainy and Censoriousness of Mankind, second, the Futility of all human Hopes, and third, the Enjoyment of being content in whatever Station it pleases Providence to place me in. In short, it has made [me] more of a Philosopher than many Years of a Life spent in Ease and Pleasure could have done. Should you receive this, do assure my ever honored and much respected Friend Mr. Betham of my Innocence of the Crime which I imagine has been laid to my Charge. His disinterested Kindness to me is deeply rooted in my Mind. Make him acquainted with the Reason of my remaining in the Ship. Perhaps his Assistance in interceding with his Son in Law Mr. Bligh in my Behalf might undeceive him in his groundless ill Opinion of me, and prevent his proceeding to great Lengths against me at my approaching Trial. If you should likewise apply to my Uncle Pasley and Mr. Heywood of Plymouth, their timely Aid and friendly Advice might be the Means of rescuing me from an ignominious Lot! As they will no doubt proceed to the greatest Lengths against me (being the only surviving Officer), and being more inclined to believe a prior Story, all that can be said to confute it will be looked upon as mere falsity and Invention, which, should it be my unhappy Case, and they should be resolved upon my Destruction as an Example to Futurity, may God enable me to bear my Fate with the Fortitude of a Man, conscious that Misfortune, not any Misconduct of mine, can have brought it upon me, and assured that my God and my Conscience can assert my Innocence. Yet, why should I despond—I have, I hope, still a Friend in that Provi-

This explicit rendering of the interior of "Pandora's Box" reveals how the captured *Bounty* crew were shackled by wrist and ankle, enduring five months of imprisonment in grueling conditions. According to prisoner Peter Heywood "[We] were treated with great Rigour, not being allowed ever to get out of this Place, and being obliged to eat, drink, sleep, and obey the Calls of Nature here" (© Queensland Museum, Robert Allen).

dence which has preserved me in many greater Dangers, and will always protect those who are deserving of it, and on whom alone I now depend for Safety. These are the sole Considerations which have enabled me to make myself easy and content under my past Misfortunes, the Relation of which I shall now continue up to the present Time.

Twelve more of the People who were at 'Taheite having delivered themselves up, there was a sort of Prison built upon the after Part of the Quarter Deck, into which we were all put in close Confinement, with both Legs and both Hands in Irons, and were treated with great Rigour, not being allowed ever to get out of this Place, and being obliged to eat, drink, sleep, and obey the Calls of Nature here you may form some Idea of the disagreeable Situation I must have been in (unable to help myself, being deprived of the use of both my Legs and Hands), but by no means adequate to the Reality, such as I am unable to represent…

From The Journal of James Morrison, Boatswain's Mate of the Bounty

We went on shore to Tommarees to Breakfast but were scarcely sat down when a Friend of Heeteheetes arrived in haste, telling us that a ship had anchord at Maatavye since we had left it, that those who we had left there were gone on board, and that the Boats Mand and Armd were then at Atahooroo in their Way after us, that Heete-heete who was their Pilot had sent him to give us Notice that we might know how to act. No time was now to be lost in fixing on the best plan, and it was agreed to avoid seeing the Boats: and for this reason we got on board leaving Brown & Byrn on shore, and Got under way stood out with a fresh Breeze at E S E standing to the Southward on a Wind.—we hoped by keeping out of sight of the Boats to reach the Ship and go on board of our own accord, hoping thereby to have better treatment then if we stayd to be made prisoners, and Heete-heetes Messenger had given us a very unfavourable account of the Treatment of those who went on board from Maatavye.

When we were about a league from the land we saw two sail to leeward, but could not disern whether they were Boats or Canoes, but as we left them apace we thought they could be no other then Fishing Canoes. Soon after noon we lost sight of them, and at 4 oClock we hove about & stood in, but it was Sunday the 27th before we could fetch in, owing to the Contrary winds & light airs which prevailed.

When we Anchord we were informd that Mr. Hayward, formerly of the Bounty, was Officer of one of the Boats, which proved to be the same we had seen, who finding they were not like to come up with the Chase had returned to the ship; we also learnt that Byrn had gone to the Ship and Brown having plunder'd Burketts house of all that he could, was gone on board also.

Tommaree, seeing Brown seizing on all that he could find, had sent evry thing back into the Mountains where Burkett, Sumner, Muspratt, Heildbrandt, McIntosh & Millward, went after them, leaving Norman, Ellison and Myself to take Care of the Vessel; in the Mean time I went on shore to get some Cocoa Nuts & some provisions dressd, leaving Norman and Ellison on board, and as the surf run high on the Beach I took no arms with me, when I left the Vessel, when I went to Tommaree he promised that I should have what I wanted Imediately. I told Him that we must go to the Ship, when he said 'if you do Hayward will kill you for He is very angry.' He ordered some hands to carry off Cocoa Nuts and in the Mean time pressd me to stay with him, saying 'if you will go into the Mountains they will never be able to find you'; but I still denyd him; telling him that I must go to the ship. He then upbraided me with deceiving him, and told me that I should not go, and at the same instant I observed several of the Natives on board the Schooner (where they had gone by Tommarees order and under pretence of carrying Cocoa Nuts on board) had taken the Opportunity of Seizing Norman and Ellison and throwing them overboard. I then begd Tommaree to prevent them from being hurted, when he told me that there was no fear of them, and in a few minutes after they landed and were Conducted to Me amidst a Thousand or More of the Natives, when they Pourd so fast on board the Schooner that they bore her down on one side and she rolld the most of them overboard; however they soon stripd her of evry thing that they could remove and brought the things on shore, unbending the Sails & unreeving the rigging which they brought away with them.

We askd Tommaree what was the Meaning of this Treatment, and seeing nothing of our Companions and being unarmed ourselves we hardly knew what to think of our situation; he told us it was because we wanted to leave Him, and told us we must go and secure ourselves in the Mountains and keep away from the Ship and we should have our arms and evry thing restored, and he would make good all our damages. We still refused; when he said 'then I'll make you go,' and his men Seized us and was proceeding in land with us when we begd of Tommaree to let us see some of our Shipmates before we went, which he agreed to & a Guard was placed over us, till he should return. We were conducted to the house of Tayreehamoedooa where we had provisions prepared in abundance. We staid here all Night, and next day, When we proposed to make our escape, and a Trusty friend who had lived with me all the time I had been on the Island, being one of Poenos Men, found us out and promised to have a Canoe ready by Midnight to carry us to Maatavye, where he said that Poeno waited with impatience to see us. As soon as it was night, he took his station on the Beach, and about 10 oClock brought Brown into the House; we asked him if he had any arms, when he produced a Pistol which he said he had brought from the Ship with two hatchets & a knife, these He delivered into Normans hands, and asked us what we meant to do, & where the rest were, to which we answerd that we had not seen the others since they landed and we were going to the Ship and askd Him the Name of the Ship & her Commander; but the only account he could give was that she was an English Ship of War and Could inform us No farther. He also Produced a Bottle with some hollands Geneva of which he offered each a Dram, but the smell proved sufficient for Me and the other two drank but sparingly. Brown told us that He had been Landed at the North Side of the Isthmus by the Ships Boat of which Mr. Hayward had Command, and was sent to Papaara with presents for Tommare, but had not seen him, he said he had been beset near the Morai and narrowly escaped being Killd, his Pistol being wet would not fire, and was forced to shelter himself in the thick Brush near the Morai, and was proceeding to return to the Ship when he was met on the Beach by our Man.

The Canoe being ready we armd, Norman & Myself with a hatchet each Ellison the large Knife, and left the Pistol with Brown, who fresh Primed it, & we set forward; having got to the Canoe without interuption we got in and paddled to Attahooroo, landing about 6 Miles from Papaara on a sandy Beach, which being white was of some help to us in Travelling; here we left the Canoe and proceeded alongshore for 12 or 14 Miles and reachd Pohooatayas House at Tyetabboo about 4 in the Morning of the 29th. Here we found a launch at anchor near the beach, and some Canoes hauld up near the House. We haild the boat but received no answer; those on board being all fast a sleep, as were those who were on shore in the Canoes. On Enquirey we found that the Canoes belong'd to Areepaeea, who was Here with them, and the Officer Commanding the Boat was Mr. Robert Cornor (Second Lieut of His Majestys Ship Pandora Captain Edwards) who being asleep in one of the Canoes we waked him and delivered our selves up to Him, telling Him who we were, and delivering the Hatchets to Brown when he came up, also the Pistol and amunition which he had given to Norman by the Way.

Having informed Mr. Cornor where the Schooner was, and what had happend to us, he left us in the Launch with Mr. Rickards, Masters Mate of the Ship, and Six Men, and with 18 more he set out (as soon as daylight enabled him to proceed) by land for Papaara, taking Brown with him, we remain'd here till two in the afternoon when Mr. Hayward (who we found was Third Lieutenant of the Ship) arrived with the Pinnace and 20 Men Armd, and by his orders we had our hands tyed and Mr. Rickards being ordered into the Pinnace, Mr. Sevill a Midshipman was put on board the Launch & ordered to proceed to the Ship then 25 or 30 miles distant. Mr. Hayward askd us no other question but where the others were, which we could not answer not knowing ourselves. We parted from the Pinnace about 3 oClock, and during the Passage up, Mr. Sevill gave each of us half a Pint of Wine and from Him we learnt the Fate of the Bountys Launch, and he also informd us that

Lieut. Bligh was made Post Captain. He also enquired what was become of the Bounty and who was in her, which we answerd to the best of our knowledge, and we reach'd the Ship at 9 oClock when we were handed on board and put both legs In Irons, under the Half Deck, after which our hands were cast loose; there being no Marines, two Seamen & a Midshipman were posted over us with Pistols & bayonets.

Here we found in Irons Geo. Stuart, Peter Heywood, Josh. Coleman, Richd. Skinner, & Michl. Byrn, who informd us that Handcuffs were Making by the Armourer which were next day put on, and orders Given to the Centinals not to suffer any of the Natives to speak to us, and to shoot the first Man that spoke to another in the Taheite Language. We remaind under the Half Deck some days, during which time we had full allowance of evry thing but grog, which we did not then want, having plenty of Cocoa Nuts provided for us by our friends, who were not sufferd to speak or look at us, any who lookd pitifully toward us were ordered out of the Ship.

In the Meantime a hammock was given to each to spread under us and a shirt & Trowsers given to each of us but these were of no use as we could not get them on and off, our Irons being Clenchd fast. The Carpenters were now set to work to erect a kind of Poop on the Quarter Deck for our reception.

On the 9th of April the Schooner was brought to the Ship by Mr. Hayward, and in her came Thos. Burkett, Jno. Sumner, Thos. McIntosh, Willm. Muspratt, Jno. Millward, & Henry Heildbrand who were Iron'd Hand and foot in the Same manner as we were as soon as they came on board.

The Poop or Roundhouse being finishd we were Conveyd into it and put in Irons as before. This Place we Stiled Pandoras Box, the entrance being a Scuttle on the top of 18 or 20 inches Square, Secured by a bolt on the top thro' the Coamings, two Scuttles of nine inches square in the Bulk head for air with Iron Grates, and the Stern ports bar'd inside and out with Iron; the Centrys were placed on the top while the Midshipman walkd aCross [sic] by the Bulk head. The length of this Box was 11 feet upon deck and 18 wide at the Bulk head, and here no person was suffered to speak to us but the Master at Arms, and His orders were not to speak to us on any score but that of our provisions.

The Heat of the place when it was calm was so intense that the Sweat frequently ran in Streams to the Scuppers, and produced Maggots in a short time; the Hammocks being dirty when we got them, we found stored with Vermin of another kind, which we had no Method of erradicating but by lying on the Plank; and tho our Freinds would have supplyd us with plenty of Cloth they were not permitted to do it, and our only remedy was to lay Naked,—these troublesome Neighbours and the two necessary tubbs which were Constantly kept in the place helpd to render our situation truely disagreeable.

During the time we staid, the Weomen with whom we had cohabited on the Island Came frequently under the Stern (bringing their Children of

> 1791
> April
>
> On the 9th of April the Schooner was brought to the Ship by Mr. Hayward, and in her came Thos. Burkett, Jno. Sumner Thos. McIntosh, Willm. Muspratt, Jno. Millward, & Henry Hildbrandt who were Iron'd Hand and foot in the Same Manner as we were as soon as they came on board.
>
> The Poop or Roundhouse being finished we were convey'd into it and put in Irons as before. This Place we Stiled Pandora's Box the entrance being a Scuttle on the top of 18 or 20 inches Square, Secured by a bolt on the top thro' the Coamings, two Scuttles of nine inches Square in the Bulk head for air with Iron Grates, and the Stern ports bar'd inside and out with Iron. The Centrys were placed on the top while the Midshipman walked across by the Bulkhead. The length of this Box was 11 feet upon deck and 18 wide at the Bulk head; and here no person was suffered to speak to us but the Master at Arms, and his Orders were not to speak to us on any Score but that of our provisions —
>
> The Heat of the Place when it was calm was so intense that the Sweat frequently ran in Streams to the Scuppers, and produced Maggots in a short time; The Hammocks being dirty when we got them, we found stored with vermin of another kind, which we had no Method of erradicating but by lying on the Plank; and tho our friends would have supply'd us with plenty of Cloth they were not permitted to do it, and our only remedy was to lay Naked.— These troublesom Neighbours and the two

Manuscript Leaf No. 181 of James Morrison's *Journal* describes the arrival of the captured *Bounty* crew in Matavy Bay, Tahiti, and the horrors of "Pandora's Box" (courtesy State Library of New South Wales).

which there were 6 born, Four Girls & two Boys, & several of the Weomen big with Child) Cutting their Heads till the Blood discolloured the water about them, their Female friends acting their part also and making bitter lamentations,—but when they came to be known, they were always driven away by the Captains orders and none of them sufferd to come near the Ship. Notwithstanding which they continued to come near enough to be observed, and there performd their Mourning rites which on the day the Ship Weighd, were sufficient to evince the truth of their Grief & melt the most obdurate Heart.

It being Customary for the Officer of the Watch to examine our Irons before he was releived, McIntosh happening to have a large Shackle had got one of his legs out in the Night, which was reported to the Captain and a general examination took place, when the leg Irons were reduced to fit close, and Mr. Larkan the First Lieut. in trying the Handcuffs took the Method of setting his foot against our breasts and hauling the Handcuffs over our hands with all his Might, some of which took the Skin off with them, and all that could be hauld off by this Means were reduced, and fitted so close, that there was no possibility of turning the Hand in them, and when our wrists began to swell he told us that 'they were not intended to fit like Gloves.'

However Colemans legs being much swelld he was let out of Irons as was also Norman & Byrn on their falling sick, but they were always handcuffd at night. McIntosh & Ellisons arms being much galld by their Irons Had them taken off till they should get well, but their legs were still kept fast.

From George Hamilton, A Voyage Round the World in His Majesty's Frigate Pandora

Next day the king, his two queens, and retinue, came on board to pay us a formal visit, preceded by a band of music. The ladies had about sixty or seventy yards of Otaheitee cloth[35] wrapt round them, and were so bulky and unweildy with it, they were obliged to be hoisted on board like horn cattle: hogs, cocoa nuts, bananas, a rich sort of peach, and a variety of ready dressed puddings and victuals, composed their present to the Captain.

As soon as they were on board, the Captain debarassoit the ladies, by rolling their linen round his middle: an indispensable ceremony here in receiving a present of cloth: and Medua, wife to Oripai the king's brother, took a great liking to the Captain's laced coat, which he immediately put on her with much gallantry; and that beautiful princess seemed much elated with her new finery. I cannot ommit a circumstance of this lady's attachment to dress. There was a custom which had prevailed for a long time, to present the god with all red feathers that could be procured; but thinking she would become red feathers full as well as his godship, immediately employed all her domestics making them up into fly flaps, and other personal ornaments, to prevent the altar making a monopoly of all the good things, in this, as well as in other countries.

A grand Hæva was next day ordered for our entertainment ashore, on Point Venus, and on our landing we were preceded by a band of music, and led to where the king and his levee were in waiting to receive us. The course was soon cleared by the chiefs, and the entertainment began by two men, who vied with each other in filthy lascivious attitudes, and frightful distortions of their mouths. These having performed their part, two ladies, pretty fancifully dressed, as described in Captain Cook's Voyages, were introduced after a little ceremony. Something resembling a turkey-cock's tail, and stuck on their rumps in a fan kind of fashion, about five feet in diameter, had a very good effect while the ladies kept their faces to us; but when in a bending attitude, they presented their rumps, to shew the wonderful agility of their loins; the effect is better conceived than described. After half an hours hard exercise, the dear creatures had remüe themselves into a perfect fureur, and the piece concluded by the ladies exposing that which is better felt than seen; and, in that state of nature, walked from the bottom of the theater to the top where we were sitting on the grass, till they approached just by us, and then we complimented them in bowing, with all the honours of war.

These accomplishments are so much prized amongst them, that girls come from the interior parts of the country, to the court residence, for improvement in the Hæva: just as country gentlemen send their daughters to London boarding-schools.

This may well be called the Cytheria of the southern hemisphere, not only from the beauty and elegance of the women, but their being so deeply versed in, and so passionately fond of the Eleusinian mysteries; and what poetic fiction has painted of Eden, or Arcadia, is here realized, where the earth without tillage produces both food and cloathing, the trees loaded with the richest of fruit, the carpet of nature spread with the most odoriferous flowers, and the fair ones ever willing to fill your arms with love.

It affords a happy instance of contradicting an opinion propagated by philosophers of a less bountiful soil, who maintain that every virtuous or charitable act a man commits, is from selfish and interrested views. Here human nature appears in more amiable colours, and the soul of man, free from the gripping hand of want, acts with a liberality and bounty that does honour to his God.

A native of this country divides every thing in common with his friend, and the extent of the word friend, by them, is only bounded by the universe, and was he reduced to his last morsel of bread, he cheerfully halves it with him; the next that comes has the same claim, if he wants it, and so in succession to the last mouthful he has. Rank makes no distinction in hospitality; for the king and beggar relieve each other in common.

The English are allowed by the rest of the world, and I believe with some degree of justice, to be a generous, charitable people; but the Otaheiteans could not help bestowing the most contemptuous word in their language upon us, which is, Peery, Peery, or Stingy.

In becoming the Tyo, or friend of a man, it is expected you pay him a compliment, by cherishing his wife; but, being ignorant of that ceremony, I very innocently gave high offence to Matuara, the king of York Island, to whom I was introduced as his friend: a shyness took place on the side of his Majesty, from my neglect to his wife; but, through the medium of Brown the interpreter, he put me in mind of my duty, and on my promising my endeavours, matters were for that time made up. It was to me, however, a very serious inauguration: I was, in the first place, not a young man, and had been on shore a whole week; the lady was a woman of rank, being sister to Ottoo, the king of Otaheitee, and had in her youth been beautiful, and named Peggy Ottoo. She is the right hand dancing figure so elegantly delineated in Cook's Voyages. But Peggy had seen much service, and bore away many honourable scars in the fields of Venus. However, his Majesty's service must be done, and Matuara and I were again friends. He was a domesticated man, and passionately fond of his wife and children; but now became pensive and melancholy, dreading the child should be Piebald; though the lady was six months advanced in her pregnancy before we came to the island.

The force of friendship amongst those good creatures, will be more fully understood from the following circumstance: Churchhill, the principal ringleader of the mutineers, on his landing, became the Tyo, or friend, or a great chief in the upper districts. Some time after the chief happening to die without issue, his title and estate, agreeable to their law from Tyoship, devolved on Churchhill, who having some dispute with one Thomson of the Bounty, was shot by him. The natives immediately rose, and revenged the death of Churchhill their chief, by killing Thomson, whose skull was afterwards shown to us, which bore evident marks of fracture.

Oedidy, although perfectly devoted to our interest, on being appointed one of the guides in the expedition against the mutineers, expressed great horror at the act he was going to commit, in betraying his friends, being Tyo to one of them.

They are much less addicted to thieving than when Capt. Cook visited them; and when things were stolen, by applying to the magistrate of the district, the goods were immediately returned; for, like every other well regulated police, the thief and justice were of one gang.

Sometimes we slightly punished the offenders, by cutting off their hair. A beautiful young creature, who lived at the Observatory[36] with one of our young gentlemen, slipped out of bed from him in the night, and stole all his linen. She was punished for the theft, by shaving one of her eye-brows, and half of the hair off her head. She immediately run into the woods, and used to come once or twice a day to the tent, to request looking at herself in the glass; but the grotesque figure she cut, with one side entirely bald, made her shriek out, and run into the woods to shun society.

With respect to agriculture, in a soil where nature has done so much, little is left to human industry; but had there been occasion for it, abilities would not be wanting. It is much to be lamented, that the endeavours of the philanthropic Sir Joseph Banks[37] were frustrated, by their razing of every thing which he took so much pains to rear amongst them, a few shaddocks excepted. Tobacco and cotton have escaped their ravage; and they are much mortified that they cannot eradicate it from their grounds: but were a handloom on a simple construction, as used by the natives of Java, introduced amongst them, they could soon turn their cotton to good account. An instance of their ingenuity and imitative powers in matting, was a thing perfectly unknown amongst them til Captain Cook introduced it from Anamooka, one of the Friendly Isles: but in that branch of manufacture they now far surpass their original. They have likewise abundance of fine sugar canes, growing spontaneously all over the island, from which rum and sugar might be extracted. Indeed an attempt was made by Coleman, the armourer of the Bounty, who made a still, and succeeded; but, dreading the effects of intoxication, both amongst themselves and the natives, very wisely put an end to his labours, by breaking the still.

Captain Bligh has likewise planted Indian corn, from which much may be expected. On our landing, as soon as public business of more importance would permit, our gentlemen were indefatigable in laying out a piece of garden ground, and ditching it round. Lemons, oranges, limes, pine apples, plants of the coffee tree, with all the lesser class of things, as onions, lettuces, peas, cabbages, and every thing necessary for culinary purposes, were planted.

In order that they might not meet the same fate of the things planted by Sir Joseph Banks, Captain Edwards made use of every stratagem to make the chiefs fond of the oranges and limes, by dipping them in sugar, to cover the acid before it be presented to them to eat. Messrs. Corner and Hayward were equally zealous in using the most persuasive arguments with the chiefs to take care of our garden, and rear and propagate the plants when we were gone; to all which they lent a deaf ear, and treated the subject with much levity, saying, they might be very good to us, but that they were already plentifully supplied with every thing they wished or wanted, and had not occasion for more. But on the Lieutenant's representing, that if, on our return, they could supply us with plenty of such articles as we left with them, they in exchange would receive hatchets, knives, and red cloth, they seemed more favourably inclined to our project; and I have no doubt but that some after navigators will reap the benefit of their industry.

The Bread-fruit, although the most delicate and nourishing food upon earth, is, with people like them, liable to inconveniencies; for in such a group or Archipelago of islands, whose inhabitants are in such various gradations of refinement, from the gentle and polished Otaheitean, to the savage and cannibal Feegee, a war amongst them is often attended with devastation as well as famine. By cutting round the bark of the Bread-fruit tree, a whole country

A Tahitian woman lifts her baby, hoping that the father, a prisoner in "Pandora's Box," catches a glimpse of their child. James Morrison vividly described such a scene in his *Journal*: "...the Weomen with whom we had cohabited on the Island Came frequently under the Stern (bringing their Children of which there were 6 born, Four Girls & two Boys, & several of the Weomen big with Child) Cutting their Heads till the Blood discoloured the water about them, their Female friends acting their part also and making bitter lamentations" (Roy Andersen/ National Geographic Creative).

may be laid waste for four or five years. Young trees not bearing in less time, such as Indian corn, English wheat and peas, that have been left amongst them, can in time of war be stored in granaries on the top of their almost inaccessible mountains.

While speaking of the Bread-fruit tree, I can exemplify my subject from what happened to an island contiguous to Otaheite, whose coast abounded with fine fish; and the Otaheitans, being themselves too lazy to catch them, destroyed all the Bread-fruit trees on this little island; by which act of policy, they are obliged to send over boats with fish regularly to market, to be supplied with bread in barter from Otaheite. To this island they likewise send their wives, thinking they become fair by living on fish, and low diet. They also send boys for the same reason, whom they keep for abominable purposes.

As to the religion of this country, it is difficult for me to define it. Their tenets although equally ignorant of heathen mythology or theological intricacies, seem to partake of both; and, like other nations, in the early ages of society, are rendered subservient to political purposes, as by the machinery of deification, the person of the king is sacred and inviolable. Notwithstanding the king be a broad shouldered strapping fellow, three sturdy stallions of cecisbeos, or lords in waiting, are kept for the particular amusement of the queen, when his majesty is in his cups. Yet the royal issue is always declared to be sprung from the immortal Gods; and the heir-apparent, during his minority, is put under the tuition of the high priest. Their God is supposed to be omnipresent, and is worshipped in spirit, idolatry not being known amongst them. The sacred mysteries are only known to the priests or augurs, the king, princes, and great chiefs, the common people only serving as victims, or to fill up the pageantry of a religious procession. One of our gentlemen expressing a wish to the high priest, of carrying from amongst them that God whose altars craved so much human blood, he, like a true priest, had his subterfuge ready, by saying, there were more of the same family in the other islands, from whence they could easily be supplied. On all great occasions, each district sends a male victim; and the island containing forty districts, it may be presumed the mortality is great. Between the sacrifices and the ravages of war, a preponderating number of females must have taken place; to counteract which, a law passed, that every other female child should be put to death at birth; and the husband always officiating as acoucheur to his wife, the child is destroyed as soon as the sex is discovered.

The absurdity of this inhuman law is now pretty evident. Women are become more scarce, and set a higher value on their charms, which occasions many desperate battles amongst them. Some with fractured skulls were sent on board of us, which had been got in amorous affrays of that kind.

It may naturally be supposed, that people of such gentle natures make no conspicuous figure in the theater of war.

Their war-canoes are very large, on which a platform is placed, capable of containing from a hundred and fifty to two hundred men. But their taste in decorating the prow of their men of war, plainly indicates they are more versed in the fields of Venus than Mars, every man of war having a figure head of the god Priapus, with a preposterous insignia of his order; the sight of which never fails to excite great glee and good humour amongst the ladies.

It is customary with those nations at war, that the treaty of peace be confirmed by the conquerors sending a certain number of their women to cohabit with the nation that is vanquished, in order to conciliate their affection by a bond more lasting than wax and parchment. It was the unhappy lot of Otaheite to be overcome by a nation whose women were too masculine for them; they being accustomed to the amorous dalliance of their own beautiful females, were averse to familiar intercourse with strangers. The ladies returned with all the rage of disappointed women, and the war was renewed with all its horrors.

They are well acquainted with the bow and arrow, but use it as an amusement. The only missive weapons they use are the sling and spear. They have now amongst them about twenty stand of arms, and two hundred rounds of powder and ball. They can take a musket to pieces, and put it up again; are good marksmen, take proper care of their arms and ammunition; and are highly sensible of the superior advantage it gives them over the neighbouring nations.

In the preparing and printing their cloth, the women display a great share of ingenuity and good taste. Many of their figures were exactly the patterns which prevailed, as fashionable, when we left England, both striped and figured. They print their figured cloth by dipping the leaves in dye-stuffs of different colours, placing them as their fancy directs. Their cloth is of different texture of fineness, from a stuff of the same nature in quality as the slightest India paper, to a kind as durable as some of our cottons; but they will not bear water, and of course become troublesome and expensive. They are generally made up in bales, running about two yards broad, and twenty or thirty yards long. We had some thousands of yards of it sent on board as presents.

Their sumptuary laws, at first sight, may appear severe towards the fair sex, who are not permitted to eat butcher-meat, nor to eat at all, in the presence of their husbands. It certainly does not convey the most delicate ideas, to a mind impressed with much sensibility, to see a fine woman devouring a piece of beef; and those voluptuaries, who may be said to exist only by their women, would naturally endeavour to remove the possibility of presupposing a disgusting idea, in that object in which all their happiness centres.

Every woman, the queen and royal family excepted, on the approach of the king, is denuded down to the waist, and continues so whilst his majesty is in sight. Should the king enter a woman's house, it is immediately pulled down. The king is never permitted to help himself with meat or drink, which makes him a very troublesome visitor, as he is never quiet whilst a bottle is in sight, till he has had the last drop of it.

Their houses are well adapted to the temperate climate they inhabit, and generally consist of three chambers, the interior one of which the chief retires to, after he has drank his cava.[38] A profound silence is observed during his repose; for should they be suddenly awaked, it produces violent vomiting, and a train of uneasy sensations; but, otherwise, if undisturbed, it proves a safe anodyne, creates amorous dreams, and a powerful excitement to venery. In the adjoining chamber, his fair spouse waits, with eager expectation, to avail herself of the happy moment when her lord should awake, which is by slow degrees; and he is roused from Elysium, by her gentle offices, in tenderly embracing every part of his body, until his ideal scenes of bliss are realised; and when fully sated with the luscious banquet, they retire to the bath, to gather fresh vigour for a renewal of similar joys. In this mazy round of chaste dissipation, the hours glide gently on, and the evening is spent in dancing to the music of Pan's pipes, the flute, and hæva drum. They then go to the bath again, and the festivity of the evening is concluded with a repast of fruit, and young cocoanut milk. The whole village indiscriminately join the feast; and the demon of rank and precedence, with their appendages malevolence and envy, has never yet disturbed their happy board.

Happy would it have been for those people, had they never been visited by Europeans; for, to our shame be it spoken, disease and gunpowder is all the benefit they have ever received from us, in return for their hospitality and kindness. The ravages of the venereal disease is evident, from the mutilated objects so frequent amongst them, where death has not thrown a charitable veil over their misery, by putting a period to their existence.

A disease of the consumptive kind has of late made great havoc amongst them; this they call the British disease, as they have only had it since their intercourse with the English.

In this complaint they are avoided by society, from a supposition of its being contagious; and in every old out-house, you will find miserable objects, for want of medical assistance, abandoned to their wretched fate. From what we could learn, it generally terminates fatally in ten or twelve months; but I am led to believe, that in many cases it originates from the venereal disease.

The voice of humanity, honour, and justice, calls upon us as a nation to remedy those evils, by sending some intelligent surgeon to live amongst them. They at present pant for the pruning-hand of civilization and the arts, love and adore us as beings of a superior nature, but gently upbraid us with having left them in the same abject state they were at first discovered.

We had buoyed many of them up with the hopes of carrying them to England with us, in order to secure their fidelity and honesty, especially those who were most useful in our domestic concerns; but on explaining to them, that even bread was not to be obtained in England without labour, they lost hopes of their favourite voyage.

Large presents were now brought us for our sea-store; and notwithstanding Mr. Bentham our purser having most liberally supplied the ship with four pounds of fresh pork per man each day, it made no apparent scarcity; beside salting some thousand weight, and a prodigious number of goats, fowls, and other things. Could we have made it convenient to have staid another week, some cows were promised to have been sent us from a neighbouring island. Capt. Cook had left with them a horse and mare, a cow with calf, and a bull; but, from some mistake, they killed a horse instead of one of the cows, and found it very tough, disagreeable eating, by which means they were disgusted with all the horned cattle, and drew an unfavourable conclusion, that their meat was all of the same texture. Had some pains been taken with them, to get the better of a dislike they have to milk, and explained to them how variously it might be employed as food, I have no doubt but they would have paid more attention to the horned cattle. They used to persist in saying, that milk was urine; but on pointing to a woman that was suckling her child, and pushing their own argument, they seemed convinced of their error. We have left them a goose and a gander, which they take great delight in.

Edea the Queen endeavoured to conquer that absurd dislike, and at last became fond of milk in her tea.

PART FOUR

Searching for Fletcher Christian

From Captain Edwards' Report

Christian had been frequently heard to declare that he would search for an unknown or uninhabited Island in which there was no harbour for Shipping, would run the Ship a Shore, and get from her such things as would be useful to him and settle there, but this information was too vague to be follow'd in an immense Ocean strew'd with an almost innumerable number of known & unknown Islands. Therefore after the Ship was caulked which I found necessary to be done, the Rigging overhauled and in other respects refitted then for sea & fitted the Pirates Schooner as a Tender & put onboard two petty officers & seven Men to Navigate her, conceiving she would be of considerable use in Covering the Boats in my future search for the Bounty, as well as for reconnoitering the Passage through the Reef leading to Endeavour Straits. I sailed from Otaheite on the 8th of May with a view to put the remainder of my Orders into Execution. Oediddee was desirous to go in the Pandora to Ulietia & to Bolabola and as I thought he would be useful as a guide for the Boats I took him with me & steered for Huahaine which we saw the next Morning.

From George Hamilton, A Voyage Round the World in His Majesty's Frigate Pandora

A painting of Capt. Cook, done in oil by Webber, which had been delivered to Capt. Edwards on his first landing, was now returned to them. It is held by them in the greatest veneration; and I should not be surprised if, one day or other, divine honours should be paid to it. They still believe Capt. Cook is living; and their seeing Mr Bentham our purser, whom they perfectly recollected as having been [on] the voyage with him, and spoke their language, will confirm them in that opinion.

The harbour was surveyed by Mr. Geo. Passmore the master, an able and experienced officer.

Part Four. Searching for Fletcher Christian

Our officers here, as at Rio Janeiro, showed the most manly and philanthropic disposition, by giving up their cabins, and sacrificing every comfort and convenience for the good of mankind, in accommodating boxes with plants of the Bread-fruit tree, that the laudable intentions of government might not be frustrated from the loss of his majesty's ship Bounty.

We had now completed our water from an excellent spring, out of a rock close to the water's edge, at Ossaree.

King Ottoo, and his queen Edea, came on board, and were very importunate in their solicitations to Capt. Edwards, requesting him to take them to England with him. Aeredy the concubine likewise requested the same favour; but she more generously begged they might all three go together. But Oripai, and the other chiefs, remonstrated against his going, as they were on the eve of a war.

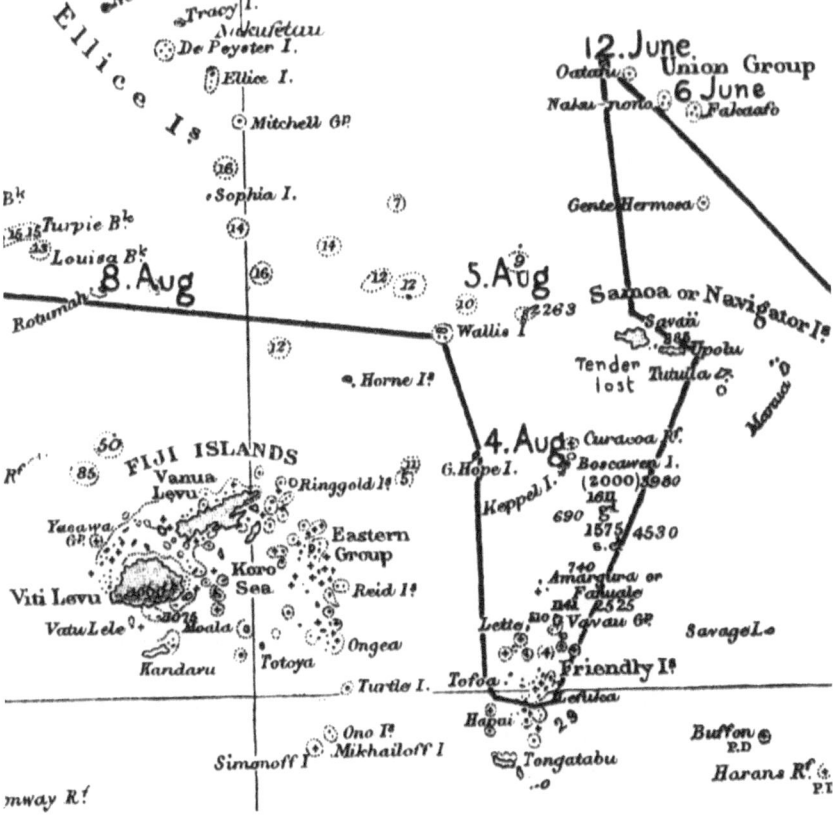

This section of a map published in the 1915 edition of Captain Edward Edwards' *Voyage of H.M.S. Pandora* traces the route he was directed to take after leaving Tahiti in search of H.M.S. *Bounty* and Fletcher Christian's band of mutineers.

We were now perfectly ready for sea; and as Capt. Cook's picture is presented to all strangers, it is customary for navigators to write their observations on the back of it; so our arrival and departure was notified upon it.

The ship was filled with cocoa-nuts and fruit, as many pigs, goats, and fowls, as the decks and boats would hold. The dismal day of our departure now arrived. This I believe was the first time that an Englishman got up his anchor, at the remotest part of the globe, with a heavy heart, to go home to his own country. Every canoe almost in the island was hovering round the ship; and they began to mourn, as is customary for the death of a near relation. They bared their bodies, cut their heads with shells, and smeared their breasts and shoulders with the warm blood, as it streamed down; and as the blood ceased flowing, they renewed the wounds in their head, attended with a dismal yell.

Ottoo now took leave of us; and, with the tears trickling down his cheeks, begged to be remembered to King George. The tender was put in commission, and the command of her given to Mr. Oliver the master's mate, Mr. Renouard a midshipman, James Dodds a quartermaster; and six privates were put on board of her. She was decked, beautifully built, and the size of a Gravesend boat.

With a pleasant breeze, on the evening of the 8th of May, passed Emea or York Island, contiguous to, and in sight of Otaheite. It is governed by Matuara, brother-in-law to Ottoo. It is a pleasant romantic looking spot, with very high hills upon it, and about twelve miles in circumference. They were lately attacked by some neighbouring power, and Matuara requested the lend of a musket from his friend and ally. When peace was restored, Ottoo sent for his musket. Matuara represented, that as a man, from a sense of honour, he wished to return it; but that as a king, the love he bore his subjects prevented him complying with the request. That single musket, and a few cartridges, gives him no small degree of consequence, and are retained as the royal dower of his wife.

Next morning we reached Huaheine, and sent the boats on shore in Owharre Bay. As Oedidy the chief requested to go with us to Whytutakee, he went on shore with the officers, in their search for intelligence of the mutineers; but they returned without success.

Here we learned the fate of Omai, the native of Otaheite, whom Captain Cook brought from England. On his return here, he had wealth enough to obtain very fine woman on the island; and at last fell a martyr to Venus, having finished his career by the venereal disease, two years after his landing. His house and garden are still standing; but his musket occasioned a war after his death, and was found in the possession of a native of Ulitea. His servant was on board of us, but had not retained a single article of his property.

On the 10th, we examined Ulitea and Otaha, interchanged presents with the natives, and landed in Chamanen's Bay; but got no information.

We examined Bolobola on the 11th; and Tatahu, the king, honoured us with a visit. The people of this island are of a more warlike disposition than any other of the Society Islands; and on account of that national ferocity of character, are much caressed by the Otaheitans and neighbouring islands. They are sensible of their pre-eminence, and boast of their country, in whatever island you meet them. They are tatooed in a particular manner; and whether they may have spread their conquests, or other nations imitated them, I could not learn; but a prodigious number, in islands we afterwards visited, were tatooed in their fashion. What was most singular, we saw some with the glans of the penis entirely tatooed; and our men, from being tatooed in the legs, arms, and breast, places of much less sensation, were often lame for a week, from the excruciating torture of the operation. Tatahu likewise informed us there were no white men on Tubai, a small island to the northward of Bolobola, and under his jurisdiction; nor upon Mauruah, another island in sight, and to the westward of Bolobola. He also mentioned another island, which he called Mopehah. Here Oedidy went on shore; but getting drunk in meeting some of his old friends, he fell asleep, and lost his passage. On the 12th we left Mauruah, and on the 13th lost sight of the Society Islands.

Here one of the prisoners begged to speak with the Captain, and gave information of Mr. Christian's intended rout[e].

We now shaped our course to fall in to the eastward of Whytutakee, an island discovered by Capt. Bligh, and on the 19th made the island. We sent the boat on shore, covered by the tender, to examine it; but found it a thing impossible for the Bounty to have been there; and the natives said they had seen no white people. They were very shy, and we could not coax them on board. One of them recollected having seen Lieut. Hayward on board the Bounty. Here we purchased from the natives a spear of most exquisite workmanship. It was nine feet long, and cut in the form of a Gothic spire, all its ornaments being executed in a kind of alto relievo; which, from the slow progress they made with stone tools, must have been the labour of a man's whole life.

Here nature begins to assume a ruder aspect; and the silken bands of love gives way to the rustic garniture of war. The natives of either sex wear no cloathing, but a girdle of stained leaves round their middle, and the men a gorget, of the exact shape and size as at present wore by officers in our service. It is made of the pearl oyster-shell. The centre is black, and the transparent part of the shell is left as an edge or border to it, which gives it a very fine effect. It is flung round their neck with a band of human hair, or the fibres of cocoa nut-shell, of admirable texture, and a rose worked at each corner of the gorget, the same as the military jemmy of the present day.

We now began to discover, that the ladies of Otaheite had left us many warm tokens of their affection.[39]

Instructions were given to the commander of the tender to be particular in guarding against surprise, and a rendezvous established, in case of separation; and on Sunday, the 22d of May, made Palmerston's Islands.

The tender's signal was made to cover the boats in landing; and some natives were seen rowing across the lagoon to a considerable distance. Soon after their landing, Lieut. Corner and his party discovered a yard and some spars marked Bounty, and the broad arrow upon them. When this intelligence was communicated to the ship, a signal was made to the party on shore to advance with great circumspection, and to guard against surprise. Mr. Rickards, the master's mate, went in the cutter, and made a circuit of the island.

Lieuts. Corner and Hayward landed on the different isles with cork-jackets; but the surf running very high all round, rendered it exceedingly dangerous, and in many places impracticable. Had they not been expert swimmers, in duty of this kind, they must have certainly been drowned, as they had not only themselves and the party to take care of, but the arms and ammunition to land dry.

About four o'clock in the afternoon, Mr. Sival the midshipman came on board in the jolly-boat, and brought with him several very curious stained canoes, representing the figure of men, fishes, and beasts. He had committed some mistake in the orders he was sent to execute, and was ordered to return immediately to rectify it; but the boat did not come back again. A few minutes after she left the ship, the weather became thick and hazy, and began to blow fresh; so that, even with the assistance of glasses, they could not see whether she made the shore or not. It continued to blow during the night, so as to prevent the party on shore from coming on board. They had been employed during the day in searching all the islands with particular attention, having every reason to suspect the mutineers were there, from finding the Bounty's yard and spars. But at last, wore out with fatigue in marching, and swimming through so many reefs, and having no victuals the whole day, in the evening they began to forage for something to eat. The gigantic cockle was the only thing that presented. Of the shell of one they made a kettle, to boil some junks of it in. (It may be necessary here to remark, for the information of those who are not acquainted with it, that there are some of them larger than three men can carry.) Of this coarse fare, and some cocoa-nuts, they made shift, with the assistance of a good appetite, to make a tolerable hearty supper; they then set the watch, and went to sleep. They had thrown a large nut on the fire before they lay down, and forgot it; but in the middle of the night, the milk of the cocoa-nut became so expanded with the heat, that it burst with a great explosion. Their minds had been so much engaged in the course of the day with the enterprise they were employed in, expecting muskets to be fired at them from every bush, that they all jumped up, seized their arms, and were some time before they could undeceive themselves, that they were really not attacked.

In the morning the boats returned; and we were much concerned to hear that they had seen nothing of the jolly-boat. The tender received a fresh supply of provisions and ammunition; at the same time they had orders to cruise in a certain direction, to look for the jolly-boat; and Palmerston's Isles was appointed as a rendezvous to meet again. Lieut. Corner now came on board, in a canoe not much bigger than a butcher's tray. The cutter was sent a second time to search the reefs, but returned without success. We then run down with the ship in the direction the wind had blown the preceding day, in hopes of finding the boat; but after a whole day's run to leeward, and working up again by traverses to the Isles, saw nothing of her. The tender hove in sight in the evening, and we again searched the Isles without success. All further hopes of seeing here [sic] were given up, and we proceeded on our voyage. It may be difficult to surmise what has been the fate of these unfortunate men. They had a piece of salt-beef thrown into the boat to them on leaving the ship; and it rained a good deal that night and the following day, which might satiate their thirst. It is by these accidents the Divine Ruler of the universe has peopled the southern hemisphere.

Here are innumerable islands in perpetual growth. The coral, a marine vegetable, with which the South Seas in every part abounds, is continually shooting up from the bottom to the surface, which at first forms lagoon islands; and the water in the centre is evaporated by the heat of the sun, till at last a terra firma is completed. In this state it would for ever remain a barren sand, had not Divine Providence given birth to the cocoa-nut tree, whose fruit is so protected with a hard shell, that after floating about for a twelve-month in the sea, it will vegetate, take root, and grow in those salt marshes, lagoons, incipient islands, or what you please to call them. Their roots serve to bind the surface of the coral; and the annual shedding of their leaves, in time creates a soil which produces a verdure or undergrowth. This affords a favourite resting-place to sea-fowls, and the whole feathered race, who in their dung drop the seeds of shrubs, fruits, and plants; by which means all the variety of the vegetable kingdom is disseminated. At last the variegated landscape rises to the view; and when the divine Architect has finished his work, it becomes then a residence for man.

From the various accidents incident to man in the early stages of society, their wants, and the restless spirit inherent in their natures, they are tempted to dare the elements, either in fishing, commerce, or war; and from their temerity are often blown to remote and uninhabited islands. Distressing accidents of this nature often happening to inhabitants of the South Seas, they now seldom undertake any hazardous enterprise by water without a woman and a sow with pig, being in the canoe with them; by which means, if they are cast on any of those uninhabited islands, they fix their abode.

Their remote situation from European powers has deprived them of the culture of civilized life, as they neither serve to swell the ambitious views of conquest, nor the avarice of commerce. Here the sacred finger of Omnipotence has interposed, and rendered our vices the instruments of virtue; and although that unfortunate man Christian has, in a rash unguarded moment, been tempted to swerve from his duty to his king and country, as he is in other respects of an amiable character, and respectable abilities, should he elude the hand of justice, it may be hoped he will employ his talents in humanizing the rude savages; so that, at some future period, a British Ilion may blaze forth in the south with all the characteristic virtues of the English nation, and complete the great prophecy, by propagating the Christian knowledge amongst the infidels. As Christian has taken fourteen beautiful women with him from Otaheite, there is little doubt of his intention of colonizing some undiscovered island.

On the 6th day of June, we discovered an island, which was named the Duke of York's island. Lieuts. Corner and Hayward were sent out to examine it in the two yauls, covered by the tender. Some huts being discovered by the ship, a signal was immediately made for the party on shore to be on their guard, and to advance with caution.

Soon after their arrival on shore, a ship's wooden buoy was discovered. On searching the huts, nets of different sizes were found hanging in them, and a variety of fishing utensils. Stages and wharfs were likewise discovered in different parts of the creek, which led us to imagine it was only an island resorted to in the fishing season, by some neighbouring nation. The skeleton of a very large fish, supposed to be a whale, was found near the beach; and a place of venerable aspect, formed entirely by the hand of Nature, and resembling a Druidical temple, commanded their attention. The falling of a very large old tree, formed an arch, through which the interior part of the temple was seen, which heightened the perspective, and gave a romantic solemn dignity to the scene. At the extreme end of the temple, three altars were placed, the centre one higher than the other two, on which some white shells were piled in regular order.

After traversing the island, they returned to the huts, and hung up a few knives, looking-glasses, and some little articles of European manufacture, that the natives, on their return, might know the island had been visited.

On the 12th, we discovered another island, which was named the Duke of Clarence's island. In running along the land, we saw several canoes crossing the lagoons. The tender's signal was made, to cover the boats in landing, and Lieuts. Corner and Hayward sent to reconnoitre the beach, to discover a landing-place. In this duty, they came pretty near some of the natives in their canoes, who made signs of peace to them; but, either from fear or business, avoided having any intercourse with us. Morais, or burying-places, were likewise found here, which indicated it to be a principal residence. Here they find some old cocoa trees hollowed longitudinally, as tanks or reservoirs for the rain water.

On the 18th, we discovered an island of more considerable extent than any island that has hitherto been discovered in the south; and as there were many collateral circumstances which might hereafter promise it to be a discovery of national importance, in honour of the first lord of the admiralty, it was called Chatham's Island. It is beautifully diversified with hills and dales, of twice the extent of Otaheite, and a hardy warlike race of people. The natives described a large river to us, which disembogued itself into a spacious bay, that promises excellent anchorage. Here we learned the death of Fenow, king of Anamooka, from one of his family, of the same name, who had a finger cut off in mourning for him. After trading a whole day with the natives, who seemed fair and honourable in their dealings, we examined it without success, and proceeded on our voyage.

On the 21st, we discovered a very considerable island, of about forty miles long. It was named by the natives Otutuelah. Capt. Edwards gave no name to it; but should posterity derive the advantages from it which it at present promises, I presume it may hereafter be called Edwards's island.

It is well wooded with immense large trees, whose foliage spreads like the oak; and there is a deal of shrubbery on it, bearing a yellow flower. The natives are remarkably handsome. Some of them had their skins tinged with yellow, as a mark of distinction, which at first led us to imagine they were diseased. Neither sex wear any cloathing, but a girdle of leaves round their middle, stained with different colours. The women adorn their hair with chaplets of sweet-smelling flowers and bracelets, and necklaces of flowers round their wrists and neck.

On their first coming on board, they trembled for fear. They were perfectly ignorant of fire arms, never having seen a European ship before. They made many gestures of submission, and were struck with wonder and surprise at every thing they saw. Amongst other things, they brought us some most remarkable fine puddings, which abounded with aromatic spiceries, that excelled in taste and flavour the most delicate seed-cake. As we have never hitherto known of spices or aromatics being in the South Seas, it is certainly a matter worthy the investigation of some future circumnavigators. We traded with them the whole day, and got many curiosities. Birds and fowls, of the most splendid plumage, were brought on board, some resembling the peacock, and a great variety of the parrot kind.

One woman amongst many others came on board. She was six feet high, of exquisite beauty, and exact symmetry, being naked, and unconscious of her being so, added a lustre to her charms; for, in the words of the poet, "She needed not the foreign ornaments of dress; careless of beauty, she was beauty's self."[40]

Many mouths were watering for her; but Capt. Edwards, with great humanity and prudence, had given previous orders, that no women should be permitted to go below, as our health had not quite recovered the shock it received at Otaheite; and the lady was obliged to be contented with viewing the great cabin, where she was shewn the wonders of the Lord on the face of the mighty deep. Before evening, the women went all on shore, and the men began to be troublesome and pilfering. The third lieutenant had a new coat stole out of his cabin; and they were making off with every bit of iron they could lay hands on.

It now came on to blow fresh, and we were obliged to make off from the land. Those who were engaged in trade on board were so anxious, that we had got almost out of sight of their canoes before they perceived the ship's motion, when they all jumped into the water like a flock of wild geese; but one fellow, more earnest than the rest, hung by the rudder chains for a mile or two, thinking to detain her.

This evening, at five o'clock, we unfortunately parted company, and lost sight of our tender. False fires were burnt, and great guns and small arms were fired without success, as it came on thick blowing weather.

We cruised for her all the 23d and 24th, near where we parted company, which was off a piece of remarkable high land. What was most unfortunate, water and provisions were then on deck for her, which were intended to have been put on board of her in the morning. She had the day before received orders, in case of separation, to rendezvous at Anamooka, and to wait there for us. A small cag of salt, and another of nails and iron-ware, were likewise put on board of her, to traffic with the Indians, and the latitudes and longitudes of the places we would touch at, in our intended rout. She had a boarding netting fixed, to prevent her being boarded, and several seven-barrelled pieces and blunderbusses put on board of her.

As we proceeded to the eastward, we saw another island, which we knew to be one of the navigator's isles, discovered by Mons. Bougainville. On the 28th, in the morning, saw the Happai Islands, discovered by Capt. Cook, and before noon, the group of islands to the eastward of Anamooka, and sailed down between Little Anamooka and the Falafagee Island.

On the 29th, we anchored in the road of Anamooka. Immediately on our arrival, a large sailing canoe was hired, and Lieut. Hayward and one private sent to the Happai and Feegee Islands, to make inquiry after the Bounty and our tender; but received no intelligence. Here they found an axe, which had been left by Capt. Cook, and bartered with the natives of the different islands for hogs, yams, &c.

The people of Anamooka are the most daring set of robbers in the South Seas; and, with the greatest deference and submission to Capt. Cook, I think the name of Friendly Isles is a perfect misnomer, as their behaviour to himself, to us, and to Capt. Bligh's unfortunate boat at Murderer's Cove,[41] pretty clearly evinces. Indeed Murderer's Cove, in the Friendly Isles, is saying a volume on the subject.

Part Four. Searching for Fletcher Christian

Two or three of the officers were taking a walk on shore one evening, who had the precaution to take their pistols with them. They seemed to croud round us with more than idle curiosity; but, on presenting the pistols to them, they sheered off. The Captain soon joined us, and brought his servant with him, carrying a bag of nails, and some trifling presents, which he meant to distribute amongst them; but he took the bag from him, and dispatched him with a message to the boat, on which the crowd followed him. As soon as he got out of our sight, they stripped him naked, and robbed him of his cloaths, and every article he had, but one shoe, which he used for concealing his nakedness. At this juncture Lieut. Hayward arrived from his expedition, and called the assistance of the guard in searching for the robbers. We saw the natives all running, and dodging behind the trees, which led us to suspect there was some mischief brewing; but we soon discovered the great Irishman, with his shoe full in one hand, and a bayonet in the other, naked and foaming mad with revenge on the natives, for the treatment he had received. Night coming on, we went on board, without recovering the poor fellow's cloaths.

Next day we were honoured with a visit from Tatafee, king of Anamooka, who is of lineal descent from the same family that reigned in the island when discovered by Tasman, the Dutch circumnavigator; and the story of his landing and supplying them with dogs and hogs, is handed down, by oral tradition, to this day.

Here society may be said to exist in the second stage with respect to Otaheite. As land is scarcer, private property is more exactly ascertained, and each man's possession fenced in with a beautiful Chinese railing. Highways, and roads leading to public places, are neatly fenced in on each side, and a handsome approach to their houses by a gravel-walk, with shrubbery planted with some degree of taste on each side of it. Many of them had rows of pine apples on each side of the avenue. Messrs. Hayward and Corner, with their usual benevolence, took much pains in teaching them the manner of transplanting their pine-apples; which hint they immediately adopted, and were very thankful for any advice, either in rearing their fruit, or cultivating their ground. The shaddocks are superior in flavour to those of the West Indies; and they will soon have oranges from what we have left amongst them.

The women here are extremely beautiful; and although they want that feminine softness of manners which the Otaheite women possess in so eminent a degree, their matchless vivacity, and fine animated countenances, compensate the want of the softer blandishments of their sister island.

There is a favourite amusement of the ladies here, (the cup and ball), such as children play at in England. It serves to give them a dégagé kind of air, by which means you have a more elegant display of their charms. They are well aware of their fascinating powers, and use them with as much address as our fine women do notting, and other acts of industry. Trade went briskly on. They brought abundance of hogs, and several ton weight of very excellent yams. We found that the pork took salt, and was cured much better here than at Otaheite.

Many beautiful girls were brought on board for sale, by their mothers, who were very exorbitant in their demands, as nothing less than a broad axe would satisfy them; but after standing their market three days, *la pucelage* fell to an old razor, a pair of scissars, or a very large nail. Indeed this trade was pushed to so great a height, that the quarter-deck became the scene of the most indelicate familiarities. Nor did the unfeeling mothers commiserate with the pain and suffering of the poor girls, but seemed to enjoy it as a monstrous good thing. It is customary here, when girls meet with an accident of this kind, that a council of matrons is held, and the noviciate has a gash made in her fore finger. We soon observed a number of cut fingers amongst them; and had the razors held out, I believe all the girls in the island would have undergone the same operation.

A party was sent on shore to cut wood for fuel, and grass for the sheep; but they would not permit a blade of grass to be cut till they were paid for it.

The watering party shared the same fate; and notwithstanding a guard of armed men were sent to protect the others whilst on that duty, the natives were continually harassing them, and committing depredations. One of them came behind Lieut. Corner, and made a blow at him with his club, which luckily missed his head, and only stunned him in the back of the neck; and, while in that state, snatched his handkerchief from him; but Mr. Corner, recovering before the thief got out of sight, leveled his piece and shot him dead.

Tatafee the king was going to collect tribute from the islands under his jurisdiction, and went in the frigate to Tofoa; but previous to our sailing, a letter was left to Mr. Oliver, the commander of the tender, should he chance to arrive before our return, with Macaucala, a principal chief. In the night, the burning mountain [volcano] on Tofoa exhibited a very grand spectacle; and in the morning two canoes were sent on shore, to announce the arrival of those two great personages, Tatafee and Toobou, who went on shore in the Pandora's barge, to give them more consequence; but the tributary princes came off in canoes, to do homage to Tatafee before he reached the shore. They came alongside the barge, lowered their heads over the side of the canoe, and Tatafee, agreeable to their custom, put his foot upon their heads. When on shore, what presents he had received from us, he distributed amongst his subjects, with a liberality worthy of a great prince.

Some of the people were here who behaved with such savage barbarity to Capt. Bligh's boat at Murderer's Cove. They perfectly recollected Mr. Hayward, and seemed to shrink from him. Captain Edwards took much pains with Tatafee, the king, to make him sensible of his disapprobation of their conduct to Capt. Bligh's boat. But conciliatory and gentle means were all that could be enjoined at present, lest our tender should fall in amongst them.

The wind not permitting us to visit Tongataboo, we proceeded to Catooa and Navigator's Isles, the loss of our tender having prevented us from doing it before, and endeavoured to fall in with the easternmost of these islands.

On the morning of the 12th of July, we discovered a cluster of islands in the N. N. W. quarter; but the wind being favourable for us, left examining of them till our return to the Friendly Isles. On the 14th, in the forenoon, saw three isles, supposed to be the cluster of isles called, by Bougainville, Navigator's Isles. The largest the natives called Tumaluah. We passed them at a little distance, and found much intreaty necessary to bring them on board.

On the 15th, we saw another island, which proved to be Otutuelah, which has been already described. Here we found some of the French navigator's cloathing and buttons; and there is little doubt but they have murdered them.

On the 18th, saw the group of islands we discovered on our way here; and on the 19th, ran down the north side till we came to an opening, where we saw the sea on the other side. A sound is formed here by some islands to the south east and north west, and interior bays, which promises better anchorage than any other place in the Friendly Isles. The natives told us there were excellent watering-places in several different parts within the sound. The country is well wooded. Several of the inferior chiefs were on board, one of the Tatafee, and one of the Toobou family; but the principal chief was not on board. We supposed he was coming off just as we sailed. The natives in general were very fair and honourable in their dealings. They were more inoffensive and better behaved than any we had seen for some time. They have frequent intercourse with Anamooka, and their religion, customs, and language, are the same.

A number of beautiful paroquets were brought off by the natives, all remarkable for the richness and variety of their plumage.

The group of islands was called Howe's Islands, but were particularly distinguished by the names of Barrington's, Sawyer's, Hotham's, and Jarvis's Islands. The sound itself was called Curtis's Sound. Under the general denomination of Howe's Islands, were included several islands to the south east, to which we gave no particular name, and two more islands to the westward, called Bickerton's Islands, including two small islands near the above. There seems to be a tolerable landing-place on the north-west side of Gardner's Island. All this part of the island has a most barren aspect. There were evident marks of volcanic eruptions having happened. The very singular appearance which this part of the islands presented, I cannot omit mentioning; it bore the figure of a piece of flat table-land, without the slightest eminence or indentation, and smoke was issuing from the edges, round its whole circumference.

On the 23d, we passed an inhabited island, which we supposed to be the Pylestaart island. It has two remarkable high peaks upon it.

On the 26th, we saw Middleburg Island, and run down between it and Euah; examined it without success; passed Tongatabu; got some provisions here, but found the water brackish.

On the 29th, we anchored again in the road of Anamooka. We were sorry to hear the tender had not been there. On the 5th of August, we again proceeded on our voyage. As the occurrences at this time bore some semblance to the transactions in our last visit, to avoid wounding the delicate, or satiating the licentious, we shall conclude in the torpid phraseology of the log, with ditto repeated.

Every thing being ready for sea on the 3d day of August, we sailed from Anamooka; and on the 5th, discovered an island of some considerable extent, called by the natives Onooafow, which we called Proby's Island, in honour of Commissioner Proby. We traded with the inhabitants for some hours. The land was hilly, and the houses of much larger construction than we had observed in those seas.

We were now convinced that we were further to the westward than we imagined, and therefore shaped a course to fall in to the eastward of Wallis's Island; and next day fell in with it. We gave presents, as customary, to the first boat; who, from a theft they committed, were afraid to return. Their cheek-bones were much bruised and flattened, and some had both their little fingers cut off.

We now bore away, intending to steer in the track of Carteret and Bligh, between Spirito Santo and Santa Cruz; and on the 8th, saw land to the westward. We sounded, but found no bottom. We run down the island, and saw a vast number of houses amongst the trees. It is very hilly, and, from the great height of some of them, may be called mountains. They are cultivated to the top; the reason of which, I presume, is from its being so full of inhabitants. It is about seven miles long; and being a new discovery, we called it Grenville's Island, in honour of Lord Grenville. The name the natives give it is Rotumah. They came off in a fleet of canoes, rested on their paddles, and gave the war-hoop at stated periods. They were all armed with clubs, and meant to attack us; but the magnitude and novelty of such an object as a man of war, struck them with a mixture of wonder and fear. They were, however, perfectly ignorant of fire-arms, and seemed much startled at the report of a musket, were too shy to stand the experiment of a great gun. As they came off with hostile intentions, they brought no women with them.

They wore necklaces, bracelets, and girdles of white shells. Their bodies were curiously marked with the figures of men, dogs, fishes, and birds, upon every part of them; so that every man was a moving landscape. These marks were all raised, and done, I suppose, by pinching up the skin.

They were great adepts in thieving, and uncommonly athletic and strong. One fellow was making off with some booty, but was detected; and although five of the stoutest men in the ship were hanging upon him, and had fast hold of his long flowing back hair, he overpowered them all, and jumped overboard with his prize. There is a high promontory on this island, which we named Mount Temple.

On the 11th, no land being then in sight, we run over a reef of coral, in eleven fathom water. We were much alarmed, but passed it in five minutes; and on sounding immediately afterwards, found no bottom. This was called Pandora's Reef.

On the 12th, in the morning, we discovered an island well wooded, but not inhabited. It had two remarkable promontories on it, one resembling a mitre, and the other a steeple; from whence we called it Mitre Island. We passed it, and stood to the westward; and at ten, the same morning, discovered another island to the north west. It is entirely cultivated, and [has] a vast number of inhabitants, though only a mile in length. The beach from the east, round by the south, is a white sand, but too much surf for a boat to attempt to land. In gratitude for the many good things we had on board, and the very high state of preservation in which they kept, we called this Cherry's Island, in honour of—Cherry, Esq; Commissioner of the Victualing-office.

On the 13th of August, we discovered another island to the north west. It is mountainous, and covered with wood to the very summit. We saw no inhabitants, but smoke in many different parts of it, from which it may be presumed it is inhabited. This we called Pitt's Island.

On the 17th, at midnight, we discovered breakers on each bow. We had just room to wear ship; and as this merciful escape was from the vigilance of one Wells, who was looking out ahead, it was called Wells's Shoals. Those hairbreadth escapes may point out the propriety of a consort. In the morning, at day-light, we put about, to examine the danger we were in, and found we had got embayed in a double reef, which will very soon be an island. We run round its north west end, and on the 23d saw land, which we supposed to be the Luisiade, a cape bearing north east and by east. We called it Cape Rodney. Another contiguous to it was called Cape Hood; and a mountain between them, we named Mount Clarence.

After passing Cape Hood, the land appears lower, and to trench away about north west, forming a deep bay; and it may be doubted whether it joins New Guinea or not.

We pursued our course to the westward, keeping Endeavour Straits open, by which means we hoped to avoid the dangers Capt. Cook met with in higher latitudes.

On the 25th, saw breakers; hauled up, and passed to the westward of them; the sea broke very gently on them. To these we gave the name of

Look-out Shoals. Before noon we saw more breakers, the reef of which was composed of very large stones, and called it Stony-reef Island.

On seeing obstruction to the southward, stood to the westward, where there appeared to be an opening. We saw an island in that direction, and a reef extending a considerable way to the north west. Hauled upon the wind, seeing our passage obstructed, and stood off and on, under an easy sail in the night, till daylight; and in the morning bore away, and discovered four islands, to which the name of Murray's Islands was given. On the top of the largest, there was something resembling a fortification. We saw at the same time three two–masted boats. We kept running along the reef, and in the forenoon thought we saw an opening. Lieut. Corner was immediately ordered to get ready, to discover if there was a passage for the ship, and went to the topmasthead, to look well round him before he left us. It was judged necessary that he should take with him an axe, some fuel, provisions, a little water, and a compass, previous to his departure.

From Captain Edwards' Report

The Tender and the Boats were employ'd the 9th & part of the 10th in Examining the Harbours and Oediddee went with them as Pilot, several Chiefs came onboard and brought with them Hogs and other Articles the produce of the Island and a Servant of Omia also came onboard said that he was not then much the better for his Masters Riches however his former connections was the cause of his visit to the Ship being made very profitable to him, and all the Chiefs & their attendance received presents from me. Two of the Chiefs of this Island were desirous to go in the Ship to Ulietia and I had given them leave but when the Ship was about to make Sail they suddenly changed their minds and went onshore & took Oediddee with them. Oediddee promised to follow us there the next day but we did not see him again. I proceeded to Ulietea Otaka & Bolabola and the Tender & boats were employ'd in Examining the Bays & Harbours of these Islands but we got no intelligence of the Bounty or her People.

Tah-a-too who called himself King of Bolabola informed me that he had been a few days before at Tubai which is a small low Island situated to the Northward of Bolabola and under its Jurisdiction, and that there was no white Man upon that Island nor upon Maurua another Island in sight of & to the Westward of Bolabola, he also mentioned another Island which I thought he called Mopehah, but we know no such Island unless it be Howes Island & that seems to be situated too far to the South & to the West for the Island he attempted to describe and point out to us. The Cheifs and several other people came onboard from these Islands & brought with them the usual produce and they were at all the Islands very pressing to prevail upon us to make a longer stay with them but as I had another object particularly in view, and my people in good health I did not think it proper unnecessarily to waste my time for the sake of procuring a few articles that were in great[er] abundance at these Islands than at Otaheite. I made presents to all these Cheifs as it was my custom to do to every one that had the least pretension to preeminence and to all the people who came on board in a first Boat. After leaving Bolabola I steered for Maurua and passed it at a small distance. Howes Island was not seen by us it is a low Island and we passed to the Southward of it. I then shaped my course to get into the Latitude of & to fall in to the Eastward of Whytotackee[.] On the 14th Henry Hilbrant one of the Pirates gave information that Christian had declared to him the Evening before he left Otaheite, that he intended to go with the Bounty to an uninhabited Island discovered by Mr. Byron[42] situated to the Westward of the Islands of Danger which from discription & situation I supposed to be the Island called by Mr. Byron the Duke of Yorks Island and if they could Land would settle then Run the Ship upon the Reef & destroy her but if they could not Land or if upon examination found it would not answer their purpose he would look out for some other uninhabited Island. However I continued my course for Whytotackee being now determined to Examine that Island in preference to the following any intelligence however plausible, and on the Morning of the 19th saw the Island Whytotackee & sent the Tender in shore to sound and look out for a Harbour. At Noon sent Lieut. Hayward in a Yawl to look into a place on the NW part of the Island that had the appearance of a Harbour & to get intelligence of the Natives. In the evening he returned.

The place was so far from being fit for the reception of a Ship that he could Scarcely find a passage through the Reef for the Boat; he conversed with seven or eight different sets of people whom he met with in Canoes & they all agreed the Bounty was not, nor had not been there since Lieut. Bligh left the Island nor did any of them known any thing of her. Lt. Hayward recollected one of the Natives whom he remember'd to have seen on board the Bounty when they discovered the Island, and he saw another Savage belonging to a Neighbouring [island] who knew Capt. Cook and inquired after him, Omai & Oediddee whom he said he had seen. These people at first approached the Boat with caution & could not be prevailed on to come onboard the Ship as I was convinced the Bounty was not at this Island & as Hervey's Mangea, & Wattea Islands to the SE of Whytotackee were inhabited I did not think it probable that Christian in the Weak state the Ship was in would attempt to settle upon either of them, and as there was some plausibility in the information given by Hilbrant the Prisoner, and as the Duke of Yorks Island seemed to answer the description of such an Island Christian had been heard by others to declare he would search for and settle at, it being by Mr. Byrons account uninhabited & without an Harbour & as it was out of the common track of Ships in these Seas since our acquaintance with the Society Islands Stil made it more eligible for his purpose. From these united circumstances I thought it was probable he might make choise of the Duke of Yorks Island for his intended settlement. I therefore determined to proceed to that Island taking Palmerstons Island in my way thither as it also answered in all respects except situation the description of the other, and at Night I bore away and made Sail for Palmerstons Islands and made them on the 21st in the Afternoon. On the 22^d in the Morning sent the Schooner Tender & Cutter in shore to look for Harbours or Anchorage & soon after Lieut. Corner was sent in the Yawl for the same purpose & to look out for the Bounty and her people, at noon perceiving the Schooner & Cutter go round the Norther[n]most Island. I stood round the SE Island with the Ship in order to join the Yawl that was at a Grapnel off that Island. At 2 sent the other Yawl to join Lieut. Corner. At 4 the two Yawls returned with a quantity of Coco Nuts & Lt. Corner also returned onboard soon after & Lieut. Hayward was sent on shore in a Yawl to Examine the SW Island.

After dark we burnt several false fires as Signals to the Boat but the Weather being Thick and Squally she did not return till the Morning of the 23^d but the Tender joined us that night and informed me that she had found a Yard on the Island marked Bounty's Driver Yard and other circumstances that indicated that the Bounty was or had been there. The tender was immediately sent in shore after the Yawl. On the 23[d] Provisions, ammunition

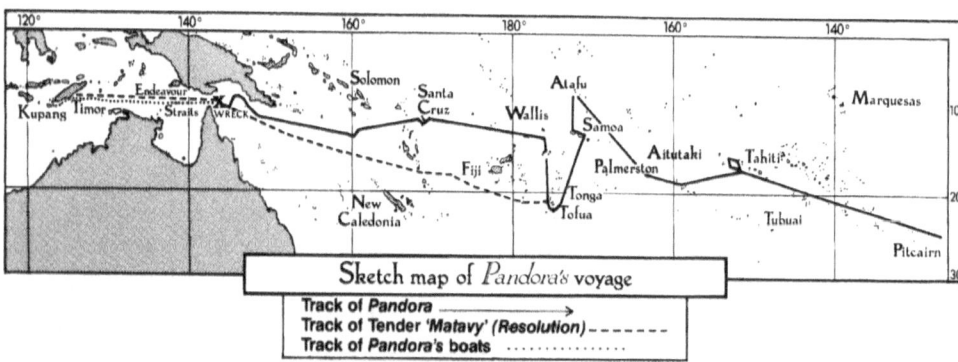

This map tracks Captain Edward Edwards' search for the *Bounty* mutineers in H.M.S. *Pandora* and the course of the schooner *Matavy* after the vessels were separated during a storm. It also shows where *Pandora* foundered and the route taken by its survivors to Timor and Kupang (Coupang) in four of the ship's boats. From *Mr. Bligh's Bad Language: Passion, Power and Theatre on the Bounty*, by Greg Dening. Copyright Cambridge University Press, 1992 (reproduced with permission of the Licensor through PLSclear).

&c. was sent onboard the Tender and Lieut Corner with a party of Men were sent with the Yawl & Tender to Land on the Northernmost Island. At 4 in the Afternoon perceived the Schooner Tender at Anchor under that Island, and the Yawl Landing the Party on a Reef Leading to it. Lieut. Corner had orders to Examine that & the Easternmost Island very minutely to see if any other traces besides the Yard could be made out of the Bounty or her people. On the 24th in the Morning sent the Cutter onboard the Tender for intelligence but she did not return till nearly 2 o'clock in the Afternoon when she brought with her seven men of Lieut. Corners party. She was sent onboard the Tender again with orders for the remainder of the party that was returned from the Search to be brought onboard the Pandora in the Yawl and for the Cutter to remain onboard the Tender to embark Lieut. Corner when he returned. The Mids. having represented to me that she answered the purpose of Landing & embarking better than a larger boat from particular circumstances of the Landing place, and I stood over for the SW Island to take onboard the other Yawl which had been sent to sound near the Reef of that Island & to procure from it some Coco Nuts &c. At 5 the Yawl came onboard & I then stood towards the Schooner in Order to take the other Yawl onboard, but the Weather became Squally with Rain & I stood out to Sea during the night.

The weather was rougher than common with an Ugly Sea & I did not get close in with them again till the 25th at Noon, soon after which the Yawl came onboard from the Schooner and informed us to my great astonishment & concern that the Cutter had not been onboard her since she left the Ship. The Tender was ordered to run down by the side of the Reef and if the Cutter was not seen there then to run out to Sea six leagues and to steer about WNW/W it being the opposite point to that on which the wind blew from the preceding Night, & I waited with the Ship to take onboard Lieut. Corner who was not then returned from the Search. He soon after appeared and was taken onboard. In his Search he found a double Canoe curiously painted, and different in make from those we had seen at the Islands we had visited, a piece of Wood burnt half through was also found. The Yard and these things lay upon the beach at high water Mark & were all eaten by the Sea Worm which is a strong presumption they were drifted there by the Waves. The Driver Yard was probably drove from Toobouai where the Bounty lost the greater part of her Spars & as no recent traces could be found on the Island of a Human being or any part of the Wreck of a Ship, I gave up all further Search and hopes of finding the Bounty or her people there. I then stood out to Sea and the Ship and the Tender cruised about in search of the cutter until the 29th in the Morning without seeing any thing of her. I being at that time well in with the Land I sent onshore once more to Examine the Reef and beach of the Northernm^t. Island but with no better success than before, as neither the Cutter or any Article belonging to her could be found there.

I then steered for the Duke of Yorks Island which we got sight of at Noon of the sixth of June and in the Afternoon the Tender & the two Yawls were sent inshore to Examine the coast. On the 7th in the Morning Lieuts. Corner & Hayward were sent onshore with a party of Men attended by the Schooner & the two yawls. We soon after saw some Hutts upon the Island and I made the Signal to the Boats to warn them of danger & for them to be upon their guard against surprize. They Landed and got Canoes within side [sic] of the Lagoon in which they made the circuit of it.

A few houses were found in Examining the Isles on the opposite side of the Lagoon, and also a Ships large Wooden Bouy; it appeared to be of foreign make & had evident Marks of its having been long in the Water. As Mr. Byron describes the Duke of Yorks Island to be without inhabitants, the sight of the Houses and a Ships Bouy before they were minutely Examined wrought so strongly on the Minds of the people that they saw many things in imagination that did not exist but attended to persuade them that the Bountys people were really upon the Island agreeable to the intelligence given by Hilbrant; but after the most minute & repeated Search no Human being of any description could be found upon the Island.

There were a number of Canoes, spare paddles, fishing Geer, and a variety of other things found in the Houses which seemed to prove that it was an occasional residence and fishery of the Natives of some Neighbouring Island. There is so great a difference in the situation of this Island as laid down in the Charts of Hawkesworths collection of Voyages & also of some others from that of Captain Cook, that there may be some doubt about its real situation. I follow'd that of Capt. Cook yet the situation of this Island by our Account did not exactly agree with him. He lays it down in Lat. 8° 41' S°. & Long. 173° 34' W. and the Center of the Island by our account lies Lat. 8°. 34' S°. & Long. pr Obs. 172° 6' and by Time Keeper 172°. 39' W^t. By our estimation this Island is not so large as it is by Mr. Byrons in other respects except the Houses it answers his description very well. I should have stood further to the Westward to have seen if there were any other Islands in that direction but I was apprehensive by so doing I might have had deficulty in fetching the Islands I had then to visit, and as the wind was unfavourable to stand to the Southward when I left the Island, I therefore satisfied myself in passing to the Westward of it, and stretching to the Northward so far as to know there was no Island within 30 miles of it on that point of the compass, and also to pass to windward of the Island when I put about & stood to the Southward.

In standing to the Southward I discovered an Island on the 12th of June, we soon perceived it was a Lagoon Island formed by a great many small Islands connected together by a Reef of Rocks forming a circle round the Lagoon in its Center. It is low but well Wooded amongst which the Coco Nut Tree is conspicuous both from its height & peculiar form; As we approached the Land we saw several Natives on the Beach. Lieut. Hayward was sent with the Tender & Yawl in shore to reconnoitre & to endeavour to converse with the Natives, and if possible to bring about a friendly entercourse with them.

They made signs of Friendship and beckoned him to come onshore. Yet whenever he drew near with the boat they always retired & he could not prevail on them to come [to] her, and the surf was thought too great to venture to Land at least before the friendship of the Natives was better confirmed. We soon afterwards saw several Sailing Canoes with stages in their middle Sailing across the Lagoon for the opposite Isles, but whether it was a flight or that they were only going afishing or on some other business we were [at] that time at a loss to know. Lieut. Corner was sent to look for a better Landing place & thinking that there was the appearance of an opening into the Lagoon round the NW Island I stood that way with the Ship to take a view of it, but found that it was also barred in that part by a Reef—

Better Landing places were found but they were to Leeward and at a considerable distance from the place that seemed to be the principal residence of the Natives. The next Morning Lieuts. Corner & Hayward Landed with a strong party near the Houses which they found deserted by the Natives & they had taken with them all the Canoes except one, it appeared exactly to resemble those we had seen at the Duke of Yorks Island. The Houses, fishing Geer, and utencels were also similar to those seen there which made me suppose that these were the people who occasionally visited that Island, but this had the appearance of being the principal residence; as Morais or burying places were found at this, but none at the former.

I was very desirous to get communication with these people as I thought we might possibly get some useful information relative to the Bouy we had seen at the Duke of Yorks Island, or about the Bounty, had she touched at either of these Islands, or at others in their Neighbourhood. With that view I left in, and about the Houses Hatchets, knives, Glasses and a variety of things that I thought would be useful or pleasing to them, and also to shew them we were dispos'd to be friendly to them, and by that means I hoped they would become less shy, and that an intercourse with them would be brought about, and I stood round the Northernmost Isle to visit other parts of the Island, & on the 14th in the Morning Lieut. Corner was sent in shore with the Tender, Yawl & Canoe & he Landed to the Eastward of the Northernmost Isle and marched round to the NE Extremity of the Isles; he perceived marks of the bare feet of the Natives in different parts, but more particularly about the Coco Nut Trees, most of which were strip'd of their fruit but not a single person or Canoe could be found. He embarked again at that part of the Isles with great dificulty, by the Assistance of Cork Jackets a Rope and the Canoes. I supposed the Natives had left the Island and I bore away to join the Tender that had been sent to Search for a Channel into the Lagoon near the Northernmost Isle, and after joining her I went once more towards the place we had first Examined & seeing no Natives or any signs of them there, I gave up the Search and on the 15th stood to the Southward for Navigators Islands. I called the Island the Duke of Clarence's Island. It is considerably larger than the Duke Of Yorks Island, it lies in Lat. 9°. 9'. 30" S°. & Long. 171°. 30'. 46" [.] There are abundance of Coco Nut trees both on this and the Duke of Yorks Island, in the trunks of which holes were cut transversely to catch and preserve water, and as no other water was seen by us, we supposed it was the only means they had to procure that useful & necessary Article. On the 18th in the Forenoon we saw a very high Island, and as I supposed it to be a New discovery I called it Chathams Island, and in standing in for it I perceived a bay towards the NE End and I made a Tack to endeavuor to look into it but perceiving that I could not accomplish my intentions before Night I bore away and run along shore and sent the Tender to reconnoitre and found opposite to a Sandy beach where there was an Indian Town, she got 25 fath^{ms}. about a ¼ of a mile from the Reef which runs off the place and carried Soundings of Sand regularly in to 5 fathoms. In the Morning a Boat was sent to sound in an opening in the Reef before the Town in which 3 fathoms of water was found and 2½ fathoms within it. This Harbour is situated on the North side near the middle but rather nearest to the West End. We were told that there was a River there, and an other or 2 between it and the [South] End. We then run round the West to the SW End of the Island & in [the] bay there 25 fath^{ms}. of water was found, the Bottom rather foul & bad Landing for a Ships Boat. The Natives said there was an[other] but the boat being called onboard by Signal she did not dare to Examine into the truth of their report. We found here a Native of the Friendly Islands who called himself Fenow and a relation of the Chief of that Name of Tongataboo. Fenow said he had seen Capt. Cook and English Ships at the Friendly Islands, & that the Natives of this Island had never seen a Ship before they saw the Pandora. The Island is more than 30 miles long a high Mountain extends almost from one extremity to the other which tapers down gradually at the Ends & sides to the Sea where it generally terminates in perpendicular cliffs of moderate height, except in a few places where there is a white beach of Coral sand. The Natives called the Island Otewhy Lat. of NW point 13°. 27'. 48" S°. Long. 172°. 32'. 13" W^r. S°. Point Lat. 13°. 46'. 18" S°. Long. 172°. 18'. 20" W^r. & East point in Lat. 13°. 32'. 20" S°. & Long. 172°. 2' W^r. On the 21st we saw another Island about four Leagues to the Eastward of this, and there are two small Islands between them, a small one in the middle, and four off its East End, three of which are of considerable height. There is a greater variety of Mountains and Valleys in this than in Chathams, and it is exceedingly well Wooded, and trees of an Enormous size grow upon the very summits of the Mountains, with spreading heads resembling the Oak. The same sort of Trees were also seen in the same situation on Chathams but not in so great abundance. This Island is near 40 miles long and of considerable breadth. The Natives called it Oattooah. Their canoes (although not so well finish'd) Language and some of their Customs much resemble those of the Friendly Islands, but they have some peculiar to themselves, that of tingeing their skin Yellow & which is a mark of distinction amongst them is one of them. The Lat. of the West Point is 13°: 52': 25" S°. & Long. 171°. 49'. 13" [W.] and the SE part in Lat. 14°. 3". 30" S°. and Long. 171°.12'. 50" W^r. As this Island by our account was considerably to the Westward of the Navigators Islands we at first supposed it to be a New discovery but after visiting the other of the Navigators Islands discovered by Monsr. Bougainville and running down again upon this we had reason to suppose that the SE End of Oattooah had been seen by him at a distance & that it was the last Island of the Group that he saw. Between 5 & 6 o'clock of the Evening of the 22^d of June lost sight of our Tender in a Thick Shower of Rain. Some thought that they saw her light again at 8 o'clock but in the Morning she was not to be seen. We cruised for her in sight of the Island all the 23^d & 24th, and as I could not find the Tender near the place where she was first missed, I thought it proper to make the best of my way for Annamooka, the place appointed as a last Rendezvous, and to endeavour to get there before her, lest her small force should be a Temptation for the Natives to attack her and accordingly we stood to the Southward. When we were to the Eastward of Oattooah we saw another Island bearing from us about ESE 8 leagues. We afterwards knew that this was one of the Navigators Islands seen by Monsr. Bougainville.

On the Morning of the 28th saw the Hahpy Islands and before Noon the Group of Island[s] to the Eastward of Annamooka. We passed round to the Southward of these Islands & run down between little Annamooka and the Fallafagee Islands & on the 29th anchored in Annamooka Road. Whilst we were watering the ship &c. I sent Lieut. Hayward to the Hahpy Islands in a double Canoe which I hired of Toobow a Chief of this Island for the purpose of examining them, and to make enquiries after the Bounty & the Tender, but no intelligence could be got of either of those Vessels at this, the Islands near it or at the Happy Islands, and having compleated our Water and got a plentiful supply of Yams, & a few Hogs & fowls we Sailed from thence on 10th of July. The Natives were very daring in their thefts but some of the Articles stolen were recovered again by the Chiefs. Yet many of them were entirely lost and as I did not think proper to carry things to extremity on that account for fear that too much rigour might opperate to the disadvantage of the Tender should she arrive at the Island in our absence, which I told them I expected she would do, and that I intended to return with the Ship in about 20 days and I left a Letter of Instructions for the Tender with Moukahkahlah a resident Chief which he promised to deliver. He is not the superior Chief, but we found him the most useful to us & I thought him the most worthy of trust.

Whilst we were at Annamooka Fattahfahé the Chief of all the Islands & who generally resides at Tongataboo or Amsterdam Island came to visit us as did also a great number of Chiefs from the Adjacent Islands & to all of whom I gave presents, and also to to [sic] such of their Friends [in] attendance that were introduced for the purpose of receiving favours. A Person called Toobow was the Principal person in authority at Annamooka when we arrived there. I learnt that he belonged to Tongataboo and had but little property on the Island he governed and I supposed that he was a Deputy or Minister of Fattahfahé who is generally acknowledged to be the Superior Chief of all the Islands known under the Names of the Friendly, Hahpy, and also of many other Islands unknown to us.

Fattahfahé and Toobow were onboard the Pandora when she got under way, attended by two large double Sailing Canoe's, the Largest of which had upwards of 40 Person[s] on board. I supposed that they came onboard to take leave & in expectation of getting some additional farewell presents in which they were not disappointed. I knew that Fattahfahé was shortly going to make the tour of the Hahpy Islands, and as I perceived that he was exceedingly well pleased with what I had given him, & with his situation & accommodation onboard the Ship, I invited him to go with us to Toofoa and Kah-o two Islands I was then steering for, and which I intended to visit, as I thought he would be useful [in] procuring us a peaceable Landing at Toofoa, the Islands wh[ose] Inhabitants had behaved so treacherously to Lieut. Bligh when he put in there for refreshments in the Bounty's Launch. Before sun set we got within a small distance of the Island, but that was too late for our Boats to go on shore, and the Canoes were sent to the Islands to announce the Arrival of these great Chiefs; their coming in the Ship I m[ade] no doubt would increase their consequence, & probably also [the] tribute they might think proper to impose on the subjects. The next Morning Lieut. Corner attended by the two Chiefs was sent on shore at Toofoa to Search & to make the Necessary inquiries after the Bounty and our Tender &c. and then to cross the Channel which is about 3 or 4 miles over and to do the same at Kah-o & when I saw the Boat put off from Toofoa & stand over for the other Island I bore away with the Ship and run through the Channel between the two Islands. At 4 in the Afternoon Lieut. Corner, Fattahfahé & Toobow returned onboard without success in their search & enquiries. The two Chiefs were put onboard their Canoes and they made sail for the Hahpy Islands. I now intended to have visited Tongataboo and the other of the Friendly Islands but as the wind was southerly and unfavourable for the purpose I took the resolution once more to visit Oattooah and also the Navigators Islands in Search of the Bounty and our Tender & to endeavour to fall in to the Eastward of those Islands.

Part Four. Searching for Fletcher Christian 87

On the Morning of the 12th we discovered a Cluster of Islands bearing from W&S to NW&N but as the wind was favourable for us to proceed I did not think it proper to loose time in Examining them now, but intended to do it on my return to the Friendly Islands.

On the 14th in the forenoon we saw three Islands which we supposed to be the three first Islands seen by Monsr. Bougainville and part of the Cluster called by him Navigators Islands, the Largest of these Islands the Natives called Toomahnuah. We passed by them at a convenient distance [&] several Canoes came towards the Ship and it was with great difficulty we prevailed on them to come alongside, and stil greater to get them into the Ship. They brought very few things in their Canoes except Coco Nuts which I bought & then gave them a few things as presents before they left the Ship and after making the Necessary enquiries as far as our limited knowledge of the Language would permit us. I proceeded to the Westward and before daylight of the Morning of the 15th we saw another Island, we run down on the North side of it, and brought to occasionally to sound and to take on board Canoes. We found the same shiness amongst the Natives here as at the last Islands, but a few presents being given to them they at last ventured on board. The Island is called by them Otootooillah it is at least five leagues long, we supposed it to be another of the Islands seen by Monsr. Bougainville. We got soundings in 53 fathoms water, and the depth decreased as we stood in shore & there probably is Anchorage on this side of the Island sheltered from the prevailing winds, but we did not see the Reef mentioned by Monsr. Bougainville to Run two Leagues from the West End.

After making the usual enquiries after the Bounty & Tender & making presents to our Visiters, we steered to the Westward inclining to the North, and before Night saw Oattooah bearing WNW. The SE End of this Island was also probably seen by Monsr. Bougainville, but by his description he could only have had a distant and a very imperfect view of the Island. On the 16th we run down on the south side of it almost to the West End and had frequent communication with the Natives, but could get no information relative either to the Bounty or our Tender. We saw a few of the Natives with bluw, [sic] Mulbery and other Coloured Beads about their necks and we understood that they got them from C.[aptain] Cook at Tongataboo one of the Friendly Islands. Having finished my business here I stood to the Southward with an intention to visit the Group of Islands we had discovered in our way hither, and we got sight of them again in the Afternoon of the 18th. On the 19th in the Morning we ran down on the Northside until we came to an Openning through which we could see the Sea on the opposite side, and a kind of Sound is formed by some Islands to the NE and some other Islands of considerable size to the SW, and in the intermediate space there are several small Isles & Rocks. On the Larboard hand of the North Entrance there is a Shoal on which the Sea appears to break, although there is from 8 to 12 fathoms of water upon it. In the other part of the Entrance there is 40 fath^{ms}. of water or more. Our boat had only time to examine the Entrance and the Larboard side of the Sound in which there are interior bays w[h]ere about 30 fath^{ms}. of water is to be found within ab[out] a cables Length of the Shore. The Branches of the Sound on the Starboard side & which are yet unexamined appear to promise better anchorage than was found on the opposite shore, and should it turn out so, it will be by far the safest & best Anchorage hitherto known amongst the Friendly Islands. The Natives told us there was good Water at several places within the Sound, and there is plenty of Wood.

Several of the Inferior Chiefs were onboard us, amongst whom were one of the Fattahfahés and one of the Toobou Family, but the Principal Chief of the Islands was not onboard, but we supposed he was coming at the time we made Sail. They brought onboard Yams, Coco Nuts, some bread fruit, a few Hogs & fowls and would have supplied us with more Hogs had it been convenient for us to have made a longer stay with them, & which they intreated us much to do. We found them very fair in their dealings, very inoffensive and better behaved than any Savages we had yet seen. They have frequent communication with Annamooka, and the other Friendly Islands, and their Customs and Languages appear to be nearly the same. I called the whole group Howes Islands. The Islands on the Larboard side of the North entrance I distinguished by the Names of Barrington & Sawyer; two on the Starboard side by the Names of Hotham & Jarvis. [A] high Island a considerable way to the NW I called Gardeners Island, and another high Island to the SW was called Bickertons Island. There is a small High Isle about 4 miles to the S°.W^d. of this, and a small low Island about 5 or 6 miles to the SE & E of Gardeners Island, and several Island[s] to the SE of the Islands forming the Sound & to several small Isles within it, to which no names were given. On the 20th at 2 in the Morning we passed with in 2 miles of the small Island that lays to the SE from Gardeners Island & soon after saw Gardeners Island, on the NW side of which there appeared to be tolerable good Landing on a shingle beach and a little to the right of this place, at the upper edge of the Cliffs is a Volcano from which we observed the smoke to issue. There are recent Marks of convulsion having happened in the Island, some parts of it appear to have fallen in, and other parts to be turned upside down. This part of the Island is the most barren Land we have seen in the country. At 9 o'clock thought we saw a large Island bearing NW & I made Sail towards it and as the Weather was hazey we did not discover our mistake 'till near Noon, when I hauled the wind to the Southward. On the 23rd saw an Island from the Masthead which I supposed was one of the Pillstart Islands. On the 26th in the Morning saw the Island of Middleburgh & on 27th run in between Middleburgh, Eooa & Tongataboo. Several Canoes came onboard us from these different Islands. We were within half a mile of the last & equally near to the Shoals of the second, but not so near to Middleburgh yet we were near enough to see into English Road. At these Islands we could neither see nor get any satisfactory information relative to the objects of our Search. The Natives brought in their Canoe's Yams, Coco Nuts and a few small Hogs and I make no doubt that I should have been able to procure plenty of these Articles had it been convenient for me to have stay'd at these Islands.

The difficulty of getting in and out of the Harbour, and the indifferent quality of the water were alone sufficient objections against my stopping here. The Road at Annamooka was more convenient for getting out and in, and the Water Although not of the very best quality is reported to be better than that found at Amsterdam and Annamooka being the place I had appointed as a Rendezvous for the Tender. I did not hesitate in giving the preference to it, and accordingly made the best of my way thither, and we saw the fallafagee Islands (which lie near Annamooka) before dark and also Toofoa Kah-o & Hoonga Tonga Islands to the Westward which are visible at a greater distance. On 28th July anchored in Annamooka Road.

The Person who now had the Principal authority on shore was a Young Chief whom we had not seen before.

There was the same respect paid to him as was paid to Fattahfahé & to Toobow, neither of those Chiefs nor Moukahkahlah were now in the Island, and the Natives were now more daring in their thefts than ever, and would sometimes endeavour to take things by force, and robbed & stripped some of our people that were separated from the Party. Lieut. Corner who Commanded the Watering and Wooding parties onshore received a blow on the Head & was robbed of a curiosity he had bought & held in his hand, and with which the Thief was making off. Lieut. Corner shot the Thief in the back and he fell to the ground, at the same instant the Natives attempted to take Axes & a Saw from the Wooding party, and actually got off with two Axes one by force and the other by stealth, but they did not succeed in getting the saw. Two muskets were fired at the thieves yet it was supposed they were not hurt but we were told that the other Man died of his wound. One of the Yawls was on shore at the time and the Longboat was Landing near her with [an] Empty Cask. Lieut. Corner drew the Wooding & watering parties towards the Boats and then began to load them with the Wood that was Cut. A Boat was sent from the Ship to enquire the cause of the firing that was heard, but before she return'd a Canoe came from the Shore to inform the Principal Chief whom I had brought on board to dine with me that one of the Natives had been killed by our people. The Chief was very much agitated at the information & wanted to get out of the cabin Windows into the Canoe, but I would not suffer him to do it and told him I would go on shore with him myself in a little time in one of the Ships boats. Our Boat soon returned and gave me an account of what had passed on shore. I told the Chief that the Lieut. had been struck & that he and his party had been robb'd of several Things and that I was very glad that the Thief was shot and that I should shoot every person that attempted to rob us, but that no other person except the Thief should be hurt by us on that account. The Axes and some other things that had been stolen before were returned and very few robberies of any consequence were attempted and discover'd 'till the day of our departure. I took this opportunity to shew the Chief what Execution the Cannon & Carronades would do by firing a six-pound shot on shore and an 18 pounder Carronade with grape shot into the Sea. I afterwards went on shore with two Boats and took with me the Chief and his attendance and before I returned onboard again told him that I should send on shore the next Morning for water & for Wood, and that I should also come on Shore myself in the course of the day, all which he approved of, and desired me to do, and accordingly the next Morning the 31st of July the water and Wooding party were sent onshore, and carried on their business without interruption, and in the Afternoon I went on shore myself and made a small present to the Chief & to some other people. On the 2^d of August having compleated my water &c and thinking it time to return to England, I did not think proper to wait any longer for the Tender, but left instructions for her Commander should she happen to arrive after my departure, and I sailed from Annamooka attended by a number of Chiefs and Canoes belonging to this and the surrounding Islands. After the ship was under way some of the Natives had the address to get in at the Cabin Windows, and stole out of the Cabin some books and other things and they had actually got into their Canoes before they were discovered. The thieves were allow'd to make their Escape but the Canoes that had the stolen things in, were brought alongside & broke up for firewood. During this transaction the other Natives carried on their trafic alongside with as much unconcern as if nothing had happen'd. I made farewell presents to all the Chiefs and to many others of different descriptions, and after hauling round Annamooka Shoals passed to the Eastward of Toofoa and Kah-o and in the Morning saw Bickertons Island and the small Island to the Southward of it. On the 4th in the Afternoon saw Land bearing NNW. At first we took it for Keppels & Boscawens Islands which I intended to visit & by account was only a few miles to the Westward of them. As we approached the Land we perceived that it was only one Island and as I supposed it was a New discovery I called it Proby's Island. The Hills of which there are a great many of different heights & forms are planted with Coco Nuts, and other trees and Houses are of a Larger size than we had usually seen on the Islands in these Seas were on the Tops of Hills of Moderate height. We passed from the SE End to the East round to the North & NW and the Landing appeared to be very indifferent until we came near the NW End, where the Land formed itself into a kind of bay & where the La[n]ding

Part Four. Searching for Fletcher Christian 91

appeared to be better. The Natives brought onboard Coco Nuts & plantains all of which I bought & made them a present of a few Articles of Iron. They told us that they had water, Hogs, fowls & yams onshore, and plenty of Wood. They spoke nearly the same Language as at the Friendly Islands. It lies in Lat. 15°. 53' S°. and Long. 175°. 51' W^r.

I was now convinced that I was rather further to the Westward than I expected, and the examining this Island had carried me still farther that way. I therefore gave up my intention of visiting Boscawens & Keppels Islands as the regaining the Easting Necessary would take up more time than would be prudent to allow at this advanced time of the Season, and as soon as I had made the Necessary enquiries &c. after the Bounty &c. our course was shaped with a view to fall in to the Eastward of Wallis Island, and the Next day the 5th a little before Noon saw that Island bearing W by S estimated by the Master at 10 leagues but I did not my self suppose it to be more than 7 leagues from us at that time. Canoes came off to us & brought Coco Nuts & fish, which they sold for Nails and I also made them a present of some small Articles which I always made a rule to do to first adventurers hoping that it might turn out advantageous to future visitors—but they went away before I had given them all I intended.

They told us there was running Water, Hogs & fowls onshore. They spoke the Language of the Friendly Islands and I observed that one of the Men had both his little fingers cut off and the flesh over his cheekbones very much bruised after the manner of the Natives of those Islands. In the Evening I bore away and made Sail to the Westward intending to run between Espirito Santo & Santa Cruz & to keep between the tracks of Capt. Carteret & Lieut. Bligh and on the 8th at ½ p[as]t 10 at night saw Land bearing from the W & S. ½ S. We had no ground at 110 fathoms.

At day light I bore away a[nd] passed round the East End and run down on the South side of the Island. There is a white beach on those parts of it on which there appears to be tolerable good Landing or better than is usually seen on the Islands in these Seas and there is probably Anchorage in different places on this side or under the small Islands of which there are several near the principal Island but as I did not hoist out a boat to Sound that still remains a doubt. There are Coco Nut Trees all along the Shore behind the beach and an uncommon number of Boughs amongst them. The Island is rather high diversified with Hills of different forms some of which might obtain the Name of Mountain but they are Cultivated up to their very summits with Coco Nut Trees or other Articles and the Island is in general as well or better Cultivated and its inhabitants more numerous for its size than any Island we have hitherto seen. The principal Island is about 7 miles long & 3 or 4 broad but including the Islands off its East & West Ends & which latter are joined to it by a Reef it is about 10 miles long. I called it Grenville Island supposing it to be a New discovery. Its Lat. is 12°. 29' and Long. 183°. 03 W^r. A great number of padling Canoes came off and view'd the Ship at a distance and I believe their intentions were at first hostile. They were all armed with Clubs and they had a great quantity of Stones in their Canoes which they use in battle, and they all occasionally joined in a kind of War Whoop. We made Signs of Peace, and offered them a variety of Toys which first drew them alongside, and then into the Ship where they behaved very quietly. Probably the unexpected presents they got from us, and our number & strength might opperate in favour of Peace, however they seemed to have the same propensity to thieving as the Natives of the other Islands, & gave us many, some of which ludicrous examples. Although at so great a distance, they said they were acquainted with the Friendly Islands and had learnt from them the use of Iron. They are Tattooed in a different manner from the Natives of the other Islands, we had visited, having the figure of a fish, Birds, and a variety of other things Marked upon their Arms. There [sic] Canoe's were not so delicately formed nor so well finish'd as at the Friendly Islands, but more resembled those of the Duke of Yorks, the Duke of Clarence & the Navigators Islands.

Neither Sailing or double Canoes came onboard nor did we see any of either of those descriptions. They told us that water and many other useful things, the usual produce of the Islands of those Seas could be procured on shore. Their Language appeared something to resemble that spoken at the Friendly Islands, and after asking them such questions as were thought Necessary some of which probably were not perfectly understood by them, or their answers by us we made Sail and continued our course to the Westward. No Women were in the canoes, that visited us—which curiosity or the hope of getting some pleasing Toys usually bring to our sight, but this is another proof that their Original intentions were hostile.

We passed the Island in so short a time, that those who neglected to come at our first appearance had not afterwards an opportunity to visit us. On the 11th at 11 O'Clock in the Morning we struck Soundings on a bank in 12 to 14 fathoms water, and at 10 Minutes after 11 had no ground at 40 fathoms. No Land was then in sight nor did we get any Soundings after in the course the day. It was called Pandora's Bank, its Lat. 12°. 11'. S°. and Long. 188°. 08' W^r.

On the next Morning saw a small Island which [was] made in two high Hummocks and a Steeple Rock of less height on the West side of the Hummocks. It obtained the name of Mitre Island. The shore appeared to be steep to, & we had no bottom at 120 fathoms within ¾ of a mile of the Shore. Saw no Landing place or any sign of Inhabitants. The Tops of the Hills were covered with Wood. There was also some on the sides but not in so great abundance they being too Steep & too bare of Soil in some places to support it. Lat. 11°. 49' S°. Long. 190. 04. 30 W^r.

By 9 O'Clock we had passed it & steered to the Westward and soon after

10 we saw another Island bearing NW&N. We hauled up to the NW to make it more distinctly it is of considerable height yet not much more than a mile long and the Top & side of the Hills very well cultivated and a number of Houses were seen near the Beach in a Bay on the South side of the Island. The beach from the East round to the South to the West End is of white Sand, but there was then too much Surf for a ships boat to Land upon it with Safety. I called it Cherrys Island. Its Lat. is 11° 37' S°. and Long. 190. 19. 30" W^r.

On the 13th of August a little before Noon saw an Island bearing about NW & N. In general it is high but to the West & NW the Mountain taper'd down to a round point of Moderate height. It abounds with Wood even the summit of the Mountains are covered with Trees. Off the SE End there was the appearance of a Harbour and from that place a Reef runs along the South side to the Westernmost extremity. In some places its distance is not much more than a mile from the Shore, in other places the distance is considerably more.

Although we were sometimes within less than a mile of the Reef we saw neither house nor people. The haziness of the Weather prevented us from seeing objects distinctly, Yet we saw smoke very plain from which it may be presumed the Island is inhabited. It is 6 or 7 leagues long and of considerable Breadth. I called it Pitts Island. Its Lat. 11°. 50'. 30" S°. South point & Long. 193°. 14'. 15" W^r. At Midnight between the 16 & 17 of Augt. Breakers were discovered ahead & upon each Bow and not a mile from us. We were lying to and heaving the Lead at the time, and had no ground at 120 fathoms. We wore Ship and stood from them & in less than an hour after more Breakers were seen extending more than a point before our Lee Beam, but we made more Sail & so got clear of them all. At day light we put about with intention to examine the Breakers we had seen in the night and we made two boards but perceiving I could not weather them without some risque I bore up & run round its NW end. It is a double Reef inclosing a space of deeper Water, like the Lagoon Islands so common in these Seas, and probably will become one in the course of time. The Sea Breaks pretty high upon it in different parts, but there is no part of the Reef absolutely above water. It is about 7 miles long in the direction of NW&W. Its breadth is not so much. Called it Wells's Shoal. It lies in Lat. 12° 20' S°. & Long. 200°. 2 W^r. We persued our Course to the Westward and on the 23^d saw Land bearing from NE to N&W. The Easternmost Land when first seen was 10 or 12 leagues from us, & it cannot be far to the Westward of the Land seen by Monsr. Bougainville & called by him the Louisiade, and probably joins to it.

A Cape in Lat. 10°. 3'. 32" S°. & Long. 212° 14' Wt. was called Cape Rodney and another Cape in Lat. 9°. 58'. S°. & Long. 212° 37' Wt. was called Cape Hood and an inland Mountain between them was called Mount Clarence. After passing Cape Hood the Land appears lower and to trench away about NNW and to form a Deep and wide bay or perhaps a passage through for we saw no other Land, and there are doubts whether it joins to New Guinea or not.

I pursued my course to the Westward between the Latitudes of 10°. and 9°. 33' S°.—keeping the Mouth of Endeavour Straits open, by which I hoped to avoid the dificulties and Dangers experienced by Capt. Cook in his passage through the Reef in a higher Latitude and also the dificulties he met with when within, in his run from thence to the Straits Mouth. On the 25th Augt. at ½ pt 9 in the Morning saw Breakers from the Masthead bearing from us W&S to WNW. I hauled up to the Southward, and passed to Eastward of them. It Runs in the direction of WSW & ENE 4' or 5' and another side runs in the direction of NW the distance unknown. The Sea broke very moderately upon it. In some places barely perceptable. In the interior part a very small Sand bank was seen from the Masthead, and no other part of the Reef was above water. It obtained the Name of lookout Shoal.

Before Noon we saw more breakers which proved to be one of those half formed Islands inclosing a Lagoon, the Reef of which was composed principally of very large Stones, but a Sand bank was seen from the Masthead extending to the Southward of it, and as I could not Weather it & seeing an

A painting by Australian artist Bronwyn Searle brings to life this description from Captain Edward Edwards' statement on the loss of H.M.S. *Pandora*: "Musquets fired from the Ship answered by the Boat by firing Musquets reciprocally to point out the place of each other's situation" (© Queensland Museum, Bronwyn Searle).

opening to the Westward I steered to the WSW—and a little before 2 O'Clock saw an Island to the Westward of us, and another Reef bearing about SW&S & I then steered W ½ N until ½ past 5 when a Reef was seen extending from the Island a considerable way to the NW the Island bearing then abt. WSW. I immediately hauled upon a wind in order to pass to the Southward of it, seeing the passage to the Northward obstructed, and I stood off & on under an easy sail during the Night, and in the Morning bore away but as we drew near, we also saw a Reef extending to the Southward from the South End of the Island. I run to the Southward along the Reef with intention and expectation of getting round it, and the whole day was spent without succeeding in my purpose, or without seeing the End of the Reef, or any break in it that gave the least hopes of a Channel fit for a Ship. The Islands which I called Murray's Islands are four in number, two of them are of considerable height may be seen 12 leagues.

The principal Island is not more than 3 miles long. It is well wooded and at the Top of the highest Hill the Rocks have the appearance of a fortified garrison. The other high Island is only a single Mountain almost destitute of Trees or Verdure. The other two are only craggy barren Rocks. We saw three two [sic] Masts boats under Sail near the Reef which we supposed belonged to the Island. Murray Isles lie in Lat. 9°. 57'. S°. and Long. 216°. 43' W^t. We kept turning to the Southward along the Reef until the 28th in search of a Channel and in the forenoon of that day we thought we saw an openning through the Reef near a White Sandy Island or Key, and a little before Lieut Corner was sent in the Yawl to Examine it. At ¾ past 4 he made the signal that there was a Channel through the Reef fit for the Ship & after the signal was made and repeated for the Boat to return onboard, and after dark, false fires and Muskets were fired from the Ship and answered with Muskets by the Boat reciprocally to point out the situation of each other. We sounded frequently but had no ground at 110 fath^{ms}.

PART FIVE

Shipwreck in Torres Strait

From Captain Edwards' Report

At abt. 20 minutes after 7 the boat was seen close under our stern, and at the same time we got soundings in 50 fathoms water. We immediately made Sail but before the Tacks were onboard and the Sails trimmed, the Ship struck upon a Reef when we were fo[und] ¼ less 2 fathoms water on the Larboard side and 3 fathoms on the Starboard side. Got out the Boats with a view of carrying out an Anchor, but before it could be effected the Ship struck so violently upon the Reef that the carpenter reported that she made 18 Inches of water in 5 Minutes, & in 5 Minutes after there was 4 feet of water in the hold. Finding the leak increasing so fast found it Necessary to turn the hands to the Pumps & to bail at the different Hatchways. She still continued to gain upon us so much that in an hour & half after she had struck there was 8½ feet of water in the hold. At 10 perceived that the Ship had beat over the Reef, where we had 10 fathoms water. We let go the small Bower & veered away a Cable & let go the best Bower under foot in 15½ fathoms water to steady the Ship. At this time the water only gained upon us in a small degree and we flattered ourselves for some time that by the Assistance of a thrummed Topsail which we were preparing and intended to haul under the Ships Bottom we might be able to free her of water, but these flattering hopes did not continue long for as she settled in the Water the leak increased, and in so great a degree that there was reason to apprehend she would sink before day light.

In the course of the night two of the Pumps were for some time rendered useless one however was repaired and we continued baling and Pumping the remainder of the Night and every effort was made to keep her afloat.

Day light fortunately appeared and gave us an opportunity to see our situation and the surrounding danger. Our Boats were kept a stern of the Ship, a small quantity of Provisions and other Necessary Articles were put into them, rafts were made, and all floating things upon Deck were unlashed. At ½ past 6 the hold was full, & water was between Decks and it also wash'd in at the upper Deck ports and there were strong indications that the ship

Part Five. Shipwreck in Torres Strait

This wood engraving of H.M.S. *Pandora* sinking, from the May 26, 1838, issue of the weekly periodical *Chronicles of the Sea*, illustrates the ship's final moments when the crew and prisoners were trying to escape the doomed vessel. "Pandora's Box," where the *Bounty* prisoners were closely confined, is depicted on the ship's quarterdeck.

was upon the very point of Sinking, and we began to leap over board and to take to the Boats and before every body could get out of her the Ship actually sunk. The Boats continued a stern of the Ship in the direction of the drift of the tide from her, and took up the people that had hold of rafts or other floating things that had been cast loose for the purpose of supporting them in the Water. We loaded two of the Boats with people and sent them to an Island or rather Key about 3 or 4 miles from the Ship, and the other two boats remained near the Ship for some time & pickd up all the people that could be seen & then followed the two first Boats to the Key, and after Landing the people &c. boats were immediately sent again to look about the Wreck & adjoining Reefs for missing people, but they returned without having found a single person. On Mustering we discovered that 89 of the Ships Company and 10 of the pirates that were prisoners onboard were saved, and that 31 of the Ships Company and four pirates were lost with the Ship.

The Boats were hauled up to secure and fit them for the intended run to Timor. An account was taken of the provision, and other Articles saved & they were spread to dry, and we put ourselves to the following allowance—to

3 Ounces of Bread which was occasionally reduced to two ounces, to ½ an Ounce of Portable soup to ½ an ounce of Essence of Malt but these two articles were not served till after we left the Key and they were at other times withheld, to two small glasses of water and one of wine. On the afternoon of the 30th sent a boat to the wreck to see if any thing could be procured. She returned with the Head of the T. G. Mast a little of the T.G. Rigging, and part of the Chain of the Lightning conductor, but without a single article of Provision. A boat was also sent to Examine the Channel through the reef &c. and was afterwards sent afishing. She lost her Grapnel but no fish was caught.

From George Hamilton, A Voyage Round the World in His Majesty's Frigate Pandora

It was now the 28th of August. It had lately been our custom to lay to in the night, M. Bougainville having represented this part of the ocean as exceedingly dangerous; and it certainly is the boldest piece of navigation that has every yet been attempted. We would gladly have continued the same custom; but the great length of the voyage would not permit it, as, after we had passed to the westward of Bougainville's track, the ocean was perfectly unexplored.

At five in the afternoon, a signal was made from the boat, that a passage through the reef was discovered for the ship; but wishing to be well informed in so intricate a business, and the day being far spent, we waited the boats coming on board, made a signal to expedite her, and afterwards repeated it. Night closing fast upon us, and considering our former misfortunes of losing the tender and jolly-boat, rendered it necessary, both for the preservation of the boat, and the success of the voyage, to endeavour, by every possible means, to get hold of her.

False fires were burnt, and muskets fired from the ship, and answered by the boat reciprocally; and as the flashes from their muskets were distinctly seen by us, she was reasonably soon expected on board. We now sounded, but had no bottom with a hundred and ten fathom line, till past seven o'clock, when we got ground in fifty fathom. The boat was now seen close under the stern; we were at the same time lying to, to prevent the ship forereaching. Immediately on sounding this last time, the topsails were filled; but before the tacks were hauled on board, and the sails trimmed, she struck on a reef of rocks, and at that instant the boat got on board. Every possible effort was attempted to get her off by the sails; but that failing, they were furled, and the boats hoisted out with a view to carry out an anchor. Before that was accomplished, the carpenter reported she made eighteen inches water in five minutes; and in a quarter of an hour more, she had nine feet water in the hold.

Part Five. Shipwreck in Torres Strait

The hands were immediately turned to the pumps, and to bale at the different hatchways. Some of the prisoners were let out of irons, and turned to the pumps. At this dreadful crisis, it blew very violently; and she beat so hard upon the rocks, that we expected her, every minute, to go to pieces. It was an exceeding dark, stormy night; and the gloomy horrors of death presented us all round, being every where encompassed with rocks, shoals, and broken water. About ten she beat over the reef; and we let go the anchor in fifteen fathom water.

The guns were ordered to be thrown overboard; and what hands could be spared from the pumps, were employed thrumbing a topsail to haul under her bottom, to endeavor to fodder her. To add to our distress, at this juncture one of the chain-pumps gave way; and she gained fast upon us. The scheme of the topsail was now laid aside, and every soul fell to baling and pumping. All the boats, excepting one, were obliged to keep a long distance off on account of the broken water, and the very high surf that was running near us. We baled between life and death; for had she gone down before day-light, every soul must have perished. She now took a heel, and some of the guns they were endeavouring to throw over board run down to leeward, which crushed one man to death; about the same time, a spare topmast came down from the booms, and killed another man.

The people now became faint at the pumps, and it was necessary to give them some refreshment. We had luckily between decks a cask of excellent strong ale, which we brewed at Anamooka. This was tapped, and served regularly to all hands, which was much preferable to spirits, as it gave them strength without intoxication. During this trying occasion, the men behaved with the utmost intrepidity and obedience, not a man flinching from his post. We continually cheered them at the pumps with the delusive hope of its being soon day-light.

About half an hour before day-break, a council of war was held amongst the officers; and as she was then settling fast down in the water, it was their unanimous opinion, that nothing further could be done for the preservation of his Majesty's ship; and it was their next care to save the lives of the crew. To effect which, spars, booms, hen-coops, and every thing buoyant was cut loose, that when she went down, they might chance to get hold of something. The prisoners were ordered to be let out of irons. The water was now coming faster in at the gun-ports than the pumps could discharge; and to this minute the men never swerved from their duty. She now took a very heavy heel, so much that she lay quite down on one side.

One of the officers now told the Captain, who was standing aft, that the anchor on our bow was under water; that she was then going; and, bidding him farewell, jumped over the quarter into the water. The Captain then followed his example, and jumped after him. At that instant she took her last heel; and, while every one were scrambling to windward, she sunk in an in-

HMS Pandora Breaking Up by John Hagan illustrates the vessel sinking, and rescue of the surviving crew and *Bounty* prisoners. The ship's cat is shown sitting on a mast-head. After the survivors reached a sandy key, Ship's Surgeon George Hamilton and prisoner James Morrison both reported how *Pandora*'s Master George Passmore returned to the wreck and rescued the ship's cat, which was "clinging to the top-gallant-mast-head" (courtesy John Hagan: Pitcairn Islands Study Center).

stant. The crew had just time to leap over board, accompanying it with a most dreadful yell. The cries of the men drowning in the water was at first awful in the extreme; but as they sunk, and became faint, it died away by degrees. The boats, who were at some considerable distance in the drift of the tide, in about half an hour, or little better, picked up the remainder of our wretched crew.

Morning now dawned, and the sun shone out. A sandy key, four miles off, and about thirty paces long, afforded us a resting place; and when all the boats arrived, we mustered our remains, and found that thirty-five men and four prisoners were lost.

After we had a little recovered our strength, the first care was to haul up the boats. A guard was placed over the prisoners. Providentially a small barrel of water, a cag of wine, some biscuit, and a few muskets and cartouch boxes, had been thrown into the boat. The heat of the sun, and the reflection from the sand, was now excruciating; and our stomachs being filled with salt water, from the great length of time we were swimming before we were picked up, rendered our thirst most intolerable; and no water was allowed to be served out the first day. By a calculation which we made, by filling the compass boxes, and every utensil we had, we could admit an allowance of two small wine glasses of water a-day to each man for sixteen days.

Part Five. Shipwreck in Torres Strait

A saw and hammer had fortunately been in one of the boats, which enabled us, with the greater expedition, to make preparations for our voyage, by repairing one of the boats, which was in a very bad state, and cutting up the floor-boards of all the boats into uprights, round which we stretched canvas, to keep the water from breaking into the boats at sea. We made tents of the boats sails; and when it was dark, we set the watch, and went to sleep. In the night we were disturbed by the irregular behaviour of one Connell, which led us to suspect he had stole our wine, and got drunk; but, on further inquiry, we found, that the excruciating torture he suffered from thirst led him to drink salt water; by which means he went mad, and died in the sequel of the voyage.

Next morning Mr. George Passmore the master was dispatched in one of the boats to visit the wreck, to see if any thing floated round her that might be useful to us in our present distressed state. He returned in two hours, and brought with him a cat, which he found clinging to the top-gallant-mast-head;

A drawing by Adam Long from the website www.seafurrers.com, dated August 29, 2016—the 225th anniversary of H.M.S. *Pandora*'s sinking—comically illustrates *Pandora*'s Master George Passmore rescuing the bedraggled ship's cat (courtesy Philippa Sandall—www.seafurrers.com, and Adam Long).

a piece of the top-gallant-mast, which he cut away; and about fifteen feet of the lightning chain; which being copper, we cut up, and converted into nails for fitting out the boats. Some of the gigantic cockle was boiled, and cut into junks, lest any one should be inclined to eat. But our thirst was too excessive to bear any thing which would increase it. This evening a wine glass of water was served to each man. A paper-parcel of tea having been thrown into the boat, the officers joined all their allowance, and had tea in the Captain's tent with him. When it was boiled, every one took a salt-cellar spoonful, and passed it to his neighbour; by which means we moistened our mouths by slow degrees, and received much refreshment from it.

From The Journal of James Morrison, Boatswain's Mate of the Bounty

Finding no opening in the Reef, we hauld to the Southward working to windward some days, and on Sunday the 28th of August the 2nd Lieut. was sent to find an Opening in the reef with the Yaul and the Ship hove too—and on Monday the 29th at 7 P M the Ship went on the Reef. Just at the time the boat returnd within hail and warnd them of the Danger, but it was now too late, the Current running fast towards the reef caused a heavy surf in which the Ship was forced on to the reef with Violent and repeated strokes and we expected evry surge that the Masts would go by the Board. Seeing the Ship in this situation we judged she would not hold long together, and as we were in danger at every stroke of killing each other with our Irons, we broke them that we might be ready to assist ourselves and keep from killing each other, and Informed the Officers what we had done. When Mr. Cornor was acquainted with it he Came aft and we told him we should attempt nothing further, as we only wanted a Chance for our lives; which he promised we should have, telling us not to fear. In the Meantime the Ship lost her rudder and with it part of the Stern post and having beat over, between 11 & 12 she was brought up in 15 fathom with both anchors, and the first news was nine feet water in the Hold! Coleman, Norman and McIntosh were ordered out to the Pumps, and the Boats got out.[43] As soon as Captain Edwards was informd that we had broke our Irons he ordered us to be handcuffd and leg Iroind again with all the Irons that could be Mustered, tho we beggd for Mercy and desired leave to go to the pumps; but to no purpose, his orders were put into execution, tho the Water in the Hold was increased to 11 feet and one of the Chain pumps broke—the Master at Arms and Corporal were now armd with each a Brace of Pistols and placed as additional Centinals over us, with Orders to fire amongst us if we made any Motion; and the Master at Arms told us that the Captain had said he would either shoot or hang to the Yard Arms those who should make any further attempt to break the Irons. We found there was no remedy but prayer, as we expected never to see Daylight and having recommended ourselves to the Almighty protection we lay down and seemd for a while to forget our Miserable Situation, tho we could hear the Officers busy getting their things into the Boats which were hauld under the stern on purpose & heard some of the Men on Deck say 'I'll be damnd if they shall go without us'. This made some of us start, and moving the Irons, the Master at Arms said 'fire upon the rascals'—as he was then Just over the Scuttle I spoke to him and said 'for gods sake dont fire, whats the matter there is none here moving'—in a few Minutes after, one of the Boats broke a drift and having but two Men in Her she could not reach the Ship again till another was sent with hands to bring her back, and now we began to think they would set off together, as it was but natural to suppose that evry one would think of himself first—however they returnd, & were secured with better Warps, and now we learnt that the Booms being Cut loose for the purpose of Making a Raft one of the Topmasts fell into the Waist and Killd a Man who was busy heaving the Guns overboard and evry thing seemd to be in great confusion—at day light in the Morning the Boats were hauld up and most of the Officers being aft on the top of the Box we observed that they were armd, and preparing to go into the Boats by the Stern ladders—we Beggd that we might not be forgort [sic], when by Captain Edwards's Order Joseph Hodges, the Armourers Mate of the Pandora, was sent down to take the Irons off Muspratt & Skinner & send them & Byrn (who was then out of Irons) up, but Skinner being too eager to get out got hauld up with his handcuffs on, and the other two following him Close, the Scuttle was Shut and Bar'd before Hodges could get to it and he in the Mean time knockd off my hand Irons & Stuarts. I beg'd of the Master at Arms to leave the Scuttle open when he answerd 'Never fear my boys we'll all go to Hell together.' The words were scarcely out of his Mouth when the Ship took a Sally and a general cry of 'there She Goes' was heard, the Master at Arms and Corporal with the other Centinals rolld overboard, and at the same instant we saw through the Stern Ports Captain Edwards astern swimming to the Pinnace which was some distance astern, as were all the Boats who had shoved off on the first Appearance of a Motion in the Ship. Burkett & Heildbrandt were yet handcuffd and the Ship under Water as far as the Main Mast and it was now begining to flow in upon us when the Devine providence directed Wm. Moulter (Boatswains Mate) to the place. He was scrambling up on the Box and hearing our Crys took out the Bolt and threw it and the Scuttle overboard, such was his presence of Mind tho He was forced to follow instantly himself. On this, We all got out except Heildbrandt and were rejoiced even in this trying scene to think that we had escaped from our prison—tho It was full as much as I could do to clear my self of the Driver boom before the Ship Sunk—the Boats were now so far off that we could not distinguish one from the other, however observing one of the Gangways Come up I swam to it and had scarcely reachd it before I perceived Muspratt on the other end of it, having brought him up with it but it falling on the Heads of several others sent them to the Bottom; here I began to get ready for Swimming and the top of our Prison having floated I observed on it Mr. P. Heywood, Burket & Coleman & the First Lieut. of the Ship, and seeing Mr. Heywood take a short plank and set off to one of the Boats, I resolved to Follow him and throwing away my trowsers, bound my loins up in a Sash or Marro after the Taheite Manner, got a short plank & followed and after having been about an hour and a half in the Water, I reachd the Blue Yaul and was taken up by Mr. Bowling, Masters Mate, who had also taken up Mr. Heywood. After taking up several others we were landed on a small sandy Key on the Reef about 2½ or 3 Miles from the Ship. Here we soon found that Four of our fellow prisoners were drown'd, two of which, Skinner and Heildbrandt, with their Handcuffs on, and Stuart and Sumner were struck by the Gangway. Burket being landed with his handcuffs on, the Captain ordered them to be taken off. We also learnt that 31 of the Pandoras Ships Company were lost, among whom were the Master at Arms & Ships Corporal—but all the Officers were Saved. A Tent was now [pitched] for the Officers & another for the Men, but we were not suffered to come near either, tho the Captain had told us, that we should be used as well as the Ships Company but we found that was not the Case, for on requesting of Captain Edwards a spare boats sail to shelter us from the sun being mostly naked it was refused tho no use was made of it; and we were ordered to keep on a part of the Island by our selves, to windward of the Tents, not being suffered to speak to any person but each other. The provision saved being very small this days allowance was only a Mouthful of Bread, and a Glass of wine; the water being but a small quantity, none could be afforded.

We staid here till Wednesday morning the 31st, fitting the Boats during which time the Sun took such an effect on us, who had been Cooped up for these five Months, that we had our skin flea'd off, from head to foot, tho we kept our Selves Covered in the Sand during the heat of the Day, this being all the Shelter that the Island affoards, the whole of it being no more then a small Bank washd up on the reef which with a Change of wind might dissapear, it being scarcely 150 Yards in Circuit and not more then 6 feet from the level at high water. There are two More of the Same kind of which this is in the Middle; between it and the one to the Southward is a Deep Channel through which a Ship might pass in safety. These Keys are laid down by Captain Edwards and their Latitude is between 10° and 11° South, about one Days run from the North Cape of New Holland.

During the Night as we found the Air very Chilly and having no covering, we threw up a bank of sand to sleep under the lee of, which proved but an indifrent barrier as we had frequent flying showers of rain sufficient to make our lodging Miserable tho not sufficient to save any to allay our thirst which was very great. We tryd for water but found none, & Mr. Cornor Making a fire got a Copper Kettle which he filld with Salt water and Making it Boil, attended it all Night saving the Drops which the Steam causes in the Cover which he put into a Cup till a spoon full was mustered. And one of the Pandoras people (Named Connell) went out of His senses drinking salt water.

On the 30th the Master went with a Boat to the Wreck, to see if any thing had come up, the Topmast heads being out of water, the Top Gallant Masts struck. He returnd with part of one of the Top Gallant Masts which he saw'd off to get clear of the Cap—and a Cat which he found sitting on the Cross trees. One of the Ships Buoys drifted passt, but was not thought worth going after tho we had no vessel to Contain water when we should find it.

Mr. Peter Heywood to Mrs. [Elizabeth] Heywood.

Batavia, November 20th, 1791.

On May 9th we left 'Taheite and proceeded to the friendly Isles, and cruised about six Weeks to the Northward and in the Neighbourhood of those Islands, in search of the *Bounty*, but without Success, in which Time we were so unfortunate as to lose a small Cutter and five Hands, and having discovered several Islands, at one of these, parted company with the Schooner which was built by our (the *Bounty*'s) People at 'Taheite and taken as a Tender by Captain Edwards (in which was an Officer and eight or nine Hands), and she was given up for lost. From the Friendly Islands we steered to the Westward, and about the Beginning of August got in among the Reefs of New Holland to endeavour at the Discovery of a Passage through, but it was not effected, for the *Pandora*, ever unlucky, and as it were devoted by Heaven to Destruction, on the 29th of August, at ½ past 7 o'Clock, was driven by a Current upon the Patch of a Reef, upon which, as there was a heavy Surf, she was almost bulged to Pieces; but having thrown all the Guns on one Side overboard, and the Tide flowing at the same Time, she beat over the Reef into a Bason encircled by the Reef, and brought up in 14 or 15 Fathom, but was so much damaged while she was on the Reef, that imagining she would go to Pieces every Moment, we had wrenched ourselves out of Irons and applied to the Captain to have Mercy on us, and suffer us to have a Chance for our Lives; but it was all in vain, and he was even so inhuman as to order us all to be in Irons again, though the Ship was expected to go down every Moment, being scarce able to keep her under with all the Pumps at Work. In this miserable Situation, with an expected Death before our Eyes, without the least Hope of Relief, and in the most trying State of Suspense, we spent the Night, the Ship being, by the Hand of Providence, kept up till Morning, in which Time the Boats had all been prepared, and as the Captain and Officers were coming upon [the] Poop or Roof of the Prison to abandon the Ship, the Water being then up to the Co[a]mings of the Hatchways, we again implored his Mercy, upon which he sent the Corporal and an Armourer down to let some of us out of Irons, when three only were suffered to go up, and the Scuttle being then clapped on, and the Master at Arms upon it, the Armourer had only time to let two People out of Irons (the Rest letting themselves out except three, two of whom went down with them on their Hands, and the third was picked up), when she began to heel over to Port so much that the Master at Arms sliding overboard and leaving the Scuttle vacant, every one tried to get up, and I was the last out but three.

The Water was then pouring in at the Bulk-head Scuttles; yet I got out and was scarce in the Water when I saw nothing above it but the Cross-trees and nothing around me but a Scene of the greatest Distress. I took a Plank (being stark naked), and swam towards an Island about three Miles off, but was picked up on my Passage by one of the Boats. When we got ashore to the small sandy Key, we found there were thirty Men drowned, four being Prisoners (one of whom was my Messmate), and ten of us and eighty nine of the *Pandora*'s saved. When a Survey was made of what Provisions had been saved, it was two or three Bags of Bread, and two or three Breakers of Water, and a little Wine; so we subsisted three Days upon two Wine Glasses of Water and two Ounces of Bread per Day...

From A Letter from Mr. Peter Heywood to Miss Nessy Heywood.

Hector, July 16th, 1792.
My dearest Nessy,

...I send you two little Sketches of the Manner in which H.M. Ship *Pandora* went down on the 29th of August, and the Appearance we who survived made upon the small sandy Key within

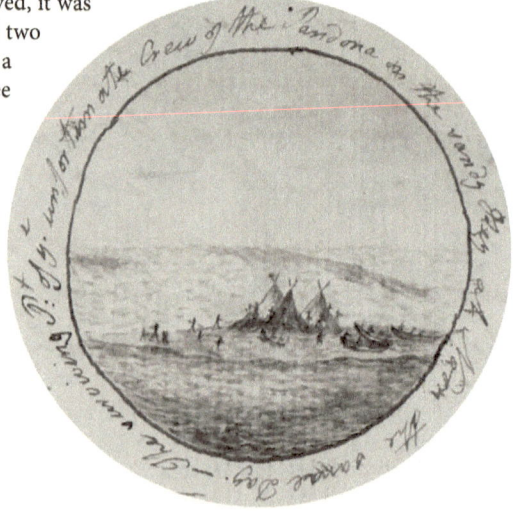

Top and above: "The Destruction of H.M.S. Pandora, August the 29th 1791 at Day break," and "P.ᵗ of yᵉ unfortunate Crew of the Pandora on the sandy Isle at Noon the same Day." Both of these miniature views are based on original drawings by Peter Heywood.

the Reef, about 90 Yards long and 60 athwart, in all 99 Souls. Here we remained three Days, subsisting on a single Wine-Glass of Wine and Water, and two Ounces of Bread a Day, with no Shelter from the Meridian and then vertical Sun. Captain Edwards had Tents erected for himself and his People, and we Prisoners petitioned him for an old Sail which was laying useless, part of the Wreck, but though in the Latitude of 11. South, he refused it, and all the Shelter we had was to bury ourselves up to the Neck in the burning Sand, which scorched the Skin (we being quite naked) entirely off our Bodies as if dipped in large Tubs of boiling Water. We were 16 Days in the same miserable Situation, before we landed at Coupang. From this you may have some faint Idea of our wretched Condition. I was in the Ship, in Irons Hands and Feet, much longer than till the Position you now see her in, the Poop alone being above the water (and that Knee-deep), when Providence assisted me to get out of Irons and from her.

PART SIX

Sailing to the Dutch East Indies

From Captain Edwards' Report

On the 31st the Boats were compleated & Launched, and we put every thing we had saved onboard of them and at ½ past 10 in the Forenoon we embarked 30 onboard the Launch 25 in the Pinnace 23 in one Yawl & 21 in the other Yawl. We steered NW&W & WNW within the Reef. This Channel through the Reef is better than any hitherto known besides the advantage it has of being situated further to the North by which many dificulties wd. be avoided when within the Reef. In the Run from thence to the Entrance of Endeavour Straits [There] is a small low white Sandy Island or Key on the Larboard hand of the Channel which lies in Lat. 11°. 23'. S°. The Tides are strong and irregular. On the 1st of September in the Morning saw Land which probably was the continent of New South Wales. The Yawls were sent in shore to Sound and look out. They saw a run of water landed and filled their two barricois which were the only Vessels of consequence they had with them, and I steered for an Island called by Lieut. Bligh Mountainous Island, and when joined by the Boats run into a Bay of that Island where we saw Indians on the beach. The Water was Shoal and the Indians waded off to the Boats. I gave them small presents & made them sensible we were in want of water. They brought us a Vessel filled with water which we had given them for the purpose & they returned to fill it again. They used many signs to Signify they wished us to Land, but we declined their invitation from motives of prudence. Just as the person was entering the water with the second Vessel of fresh water an Arrow was discharged at us by an other person which struck my boat on the Quarter and perceiving they were collecting bows and arrows, a Volley of Small Arms was fired at them, which put them to flight. I did not think it proper to Land to get Water by force, as Land was seen at that time in different directions which by appearance was likely to produce that Article, & which I flatterd myself we might be able to procure without being drove to that extremity. I therefore run close along the Shore of this Island and Landed at different places at some distance from our former Station. I also Landed

Part Six. Sailing to the Dutch East Indies

on another Island near it which I called Plum Island from its producing a Specie of that fruit but we were unsuccessful in finding the Article we were in Search and in so much want of. In the Evening we steered for Islands which we supposed were those called by Capt. Cook the Prince of Wales's Islands, and before Midnight came to a Grapnel with the Boats near one of those Islands in a large Sound—formed by Several surrounding Islands, to several of which I gave Names, and called the sound Sandwich's Sound. It is fit for the reception of Ships having from 5 to 7 fathoms water. There is plenty of wood on most of the Islands and by digging we found very good water. On the flat part of a Large Island which I called Lafory's Island situated on the Larboard hand as we entered the Sound from the Eastward—We saw a burying place and several Wolves near the watering place but we saw no natives: here we filled all our Vessels with water and made two Canvas bags in which we also put water but with this Assistance we had barely the means to take a Gallon of water for each Man in the Boats. We sent our Kettles on shore and made Tea & Portable broth, and a few Oysters were picked off the Rocks with which we made a comfortable Meal, indeed the only one we had made since the day before we left the Ship.

On the 2^d of Sept at ½ past 3 in the Afternoon we stood out of the North Entrance of the Sound. Before 5 we saw a Reef extending form [*sic*] the North to the WNW, and which appeared to run in the latter direction or more to the Westward. On the Edge of this Reef we had 3¼ fathoms water, but in hauling to the SW we soon deepen'd our Water to 5 fathoms. Besides Mountainous and West Islands seen by Lieut Bligh we saw several other Islands between the North and the West one of which I called Hawkesburys Island. We saw several large Turtle. In the Evening we saw the Northernmost Extremity of New

A view of the town and Dutch fort of Kupang (Coupang), Timor, where the H.M.S. *Pandora* wreck survivors arrived on September 18, 1791. Captain Edward Edwards reported that Governor Wanjon "received us with great humanity and goodness of Heart." Engraving by Victor Pillement and François Denis Née, after Charles-Alexandre Lesueur, from *Voyage de Découvertes aux Terres Australes*, 2nd ed., Paris: Arthus Bertrand, 1824 (courtesy National Gallery of Victoria, Melbourne, Joe White Bequest 2010 [2010.96.38]).

South Wales which forms the South side of Endeavour Straits. At Night the boats took each other in tow and we steered to the Westward. It is unnecessary to relate Our particular sufferings in the Boats during our run to Timor and is sufficient to observe that we suffered more from heat & thirst than from hunger, and that our Strength was greatly decreased. We fortunately had good Weather, and the Sea in general was not very rough, and the Boats were more Buoyant and lively in the Water than we reasonably could have expected considering the Weight and numbers we had in them.

At 7 o'clock in the Morning of the 13th September, we saw the Island of Timor bearing NW. We continued our Course to the WNW till Noon but the other boats hauled for the Land and we separated from them. At 1 o'clock we were close in with the Land and a party was sent onshore in Search of water but none was found here nor at several other places we examined as we passed along the Coast, until the next Morning when good Water was found. We also bought a few small fish which when divided afforded about 2 or 3 Ounces p. Man. Here the Launch joined us again. They informed us that they had got a supply of Water the Evening before. On the 15th in the Morning saw the Island of Rotté.[44] At ½ past 3 in the Afternoon entered the Straits of Samoa. Before Midnight we came to a Grapnel off the Fort of Coupang and found here one Ship, a Ketch & two or three small Craft.

From George Hamilton, A Voyage Round the World in His Majesty's Frigate Pandora

Every thing being ready on the following day, at twelve o'clock, we embarked in our little squadron, each boat having been previously supplied with the latitude and longitude of the island of Timor, eleven hundred miles from this place.

Our order of sailing was as follows.

In the Pinnace:
  Capt. Edwards,
  Lieut. Hayward,
  Mr. Rickards, Master's Mate,
  Mr. Packer, Gunner,
  Mr. Edmonds, Captain's Clerk,
    Three Prisoners,
    Sixteen Privates.

In the Red Yaul:
  Lieut. Larkan,
  Mr. Geo. Hamilton, Surgeon,

Part Six. Sailing to the Dutch East Indies   111

    Mr. Reynolds, Master's Mate,
    Mr. Matson, Midshipman,
        Two Prisoners,
        Eighteen Privates.

In the Launch:
    Lieut. Corner,
    Mr. Gregory Bentham, Purser,
    Mr. Montgomery, Carpenter,
    Mr. Bowling, Master's Mate,
    Mr. M'Kendrick, Midshipman,
        Two Prisoners,
        Twenty-four Privates.

In the Blue Yaul:
    Mr. Geo. Passmore, Master,
    Mr. Cunningham, Boatswain,
    Mr. James Innes, Surgeon's Mate,
    Mr. Fenwick, Midshipman,
    Mr. Pycroft, Midshipman,
        Three Prisoners,
        Fifteen Privates.

As soon as embarked, we laid the oars upon the thwarts, which formed a platform, by which means we stowed two tier of men. A pair of wooden scales was made in each boat, and a musket-ball weight of bread served to each man. At meridian we saw a key, bounded with large craggy rocks. As the principal part of our subsistence was in the launch, it was necessary to keep together, both for our defence and support. We towed each other during the night, and at day-break cast off the tow-line.

At eight in the morning, the red and blue yauls were sent ahead, to sound and investigate the coast of New South Wales, and to search for a watering-place. The country had been described as very destitute of the article of water; but on entering a very fine bay, we found most excellent water rushing from a spring at the very edge of the beach. Here we filled our bellies, a tea-kettle, and two quart bottles. The pinnace and launch had gone too far ahead to observe any signal of our success; and immediately we made sail after them. The coast has a very barren aspect; and, from the appearance of the soil and land, looks like a country abounding with minerals.

As we passed round the bay, two canoes, with three black men in each, put off, and paddled very hard to get near us. They stood up in the canoes, waved, and made many signs for us to come to them. But as they were perfectly naked, had a very savage aspect, and having heard an indifferent account of the natives of that country, we judged it prudent to avoid them.

In two hours we joined the pinnace and launch, who were lying to for us. At ten at night we were alarmed with the dreadful cry of breakers ahead. We had got amongst a reef of rocks; and in our present state, being worn out and fatigued, it is difficult to say how we got out of them, as the place was fraught with danger all round; for in standing clear of Scylla, we might fall foul of Charybdis; the horror of which, considering our present situation, may be better understood than expressed. After running along, we came to an inhabited island, from which we promised ourselves a supply of water. On our approach, the natives flocked down to the beach in crowds. They were jet black, and neither sex had either covering or girdle. We made signals of distress to them for something to drink, which they understood; and on receiving some trifling presents of knives, and some buttons cut off our coats, they brought us a cag of good water, which we emptied in a minute, and then sent it back to be filled again. They, however, would not bring it the second time, but put it down on the beach, and made signs to us to come on shore for it. This we declined, as we observed the women and children running, and supplying the men with bows and arrows. In a few minutes, they let fly a shower of arrows amongst the thick of us. Luckily we had not a man wounded; but an arrow fell between the Captain and Third Lieutenant, and went through the boat's thwart, and stuck in it. It was an oak-plank inch thick. We immediately discharged a volley of muskets at them, which put them to flight. There were, however, none of them killed. We now abandoned all hopes of refreshment here. This island lies contiguous to Mountainous Island.

It may be observed, that the channel throughout the reef is better than any hitherto known. We ascertained the latitudes with the greatest accuracy and exactness; and should government be inclined to plant trees on those sandy keys, particularly the outermost one, it would be a good distinguishing mark; and many difficulties which Capt. Cook experienced to the southward would also be avoided. The cocoa-nut tree, on account of its hardy nature, and the Norfolk and common pines, might be preferred, from their height rendering the place more conspicuous. The tides or currents are strong and irregular here, as may be expected, from the extending reefs, shoals, and keys, and its vicinity to Endeavour Straits.

We steered from these hostile savages to other islands in sight, and sent some armed men on shore, with orders to keep pretty near us, and to run close along shore in the boats. But they returned without success. This island we called Plumb Island, from its bearing an austere, astringent kind of fruit, resembling plumbs, but not fit to eat.

In the evening, we steered for those islands which we supposed were called the Prince of Wales's Islands; and about two o'clock in the morning, came to an anchor with a grappling, along side of an island, which we called Laforey's Island. As the night was very dark, and this was the last land that could afford us relief, all hands went to sleep, to refresh our woe-worn spirits.

The morning was ushered in with the howling of wolves, who had smelt us in the night, when prowling for food. Lieut. Corner and a party were sent at day-light, to search again for water; and, as we approached, the wild beasts retired, and filled the woods with their hideous growling. As soon as we landed, we discovered a foot-path which led down into a hollow, where we were led to suspect that water might be found; and on digging four or five feet, we had the ecstatic pleasure to see a spring rush out. A glad messenger was immediately dispatched to the beach, to make a signal to the boats of our success. On traversing the shore, we discovered a morai, or rather a heap of bones. There were amongst them two human skulls, the bones of some large animals, and some turtle-bones. They were heaped together in the form of a grave, and a very long paddle, supported at each end by a bifurcated branch of a tree, was laid horizontally alongst it.

Near to this, there were marks of a fire having been recently made. The ground about was much footed and wore; whence it may be presumed feasts or sacrifices had been frequently held, as there were several foot-paths which led to this spot. After having gorged our parched bodies with water, till we were perfectly water-logged, we began to feel the cravings of hunger; a new sensation of misery we had hitherto been strangers to, from the excess of thirst predominating. Some of our stragglers were lucky enough to find a few small oysters on the shore. A harsh, austere, astringent kind of fruit, resembling a plumb, was found in some places. As I discovered some to be pecked at by the birds, we permitted the men to fill their bellies with them. There was a small berry, of a similar taste to the plumb, which was found by some of the party. On observing the dung of some of the larger animals, many of them were found in it, in an undigested state; we therefore concluded we might venture upon them with safety. We carefully avoided shooting at any bird, lest the report of the muskets should alarm the natives, whom we had every reason to suspect were at no great distance, from the number of foot paths that led over the hill, and the noise we heard at intervals. Centinels were placed to prevent stragglers of our party from exceeding the proper bounds; and when every other thing was filled with water, the carpenter's boots were also filled. The water in them was first served out, on account of leakage.

There is a large sound formed here, to which we gave the name of Sandwich's Sound, and commodious anchorage for shipping in the bay, to which we gave the name of Wolf's Bay, in which there is from five to seven fathom water all round. This is extremely well situated for a rendezvous in surveying Endeavour Straits; and were a little colony settled here, a concatenation of Christian settlements would enchain the world, and be useful to any unfortunate ship of whatever nation, that might be wrecked in these seas; or, should a rupture take place in South America, a great vein of commerce might find its way through this channel.

Hammond's Island lies north west and by west, Parker's Island from north and by west to north and by east, and an island seen to the north entrance north west. We supposed it to be an island called by Captain Bligh Mountainous Island, laid down in latitude 10. 16 South.

Sandwich's Sound is formed by Hammond's, Parker's, and a cluster of small islands on the starboard hand, at its eastern entrance. We also called a back land behind Hammond's Island, and the other islands to the southward of it, Cornwallis's Land. The uppermost part of the mountain was separated from the main by a large gap. Under the gap, low land was seen; but whether that was a continuation of the main or not, we could not determine. Near the centre of the sound is a small dark coloured, rocky island.

This afternoon, at three o'clock, being the 2d of September, our little squadron sailed again, and in the evening saw a high peaked island lying north west, which we called Hawkesbury's Island. The passage through the north entrance is about two miles wide. After passing through it, saw a reef. As we approached it, we shallowed our water to three fathom; but on hauling up more to the south west, we deepened it again to six fathom. Saw several very large turtle, but could not catch any of them. After clearing the reef, stood to the westward. Mountainous Island bore N. half E; Capt. Bligh's west island, which appears in Three Hummocks, N. N. W.; a rock N. W. at the S. W. extreme of the main land, S. and by E.; and the northernmost cape of New South Wales, S. S. E.; and to the extreme of the land in sight, the eastward E. half N. a small distance from the nearest of the Prince of Wales's Islands, we discovered another island, and which we called Christian's Island. Saw Two Hummock between Hawkesbury's Island and Mountainous Island; but could not be certain whether it was one or two islands.

We now entered the great Indian ocean, and had a voyage of a thousand miles to undertake in our open boats. As soon as we cleared the land, we found a very heavy swell running, which threatened destruction to our little fleet; for should we have separated, we must inevitably perish for want of water, as we had not utensils to divide our slender stock. For our mutual preservation, we took each other in tow again; but the sea was so rough, and the swell running so high, we towed very hard, and broke a new tow-line. This put us in the utmost confusion, being afraid of dashing to pieces upon each other, as it was a very dark night. We again made fast to each other; but the tow-line breaking a second time, we were obliged to trust ourselves to the mercy of the waves. At five in the morning, the pinnace lay to, as the other boats had passed her under a dark cloud; but on the signal being made for the boats to join, we again met at day-light. At meridian, we passed some remarkable black and yellow striped sea snakes. On the afternoon of the 4th of September, gave out the exact latitude of our rendezvous in writing; also the longitude by the time-keeper at this present time, in case of unavoidable separation.

On the night between the 5th and the 6th, the sea running very cross and high, the tow-line broke several times; the boats strained, and made much water; and we were obliged to leave off towing the rest of the voyage, or it would have dragged the boats asunder. On the 7th, the Captain's boat caught a booby. They sucked his blood, and divided him into twenty-four shares.

The men who were employed steering the boats, were often subject to a *coup de soleil*, as every one else were continually wetting their shirts overboard, and putting it upon their head, which alleviated the scorching heat of the sun, to which we were entirely exposed, most of us having lost our hats while swimming at the time the ship was wrecked. It may be observed, that this method of wetting our bodies with salt water is not advisable, if the misery is protracted beyond three or four days, as, after that time, the great absorption from the skin that takes place from the increased heat and fever, makes the fluids become tainted with the bittern of the salt water; so much so, that the saliva became intolerable in the mouth. It may likewise be worthy of remark, that those who drank their own urine died in the sequel of the voyage.

We now neglected weighing our slender allowance of bread, our mouths becoming so parched, that few attempted to eat; and what was not claimed was thrown into the general stock. We found old people suffer much more than those that were young. A particular instance of that we observed in one young boy, a midshipman, who sold his allowance of water two days for one allowance of bread. As their sufferings continued they became very cross and savage in their temper. In the Captain's boat, one of the prisoners[45] took to praying, and they gathered round him with much attention and seeming devotion. But the Captain suspecting the purity of his doctrines, and unwilling he should make a monopoly of the business, gave prayers himself. On the 9th, we passed a great many of the Nautilus fish, the shell of which served us to put our glass of water into; by which means we had more time granted to dip our finger in it, and wet our mouths by slow degrees. There were several flocks of birds seen flying in a direction for the land.

On the 13th, in the morning, we saw the land, and the discoverer was immediately rewarded with a glass of water; but, as if our cup of misery was not completely full, it fell a dead calm. The boats now all separated, every one pushing to make the land. Next day we got pretty near it; but there was a prodigious surf running. Two of our men slung a bottle about their necks, jumped overboard, and swam through the surf. They traversed over a good many miles, till a creek intercepted them; when they came down to the beach, and made signs to us of their not having succeeded. We then brought the boat as near the surf as we durst venture, and picked them up. In running along the coast, about twelve o'clock, we had the pleasure to see the red yaul get into a creek. She had hoisted an English jack at her mast-head, that we might observe her in running down the coast. There was a prodigious surf, and many dangerous shoals, between us and the mouth of the creek; we, however, began to share the remains of our water, and about half a bottle came to each man's share, which we dispatched in an instant.

We now gained fresh spirits, and hazarded every thing in gaining our so much wish for haven. It is but justice here to acknowledge how much we were indebted to the intrepidity, courage, and seamanlike behaviour of Mr. Reynolds the master's mate, who fairly beat her over all the reefs, and brought us safe on shore. The crew of the blue yaul, who had been two or three hours landed, assisted in landing our party. A fine spring of water near to the creek afforded us immediate relief. As soon as we had filled our belly, a guard was placed over the prisoners, and we went to sleep for a few hours on the grass.

In the afternoon, a Chinese chief came down the creek in a canoe, attended by some of the natives, to wait upon us. He was a venerable looking old man; we endeavoured to walk down to the water-side, to receive him, and acquaint him with the nature of our distress.

We addressed him in French and in English, neither of which he understood; but misery was so strongly depicted in our countenances, that language was superfluous. The tears trickling down his venerable cheeks convinced us he saw and felt for our misfortunes; and silence was eloquence on the subject.

He made us understand by signs, that without fee or reward we should be supplied with horses, and conducted to Coupang, a Dutch East-India settlement, about seventy miles distant, the place of our rendezvous. This we politely declined, as the nature of our duty in the charge of the prisoners would not admit of it. We took leave of him for the present, after receiving promises of refreshment.

Soon after, crowds of the natives came down with fowls, pigs, milk, and bread. Mr. Innes, the surgeon's mate, happened luckily to have some silver in his pocket, to which they applied the touchstone, but would not give us any thing for guineas. However, anchor-buttons answered the purpose, as they gave us provision for a few buttons, which they refused the same number of guineas for; till a hungry dog, one of the carpenter's crew, happening to pick up an officer's jacket, spoiled the market, by giving it, buttons and all, for a pair of fowls, which a few buttons might have purchased.

All hands were busied in roasting the fowls, and boiling the pork; in the evening we made a very hearty supper. While we were regaling ourselves round a large fire, some wild beast gave a roar in the bushes. Some who had been in India before, declared it was the jackall; we therefore concluded the

Part Six. Sailing to the Dutch East Indies   117

lion could not be far off. Some were jocularly observing what a glorious supper the lord of the forest would make of us; but others were rather troubled with the dismaloes. This gave a gloomy turn to the conversation; and our minds having been previously much engaged with savages and wild beasts, and our bodies worn out through famine and watching, I believe the contagious effects of fear became pretty general. From Bligh's narrative, and others, we had been warned of the danger of landing in any other part of the island of Timor but Coupang, the Dutch settlement, as they were represented hostile and savage.

It is customary with those people, as we afterwards learnt, to do their hard work, such as beating out their rice at night, to avoid the scorching heat of the sun; and the whole village, which was about two miles off, joined in the general song, which every where chears and accompanies labour. As they had made us great offers for some cartridges of powder, which our duty could not suffer us to part with, we immediately interpreted this song into the war-hoop, and concluded, that they were going to take by force what they could not gain by entreaty. Nature, however, at last worn out, inclined to rest. The First Lieutenant and Master went on board of the boats, which were at anchor in the middle of the river, for the better security of the prisoners; and, ranging ourselves round, with our feet to the fire, went to sleep.

At dawn of day, the master gave the huntsman's hollow, which some, from being suddenly awaked, thought they were attacked by the Indians. We were all panic struck, and could not get thoroughly awaked, being so exhausted, and overpowered with sleep. Most of us were scrambling upon all fours down to the river, and crying for Christ's sake to have mercy upon them, till those who were foremost in the scramble, in crawling into the creek, got recovered from their plight by their hands being immersed in water; yet those who were foremost in running away, were not last in upbraiding the rest with cowardice, notwithstanding there were pretty evident marks upon some of them, of the cold water having produced its usual effects of micturition.

Next day we went up the creek, in one of the boats, about four miles, to one of their towns, with an intention of purchasing provisions for our sea-store. As we entered the town, the king was riding out, attended by twenty carabineers or body-guards, well mounted, and respectably armed. He passed us with all the *sang froid* imaginable, scarce deigning to glance at us.

In purchasing a pig, the man finding a good price for it, offered to traffic with us for the charms of his daughter, a very pretty young girl. But none of us seemed inclined that way, as there were many good things we stood much more in need of.

At one o'clock, being high water, we embarked again in our boats for Coupang. We sailed along the coast all day till it was dark; and, fearful lest we should overshoot our port in the night, put into a bay. After laying some time, we observed a light; and after hallooing and making a noise, the natives came down with torches in their hands, waded up alongside of us, and offered their assistance, which we accepted of, in lighting fires, and dressing the victuals we had brought with us, that no time might be lost in landing or cooking the next day.

At day break, we again proceeded on our voyage, and at five in the afternoon we landed at Coupang. The Governor, Mynheer Vanion, received us with the utmost politeness, kindness, and hospitality. The Lieutenant-Governor, Mynheer Fry, was likewise extremely kind and attentive, in rendering every assistance possible, and in giving the necessary orders for our support and relief in our present distressed state.

Next morning being Sunday, as we supposed, the 17th of September, we were preparing for church, to return thanks to Almighty God, for his divine interposition in our miraculous preservation; but were disappointed in our pious intentions; for we found it was Monday, the 18th, having lost a day by performing a circuit of the globe to the westward.

From The Journal of James Morrison, Boatswain's Mate of the Bounty

The Boats being ready, on the 31st at 10 A M we embarkd in the Following Manner, McIntosh, Ellison & Myself in the Pinnace with Captain Edwards, Lieut. Hayward and 19 officers and men, making her Compliment 24; in the Red Yaul went Burkett & Millward, with Lieut. Larkan and 19 officers & men, making her Complement 22; in the Launch, Peter Heywood, Josh. Coleman & Michl Byrn, with Lieut. Cornor & 27 officers & Men, her Complement 31, and in the Blue Yaul Norman and Muspratt, with the Master & 19 Officers and Men, Making Ninety nine souls in all—and in this situation we had a passage of between four & five hundred leagues to run before we could reach the Dutch Settlement on Timor with the Scanty allowance of 2 Musquet balls weight of Bread & hardly a Jill of water & Wine together for 24 Hours, in a Scorching hot sun now nearly vertical.

We left the Key (which was named Wreck Island) & proceeded to the N W and next morning, the 1st of September, we made the land which we supposed to be Part of New Holland and the Two Yauls were sent in with the land, while we stood on towards an Island, where we hoped to get water & in the afternoon we were Joind by the Yauls who had got Water and having filld their Vessels followed us; they having Joind us we stood into a bay to search for Water and having as we approachd the Beach found that there were some inhabitants on it, tho it was but small and did not appear very fruitful. The natives appear'd on the Beach to the amount of 18 or 19 men, women & Children, who appeard to be all of one Family; they came off freely to the Boats when we found that the Collour of their skins was heightend to a Jett Black by Means of either Soot or Charcoal, they were quite naked and their hair long & Curling but Matted like a Mopp, and some had holes in their ears which were stretchd to such a size as to receive a Mans Arm. We made signs that we wanted water which they soon understood, & a half ancker being given to one of them, & some trifles by way of encouragement, he soon returned with it almost full, which being started into a brecco and gave it to him again. He then Calld a Young Woman who stood near him and sent her for the Water. She soon returned, and with her a Man with a Bundle of Spears, when she came to the Beach the Man who had sent her went and received it, and standing up to the fork in the water, made signs for the Boats to come in, which was declined and He kept retreating. Mean while two of the Men began to prepare their Weapons, & a Javlin being thrown, struck the Pinnace, and an Arrow fired which fell close along side, both were taken up & several Musquets were fired, at which they dropd, and the Man who had the Keg let it fall & fled, but finding himself not hurt, he returnd and took it with him; they soon dissapeared and Captain Edwards ordered the Boats to follow him, putting off and standing to the westward to some other Islands then in sight. At this the First Lieut. seemd displeased, and spoke his mind so loud that Captain Edwards heard him, and desired him to be silent and obey his orders and at his Peril to say no more about the Matter—we reachd the Islands & Examined them but they afforded no water nor any thing eatable, except a sort of plumb which contains a Glutinous Gum which sticks in the Mouth teeth Throat &c.—& were by no Means a delicacy, however they were eaten; but shell fish of which we had brought some from the Key, we could not toutch for want of Water— among the shell fish found on the Key were two large Cockles of the Gigantic sort which Measured about a foot the longest way of the Shell.

Finding no water here, we bore away to the Westward and at 3 next morning made an Island where we hoped to get water, & standing in came to an anchor till day light when we weighd & got Close in, seeing no natives a Party was sent on shore to search for Water which at last they found by digging and evry vessel was filld. The Kettle was boild with Portable soup, & a pint served to each Man with as much water as we could drink, but we were reduced to many shifts to Contain water having made Canvas bags, filling a Pair of Boots & evry thing that would contain water if but for a day was filld and then the whole did not amount to 200 Gallons; a scanty allowance for 99 Men to subsist on who did not expect to reach Timor in less then 14 days and knew of no place where we could recruit till we reachd it and tho we had got an additional stock of water it was no addition to our allowance as we knew not how long the passage would be—having filled our Water we saild to the Westward and for fear of Parting Company in the Night the Pinnace took the other Boats in tow all night which was the Case evry Night through the passage.

The Heat of the Weather made our thirst insupportable and as the Canvas bags soon leakd out, no addition of allowance could take place, and to such extremity did thirst increase, that several of the men drank their own urine, and a booby being caught in the Pinnace the Blood was eagerly suckd, & the Body devided and eagerly devoured; two others were Caught by the other Boats which shared the same fate as the distress was general.

We kept a line constantly towing, but never caught any fish tho we saw several.

On the 9th as I was laying on the Oars talking to McIntosh Captain Edwards ordered me aft, and without assigning any Cause ordered me to be pinnioned with a Cord and lasshd down in the Boats Bottom, and Ellison, who was then asleep in the Boats bottom, was ordered to the same punnishment—I attempted to reason and enquire what I had now done to be thus Cruelly treated, urging the Distressd situation of the whole, but received for answer 'Silence, you Murdering Villain, are you not a Prisoner? You Piratical Dog what better treatment do you expect?' I then told him that it was a disgrace to the Captain of a British Man of War to treat a prisoner in such an inhuman Manner, upon which he started up in a Violent Rage & snatching a Pistol which lay in the Stern sheets, threatened to shoot me. I still attempted to speak, when he Swore 'by God if you speak another Word I'll heave the Log with You' and finding that he would hear no reason & my mouth being Parchd so, that I could not move my tongue, I was forced to be silent & submit; and was tyed down so that I could not move.

In this Miserable Situation Ellison & I remaind for the rest of the passage, nor was McIntosh suffered to come near or speak to either of us; however we made ourselves as easy as we could and on the 15th we made the Island of Timor, when the Boats seperated & Stood in for the land, having had a fine Breeze & fair Weather all the way. We try'd for Water at several places, but could find none till the 16th in the Morning when we found a Well near the Beach & here the Launch Joind us again when we proceeded in Company to Coupang which we reachd at Midnight and came to a Grapnel off the Fort till Morning. We found a Ship in the Road, and a Number of small Craft, and at 8 in the Morning the Captain went on shore to the Governor.

Part Seven

Passage to Batavia and England

From George Hamilton, A Voyage Round the World in His Majesty's Frigate Pandora

This [Coupang] is the Montpelier of the East to the Dutch and Portuguese settlements in India; and, from the salubrity of its air, is the favourite resort of valetudinarians and invalids from Batavia and other places. This island is fertile, variegated with hill and dale, and equally beautiful as diversified with Rotti, and its appendant isles. It is as large as the island of Great Britain. Its principal trade is wax, honey, and sandlewood; but the whole of its revenues do not defray the expence of the settlement to the Company[46]; but from the locality of its situation, it is convenient for their other islands. They had the monopoly of the sandlewood trade, which is used in all temples, mosques, and places of worship in the East, every Chinese having a sprig of it burning day and night near their household-gods.

The exclusive trade of sandlewood was valuable and convenient to the Dutch; but, from the vast extent of territory lately acquired in India, we have plenty of that commodity without going to the Dutch market. Close to the Dutch town is a Chinese town and temple. They have a governor of their own nation, but pay large tribute to the Dutch. Notwithstanding their trade is under very severe restrictions, they soon make rich; and, as soon as they become independent, return to their own country. For European and India goods, the natives barter their produce, and sell their prisoners of war, who are carried to Batavia as slaves, and the natives of Java sent from Batavia to this place in return. As they hold their tenure more from policy than strength, it would be impolitic to irritate them, by exposing their countrymen, subjugated to the lash of slavery and oppression.

An influence of this foul-couping business fell under our inspection while here. One of the petty princes, in settling his account with a merchant of this place, was some dollars short of cash. He just stepped to the door, and casting his eye on an elderly man who was near him, he laid hold of him; and, with the assistance of some of his myrmidons, gave him up as a slave, and so settled his account. We felt more interested in the fate of this poor wretch, on account of his having been a prince himself, but never before saw the face of his oppressor. He went passenger in the ship with us to Batavia.

It was a pleasing and flattering sight to an Englishman, at this remotest corner of the globe, to see that Wedgewood's stoneware, and Birmingham goods, had found their way into the shops of Coupang.

During our five weeks stay here, the Governor, Mynheer Vanion, by every act of politeness and attention, endeavoured to make us spend our time agreeably. We were sumptuously regaled at his table every day, and the evening was spent with cards and concerts. I could dwell with pleasure for an age in praise of this honest Dutchman; it is the tribute of a grateful heart, and his due. This is the third time he has had an opportunity of extending his hospitality to shipwrecked Englishmen.

About a fortnight before we arrived, a boat, with eight men, a woman, and two children, came on shore here, who told him they were the supercargo, part of the crew, and passengers of an English brig, wrecked in these seas. His house, which has ever been the asylum of the distressed, was open for their reception. They drew bills on the British government, and were supplied with every necessary they stood in need of.

The captain of a Dutch East Indiaman, who spoke English, hearing of the arrival of Capt. Edwards, and our unfortunate boat, run to them with the glad tidings of their Captain having arrived; but one of them, starting up in surprise, said, "What Captain! dam'me, we have no Captain"; for they had reported, that the Captain and remainder of the crew had separated from them at sea in another boat. This immediately led to a suspicion of their being imposters; and they were ordered to be apprehended, and put into the castle. One of the men, and the women, fled into the woods; but were soon taken. They confessed that they were English convicts, and that they had made their escape from Botany Bay.[47] They had been supplied with a quadrant, a compass, a chart, and some small arms and ammunition, from a Dutch ship that lay there; and the expedition was conducted by the Governor's fisherman, whose time of transportation was expired. He was a good seaman, and a tolerable navigator. They dragged along the coast of new South Wales; and as often as the hostile nature of the savage natives would permit, hauled their boat up at night, and slept on shore. They met with several curious and interesting anecdotes in this voyage. In many places of the coast of South Wales, they found very good coal; a circumstance that was not before known. Our men were now beginning to regain their strength; and Captain Dadleberg of the Rembang Indiaman was making every possible dispatch with his ship to carry us to Batavia.

During this time, the interment of Balthazar, King of Coupang, was performed with much funeral pomp. The Governor, Lieutenant-Governor, and all the Europeans, were invited. Six months had been spent in preparations for this fete, at which an emperor and twenty-five kings, assisted and attended in person with all their body-guards, standards, and standard-bearers, were present. When the corpse was deposited in the sepulchre, the Company's troops fired three vollies, and victuals and drink were immediately served to four thousand people.

The Dutch and English officers were invited to a very sumptuous dinner, at a table provided for the emperor and all the kings. The first toast after dinner was the dead king's health. Next they drank Mynheer Company's health, which was accompanied with a volley of small arms and paterreros. The singularity of Mynheer Company's health, led us to request an explanation; when we were informed, they found it necessary to make them believe that Mynheer Company was a great and powerful king, lest they should not be inclined to pay that submission to a company of merchants.

The inaugural ceremony at the installation of the young king, was performed by his drinking a bumper of brandy and gunpowder, stirred round with the point of a sword. After being invested with the regal dignity, he came down in state, to pay his respects to the governor. As he was preceded by music, and colours flying, every one turned out to see him. Amongst the rest was a captive king in chains, who was employed blowing the bellows to our armourer, whilst he was forging bolts and fetters for our prisoners and convicts. Here the sunshine of prosperity, and the mutability of human greatness, were excellently pourtrayed.

By a policy in the Dutch, in supplying the petty princes with ammunition and warlike stores, feuds and dissentions are kindled amongst them; and they are kept so completely engaged in civil war, that they have no time to observe the encroachments of strangers. That domestic strife serves likewise amply to supply the slave trade from the prisoners of both parties. They, however, some time since, made head against the common enemy, and forced the Dutch to retire within their trenches.

It is the custom, in this climate, to bathe morning and evening. A fine river, which runs in the centre of the town, is conveniently situated for that purpose; and we availed ourselves of it when our strength would permit. Nature has been profusely lavish, in producing, in the neighbourhood of this place, all the varied powers of landscape that the most luxuriant fancy can suggest. But, while enjoying the picturesque beauties of the scene, or sheltering in the translucent stream from the fervour of meridian heat, you are suddenly chilled with fear, from the terrific aspect of the alligator, or crested snake, and a number of venomous reptiles, with which this country abounds. There is one in particular called the cowk cowk; it is the most disgusting looking animal that creeps the ground, and its bite is mortal. It is about a foot and a half long, and seems a production between the toad and lizard. At stated periods it makes a noise exactly like a cuckoo clock. Even the natives fly from it with the utmost horror. The alligators are daring and numerous. There are instances of their devouring men and children when bathing in the shallow part of the river above the town.

The Governor, Mynheer Vanion, relates a circumstance that happened to him while hunting. In crossing a shallow part of the river, his black boy was snapped up by an alligator; but the Governor immediately dismounted, rescued the boy out of his mouth, and slew him.

The natives of Timor are subject to a cutaneous disease during their infancy, something similar to the small pox, but of longer duration. It seldom terminates fatally, and only seizes them once in their lives.

On the 6th of October, we embarked on board the Rembang Dutch Indiaman, taking with us the prisoners and convicts. Our crew became very sickly in passing the Straits of Alice. We had frequent calms and sultry weather until the 12th. In passing the Island of Flores, a most tremendous storm arose. In a few minutes every sail of the ship was shivered to pieces; the pumps all choaked, and useless; the leak gaining fast upon us; and she was driving down, with all the impetuosity imaginable, on a savage shore, about seven miles under our lee. This storm was attended with the most dreadful thunder and lightning we have ever experienced. The Dutch seamen were struck with horror, and went below; and the ship was preserved from destruction by the manly exertion of our English tars, whose souls seemed to catch redoubled ardour from the tempest's rage. Indeed it is only in these trying moments of distress, when the abyss of destruction is yawning to receive them, that the transcendent worth of a British seaman is most conspicuous. Nor would I wish, from what I have observed above, to throw any stigma on the Dutch, who I believe would fight the devil, should he appear in any other shape to them but that of thunder and lightning.

It may be remarked, that the Straits of Alice are not so dangerous as those of Sapy, and are for many reasons preferable; but it is so intricate a navigation, that a Dutchman bound from Timor to Batavia, after beating about for twelve months, found himself exactly where he first started from.

On the 21st, we got through Alice, and saw three prow-vessels, who are a very daring set of pirates that infest those seas. On the 22d, saw the islands of Kangajunk and Ulk, and run through the channel that is between them. Next day we saw the island of Madura.

On the 26th, saw the island of Java; and on the 30th, anchored at Samarang.

Immediately on our coming to anchor, we were agreeably surprised to find our tender here, which we had so long given up for lost.[48] Never was social affection more eminently pourtrayed than in the meeting of these poor fellows; and from excess of joy, and a recital of their mutual sufferings, from pestilence, famine, and shipwreck, a flood of tears filled every man's breast.

They informed us, the night they parted company with us, the savages attacked them in a regular and powerful body in their canoes; and their never having seen a European ship before, nor being able to conceive any idea of fire-arms, made the conflict last longer than it otherwise would; for, seeing no missive weapon made use of, when their companions were killed, they did not suspect any thing to be the matter with them, as they tumbled into the water. Our seven-barrelled pieces made great havoc amongst them. One fellow had agility enough to spring over their boarding-netting, and was levelling a blow with his war-club at Mr. Oliver, the commanding-officer, who had the good fortune to shoot him.

On not finding the ship next day, they gave up all further hopes of her, and steered for Anamooka, the rendezvous Captain Edwards had appointed. Their distress for want of water, if possible, surpassed that of our own, and had so strong an effect on one of the young gentlemen, that the day following he became delirious, and continued so for some months after it.

They at last made the island of Tofoa, near to Anamooka, which they mistook for it. After trading with the natives for provisions and water, they made an attempt to take the vessel from them, which they always will to a small vessel, when alone; but they were soon overpowered with the fire arms. They were, however, obliged to be much on their guard afterwards, at those islands which were inhabited.

After much diversity of distress, and similar encounters, they at last made the reef that runs between New Guinea and New Holland, where the Pandora met her unhappy fate; and after traversing from shore to shore, without finding an opening, this intrepid young seaman boldly gave it the stem, and beat over the reef. The alternative was dreadful, as famine presented them on the one hand, and shipwreck on the other. Soon after they had passed Endeavour Straits, they fell in with a small Dutch vessel, who shewed them every tenderness that the nature of their distress required.

They were soon landed at a small Dutch settlement; but the governor having a description of the Bounty's pirates from our court, and their vessel being built of foreign timber, served to confirm them in their suspicions; and as no officer in the British navy bears a commission or warrant under the rank of lieutenant, where, by seal of office, their person or quality may be identified, they had only their bare *ipse dixit* to depend on. They, however, behaved to them with great precaution and humanity. Although they kept a strict guard over them, nothing was withheld to render their situation agreeable; and they were sent, under a proper escort, to this place.

This settlement is reckoned next to Batavia, and is so lucrative, that the governor is changed every five years. The present governor's name is Overstraaten, a gentleman of splendid taste and unbounded hospitality, who lives in a princely style; and to the *otium dignitate* of Asiatic luxury, has the happiness to join an honest hearty Dutch welcome.

A regiment of the Duke of Wirtemburg is doing duty here, amongst whom were several men of rank and fashion, who shewed us much civility and politeness.

The town is regular and beautiful, and the houses are built in a style of architecture, which has given loose to the most sportive fancy. Each street is terminated with some public building, such as a great marine school, for the education of young officers and seamen; an hospital for decayed officers in the Company's service; churches; the governor's palace, &c, &c. Here the *utile dulce* has not been neglected, and those objects of national importance are placed in a proper point of view, as the just pride and ornament of a great commercial people.

Such is the effect of early prejudices, that, under the muzzle of the sun, a Dutchman cannot exist, without snuffing the putrid exhalations from stagnant water, to which they have been accustomed from their infancy. They are intersecting it so fast with canals, that in a year or two this beautiful town will be completely dammed.

In a few days, we arrived at Batavia, the emporeum of the Dutch in the East; and our first care was employed in sending to the hospital the sickly remains of our unfortunate crew. Some dead bodies floating down the canal struck our boat, which had a very disagreeable effect on the minds of our brave fellows, whose nerves were reduced to a very weak state from sickness. This was a *coup de grace* to a sick man on his *premier entree* into this painted sepulchre, this golgotha of Europe, which buries the whole settlement every five years.[49]

It is not the climate I am inveighing against; it is the Gothic, diabolical ideas of the people I indite.

Were they only Dutchmen who supplied the ravenous maw of death, it would be impertinence in me to make any comment on it; but when the whole globe lends its aid to supply this destructive settlement, and its baneful effects arising more from the letch a Dutchman has for stagnant mud than from climate, I hope the indulgent reader will pardon my spleen, when I tell them professionally, that all the mortality of that place originates from marsh effluvia, arising from their stagnant canals and pleasure-grounds.

The Chinese are here the Jews of the East, and as soon as they make their fortune, they go home. Let the amateurs of the Republican system read and learn. Be not surprised when it is observed, that these little great men, those vile hawkers of spice and nutmegs, exact a submission that the most absolute and tyrannical monarch who ever swayed a sceptre would be ashamed of. The compass of my work will not allow me to be particular; but I must instance one among many others. When an edilleer, or one of the supreme council, meets a carriage, the gentleman who meets him must alight, and make him a perfect bow in spirit; not one of Bunburry's long bows, but that bow which

Part Seven. Passage to Batavia and England

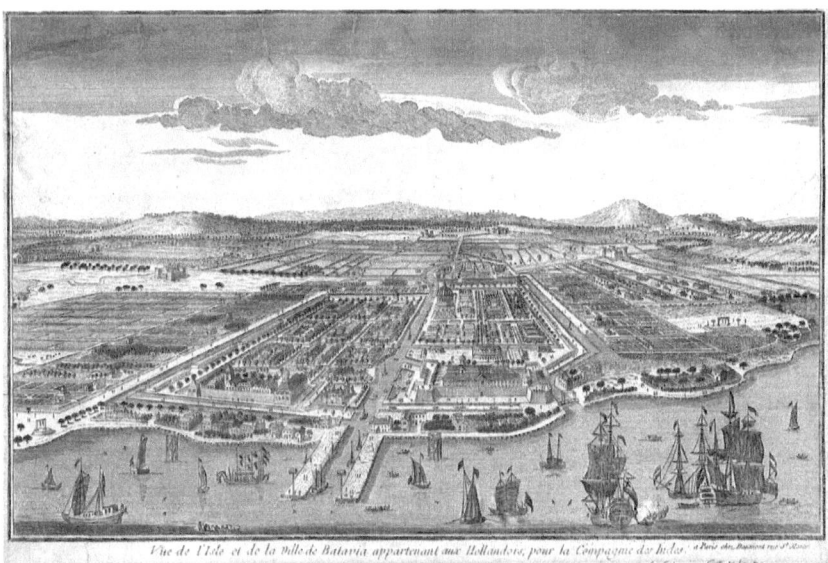

An aerial view of Batavia ca. 1780, which H.M.S. *Pandora* Ship's Surgeon George Hamilton described as a "ravenous maw of death." Batavia's marshes and filthy canals made this Dutch colonial city particularly dangerous for people in a weakened condition, including the survivors of the *Pandora*, *Bounty*, and *Matavy* open boat voyages. Published by Daumont, Paris, ca. 1780.

carries humility and submission in it, that sort of bow which every vertebræ in an English back is anchylosed against.

In our passage from this to the Cape, before we left Java, one of the convicts had jumped over board in the night, and swam to the Dutch arsenal at Honroost. In passing Bantan, we viewed the relics of Lord Cathcart. We met nothing particular in passing the island of Sumatra, but experienced great death and sickness in going through the Straits of Sunda; and after a tedious passage, arrived at the Cape of Good Hope.

Here we met with many civilities from Colonel Gordon; a gentleman no less eminent for his private virtues than his extraordinary military and literary accomplishments. From his labours, all the host of voyagers and historians of that part of the globe have been purloining; but it is to be hoped the world will, at some future period, be favoured with his works unmutilated.[50]

The town is gay, and from length of habit, the inhabitants partake much of the manners of Bath; and, for a short season, behave with the utmost attention and tenderness. Their dress and customs are more characteristic of the English than Dutch. An uncommon rage for building has lately prevailed; and although they cannot boast of that chastity of style in which Samarang is built, it is gaudy, and calculated to please the generality of observers.

Allow me to mention the singular manner in which the monkeys make depredations on the gardens here. They place a proper piquet, or advanced guard, as sentinels, when a party is drawn up in a line, who hand the fruit from one to another; and when the alarm is given by the piquet-guard, they all take flight, making sure that by the time the booty is conveyed to a considerable distance. But should the piquet be negligent in their duty, and suffer the main body to be surprised, the delinquents are severely punished.

The same ill-fated rage for canalling-murder prevails here. They have even contrived to carry canals to the top of a mountain. The boors, or country-farmers, are a species of the human race, so gigantic and superior to the rest of mankind, in point of size and constitution, that they may be called nondescripts.

Their hospital, as to scite, surpasses any in the world. It may be observed, however, that the architect, by the smallness of the windows, which only serve to exclude the light and air, seems to have studied, with much ingenuity, to render it a cadaverous stinking prison.

After being refreshed at the Cape, we passed St. Helena, the island of Ascension, and arrived at Holland; and had the happiness, through the interposition of divine Providence, to be again landed on our native shore.

The Latitudes and Longitudes of the different places touched at or discovered by his Majesty's ship Pandora, taken with the greatest accuracy from the centre of the islands.

Names of Places	Latitudes	Longitudes
Gomera	28° 5' N	17° 8' W
Canary, N.E. point	28° 13' N	15° 38' W
Teneriffe, Santa Cruz	28° 27' N	16° 16' W
Palma	28° 36' N	17° 45' W
St. Antonio, Cape de Verd Islands, crossing the Line	17° 0' N	25° 2' W
Rio Janeiro	22° 54' S	
Patagonia, Straits of Magellan		
Cape Julian, Staten Island	54° 47' 30" S	63° 58' 27" W
Cape Horn	55° 59' S	67° 21' W
Diego Ramarez		
Easter Island	27° 7' S	109° 42' W
Ducie's Island	24° 40' 30" S	124° 40' 30" W
Lord Hood's Island	21° 31' S	135° 32' 30" W
Carysfort Island	20° 49' S	138° 33' W

Part Seven. Passage to Batavia and England

Names of Places	Latitudes	Longitudes
Maitea	17° 52' S	148° 6' W
Otaheite, Matavy Bay	17° 29' S	149° 35' W
Huaheine, Owharre Bay	16° 44' S	151° 3' W
Ulitea and Otaha	16° 46' S	151° 33' W
Bolobola	16° 33' S	151° 52' W
Mauruah	16° 26' S	152° 33' W
Whytutakee	18° 52' S	159° 41' W
Palmerston's Isles	18° 0' S	162° 57' W
Duke of York's Island	8° 33' 30" S	172° 4' 3" W
Duke of Clarence's Island	9° 9' 30" S	171° 30' 46" W
Chatham's Island	13° 32' 20" S	172° 18' 20" W
Ohatooah	13° 50' S	171° 30' 6" W
Anamooka	20° 16' S	174° 30' W
Toomanuah	14° 15' S	169° 43' W
Otutuelah	14° 30' S	170° 41' W
Howe's Island	18° 32' 30" S	173° 53' W
Bickerton's Island	18° 47' 40" S	174° 48' W
Gardner's Island	17° 57' S	175° 16' 54" W
Pylestaart	22° 23' S	175° 39' W
Eoah or Middleburgh	21° 21' S	174° 34' W
Tongataboo	21° 9' S	174° 41' W
Proby's Island	15° 53' S	175° 51' W
Wallis's Island	13° 22' S	176° 15' 45" W
Grenville Island	12° 29' S	183° 3' W
" "		176° 57' E
Pandora's Reef	12° 11' S	188° 8' W
" "		171° 52' E
Mitre Island	11° 49' S	190° 4' 30" W
		169° 55' 30" E
Cherry Island	11° 37' 30" S	190° 19' 30" W
" "		169° 55' 30" E
Pitt's Island	11° 50' 30" S	193° 14' 15" W
" "		166° 45' 45" E

Names of Places	Latitudes	Longitudes
Wells's Shoal	12° 20' S	202° 2' W
" "		157° 58' E
Cape Rodney, Port of New Guinea	10° 3' 32" S	212° 14' 5" W
M. Clarence in shore "		147° 45' 45" E
Cape Hood "	9° 58' 6 S	212° 37' 10" W
" "		147° 22' 50" E
Murray's Isles	9° 57' S	216° 43' W
" "		143° 17' E
Wreck Reef	11° 22' S	216° 22' W
" "		143° 38' E
Batavia	6° 10' S	106° 51' E
Straits of Sunda	6° 36' 15 S	105° 17' 30" E
Cape of Good Hope	34° 29' S	18° 23' E
St. Helena	15° 55' S	5° 49' W
Ascension Island	7° 56' S	14° 32' W

From Captain Edwards' Report

The Launch separated from us soon after dark but got up to Coupang the next day in the forenoon. On the morning of 16th. by our account (which was the 17th in this Country) at daylight we hailed the Fort and informed them whom we were. A small Boat was sent to us and myself and Lieut. Hayward Landed at the usual place near a Chinese Temple, where we were received by the Lieut. Governor, Mr. Fruy and Mr. Bouberg, Captain Lieut. of a company Ship that Lay in the Road, and conducted by them to Governor Wanjon, who received us with great humanity and goodness of Heart. Refreshments were immediately prepared for myself & Lieutenant. Provision was provided, the People ordered to Land & they all dined in the Governors own House, and an arrangement was made for the reception and accommodation of the whole party as they arrived. The Church & the Church Yard was assigned for the use of the private Seamen, a house was hired for the Warrant and petty Officers. The People that were ill were put under the care of Mr. Timers the Surgeon General. Governor Wanjon did me & Lieut Hayward the honor to Lodge and entertain us in his own House. Mr. Corner the 2[d] Lieut. & Mr. Bentham the Purser were received in the House of Mr. Fruy. The Lieut. Governor, Lieut. Larkin and Mr. Passmore were taken into the house of Mr. Bouberg the Capt. Lieut. of a Company Ship, and Mr. Hamilton the Surgeon was accommodated in the house of Mr. Timers the Surgeon General, and Governor Wanjon did every thing in his power to supply our present Wants or that would contribute to re establishment of our health & strength and even to our amusements, and this benevolent Example was follow'd by Mr. Fruy the Lieut. Gov[r]. and the other

Gentlemen of the Place. Two Months Provision was provided for the Ship's Company & put onboard the Rembang a Dutch East India Company Ship and we embarked onboard the same Ship for Batavia on the 6th of Oct. 1791.

Before we Sailed Governor Wanjon delivered to me 8 Men, One Woman & two Children who came to Coupang in June last in a six Oared Cutter. They are supposed to be convicts and deserters from the Colony at Port Jackson.

Bill[s] were given on the different departments of the Navy for the Provisions and other Necessaries we were supplied with a[t] Coupang and also for the Maintenance & Cloathing of the Convicts. I sold one of the Yawls to the Lieut. Governor and the Longboat and the other Yawl to the Commander of the Rembang the Ship in which we embarked. The latter was not to be delivered up until I leave Batavia, and I shall make myself accountable to the Commissioners of His Majestys Navy for their amount. As I could take no more Boats with me and the Pinnace being out of repair I left her with Governor Wanjon with Permission to do with her what he thought proper.

We stopped at Samarang in the Island of Java, were [sic] we had the good Fortune to be join'd by our Tender that had separated from us off the Island Oattooah. She had all her people onboard except one Man whom they had buried a few days before.

She had been stopp'd at Java on suspicion & they were going to send her to Batavia. Mr. Overstraten the Governor of the place delivered her up to me—the Tender had contracted a small debt for Provisions &c. at Java which I shall discharge.

She fell in to the Westward of Annamooka (the Island I had appointed to Rendezvous at) without seeing it and then steered two days to the Westward nearly in its Lat. and fell in with an Island which I suppose must be one of the Feejee Islands where they waited for me five Weeks, & then proceeded through Endeavour Straits and intended to stop at Batavia. With the Iron & salt I had supplied them with, they were enabled to procure and preserve sufficient Provision for their run to Java.

I arrived at Batavia on the 7th. of Novr. and on application to the Governor & Council my People were put onboard a Dutch East India Company Ship that was lying in the Road to be kept there until they could be sent to Europe and the sick were Ordered to be received into the Company's Hospital at Batavia, and I have since agreed with the Dutch East India Company to divide my Ships Company into four parts & to embark them onboard four of their Ships for Holland at no expense to Government further than for the Officers and Prisoners and which appeared to me to be the most eligible and least expensive way of getting to England. Lieut. Larkin, two petty officers, and 18 seamen Embarked on board the Swan a Dutch East India Ship on the 19th Novr. and are sailing for Europe and myself and the remainder of the Pandora's Company and Prisoners are to embark as soon as their Ships are Manned. Myself & the Pirates are to embark onboard the Vreedenburg, Captain Christian, and I have stipulated that myself & all the Prisoners may be at Liberty to go onboard any of His Majesty's Ships or other Vessels we may meet with on mine or my Officer's application for the purpose.

Inclosed is the Latitudes & Longitudes of several Islands &c. discovered during our Voyage, the State of the Pandora's Company, a List of Pirates belonging to the Bounty taken at Otaheite and a List of Convicts & Deserters from the colony at Port Jackson.

It may be necessary to observe that these last have Several Names and that Willm: Bryant and James Cox pretend that their time of Transportation is expired. But these two men found a Boat and Money to procure Necessaries to Enable themselves and others to Escape for which I presume they are liable to punishment and think it my duty to give information.

Although I have not had the good fortune fully to accomplish the Object of my Voyage, and that is [sic] has in other respects been strongly marked with great Misfortunes, Yet I hope it will be thought that the first was not for want of perseverance, or the latter for want of care and attention of myself and those under my Command, but that the disappointment & Misfortune arose from the dificulties and peculiar circumstances of the Service we were upon.

That that of my Orders which I have been able to fulfill, with the discoveries that have been made will be some compensation for the disappointment & misfortunes that have attended us and should their Lordships upon the whole think that the Voyage will be profitable to our Country it will be a great consolation to Sir Your most obed^t. & humble Servant,

Edwd. Edwards.

Phil^p. Stevens Esqr.
Cape of Good Hope 19th March 1792
Sir

Agreeable to my intentions which I did myself the honor to signify to you in a Letter addressed from Batavia and sent by a Dutch Packet bound to Europe, I embarked the remainder of the Company of His Majesty's ship Pandora, Pirates late belonging to the Bounty and the Convicts deserters from Port Jackson on board three Dutch East India Company ships, as follows—My self, the Master, Purser, Gunner, Clerk, two Mids.^{n}, 21 seamen and Ten Pirates onboard the Vreedenburg, bound to Amsterdam.

Lieut. Corner, The Surgeon, three Mids.^{n} Fourteen Seamen and half the convicts on board the Horssen bound to Rotterdam.

and [sic] Lieut Hayward, The Boatswain, Surgeons Mate three Mids.^{n} fifteen seamen and the other half of the Convicts onboard the Hoornwey bound to Rotterdam,—Lieut. Larkan with two Petty Officers and Eighteen Seamen were embarked onboard the Zwan and Sailed from Batavia previous to the date of my former letter, and I am now informed that she has been at this Port and Sailed from hence for Europe more than a Month before my arrival.—I found His Majesty's Ship Gorgon here on her return from Port Jackson and on account both of expedition and greater Security I intend to avail myself of the opportunity [to] embark onboard of her with the Ten Pirates for England and I Request that you will be pleased to communicate the circumstances to My Lords Commissioners of the Admiralty, I have the honor to be

Sir Your most obed.^{t} and humb.^{le}

Servant—
Edw. Edwards
Philip Stephens Esq.
Admiralty Office June 19th 1792
Sir

I beg leave to inform you that I found His Majesty's Ship Gorgon at the Cape of Good Hope on my arrival at that Place in the Vreedenburg a Dutch East India

The first manuscript page of Captain Edward Edwards' dispatch to the Admiralty on H.M.S. *Pandora*'s voyage is dated November 25, 1791, Batavia. The Admiralty received it from Amsterdam on May 29, 1792 (courtesy State Library of New South Wales).

Company's Ship from Batavia, and I thought it proper to remove the Pirates late belonging to his Majesty's Armed Vessel, the Bounty, and the convicts, deserters from Port Jackson (whom I had under my Charge onboard Dutch East India Companys Ships) into His Majesty's said Ship for their greater security, and I took the same opportunity myself to embark onboard of her for England, and I hope those steps will be approved of by their Lordships. I gave you an account of my arrival at the Cape of Good Hope and of my intentions to embark on board the Gorgon with the Pirates, Convicts &c. in a Letter which I did myself the honor to address to you from thence and sent by the Baring Thomas Tingey Master, an American Ship bound to Ostend. Inclosed is the state of the Company of His Majesty's Ship Pandora at the time I left the Cape of Good Hope, and the manner in which they were disposed of on board Dutch East India Company Ships in order to be brought to Europe and also a List of the Pirates late belonging to the Bounty, and of the Convicts, deserters from Port Jackson delivered to me by Mr. Wanjon the Governor of the Dutch Settlements in the Island of Timor and now on board His Majesty Ship Gorgon. I arrived Yesterday afternoon at St. Helens left the Gorgon and Landed at Portsmouth last night and I am now at this office waiting their Lordships Command

and I have the honor to be Sir
Your most obed.^{n} humble Servant
Edw. Edwards
Philip Stephens Esq—

A view of the Cape of Good Hope, an important destination for the officers and sailors who survived the open boat voyages led by Captain William Bligh of H.M.S. *Bounty* and Captain Edward Edwards of H.M.S. *Pandora*. Colored aquatint by J. R. Hamble after William Marshall Craig, c. 1806 (courtesy Yale Center for British Art, Paul Mellon Collection).

Part Seven. Passage to Batavia and England

A list of convicts, deserters from Port Jackson, delivered to Captain Edward Edwards of His Majesty's Ship Pandora by Timotheus Wanjon, Governor of the Dutch Settlements at Timor, 5th October 1791.
  William Allen
  John Butcher
  Nathaniel Lilley, On board H.M.S. Gorgon
  James Martin
  Mary Bryant, Transported by the name of Mary Broad
  William Morton, Dd on board Dutch East India Co.'s ship, Hoornwey
  William Bryant, Dd 22nd December 1791, Hospital, Batavia
  James Cox, Dd, fell overboard Straits of Sunda
  John Simms, Dd on board Dutch East India Co.'s ship, Hoornwey
  Emanuel Bryant, Dd 1st December 1791, Batavia
  Charlotte Bryant, Dd 6th May 1792 on board H.M.S.
  Gorgon William and Mary Bryant, Children of the above
Edw. Edwards

A List of one Petty Officer and four Seamen lost in a cutter belonging to His Majesty's Ship Pandora, at Palmerston's Island on the 24th May 1791.
  John Sival, Midshipman
  James Good
  William Wasdel
  James Scott Seamen
  Joseph Cunningham
Edw. Edwards

A List of Pirates late belong[g] to His Majesty's Armed Vessel Bounty; taken by His Majesty's Ship Pandora Capt[n] Edward Edwards at Otaheite.—
  Joseph Coleman
  Peter Heywood
  Mich[l] Burn
  Ja[s] Morrison
  Ch[s] Norman, On board His Majesty's Ship Gorgon
  Tho[s] Ellison
  Tho[s] M[c]Intosh
  Will[m] Muspratt
  Tho[s] Burkett
  John Millward
  Geo Stewart, DD 29 August 1791 Lost with the Ship
  Rich[d] Skinner
  Henry Heilbrant
  John Sumner
Edw. Edwards

State of the Company of His Majestys Ship Pandora Capt[n] Edw[d] Edwards: and the manner disposed of on board Dutch East India Company Ships for their passage to Europe.

		Comm. Off. and Master.	Warr.t Officers	Petty Officers	Seamen
Zwan	Lieut.t John Larkan	1	"	2	17
Horssen	Lieut.t Rob.t Corner. M.r George Hamilton. Surgeon	1	1	2	13
Hornweg	Lieut.t Thomas Hayward, John Cunningham, Boatswain	1	1	2	14
Vreedenburg	M.r Geo. Passmore, Master. M.r Gregory Bentham, Purser, Mr. Jos.h Packer, Gunner and 1 supernumerary belong.g to H. M. Arm.d Ves.l Supply	1	2	1	18
	Hospital at Batavia				1
His Maj.tys Ship Gorgon	Capt.n Edwards	1	"	2	1
		5	4	9	64

	Whole Number borne	82
	Dead since the Ship was lost	16
	Discharged	1
	Whole N.º Ships Comp.n saved in Ship & Tender	99
	Supernum.s	
Ditto	Pirates	10
	Convicts 4 Men and 1 Woman	5

Edw. Edwards

No. 8 Craven Street Strand 9th July 1792
Sir

    I beg leave to acquaint you that I have information that the Vreedenburg and the Horssen two Dutch East India companys Ships on board of which part of the company of His Majestys Ship Pandora are embarked were off the Start on the 5th of this Month in their way to Holland and that the Hoornwey the Ship on board which the remainder of the company of the Pandora were embarked was expected to sail from

Part Seven. Passage to Batavia and England

the cape of Good Hope in about 3 Weeks after the two former Ships left that place, but the account does not mention the time they left the cape themselves—

I have the honor to be
Sir
Your most Obed.^{nt} hum.^{ble} Servant
Edw. Edwards

List of Islands and places discovered by His Majesty's Ship pandora with their Latitudes and Longitudes

Names of Islands.	Latitude South	Longitude West
Ducie Island	24° 40' 30"	124° 40' 30"
Lord Hoods Island	21° 31' 00"	135° 32' 30"
Carisfort Island	20° 49' 00"	138° 33' 00"
Duke of Clarence Island	9° 09' 30"	171° 30' 46"
Otewhy, or Chatham Islands	13° 32' 30"	172° 18' 25"
Howes Isles	18° 32' 30"	173° 53' 00"
Gardeners Island	17° 57' 00"	175° 16' 54"
Bickertons Island	18° 47' 40"	174° 48' 00"
Onooahfow or Probys Island	15° 53' 00"	175° 51' 00"
Rotuman or grenville Islands	12° 29' 00"	183° 03' 00"
Pandora's Bank	12° 11' 00"	188° 08' 00"
Mitre Island	11° 49' 00"	190° 04' 30"
Cherry Island	11° 37' 30"	190° 19' 30"
Pitts Island South point	11° 50' 30"	193° 14' 05"
Wells Shoal or Reef	12° 20' 00"	202° 02' 00"
Cape Rodney	10° 03' 32"	212° 14' 05"
Mount Clarence between the two Capes		
Cape Hood	9° 58' 06"	212° 37' 10"
Look out Shoal		
Stoney Reef Islands		
Murrays Isles	9° 57' 00"	216° 43' 00"
Wreck Reef		
Escape Key	11° 23' 00"	
Entrance Key	11° 23' 00"	

Edw. Edwards

A list of Fourteen pirates, belonging to His Majesty's late ship Bounty taken at Otaheite.

1   Joseph Coleman
Peter Heywood
Mich¹ Byrn
James Morrison
5   Charles Norman
Thomas Ellison
Thomas M‹Intosh
William Muspratt
Thomas Burkitt
10 John Millward

George Stewart DD 29 Aug¹ 1791 Drown'd
Richard Skinner DD 29   "   "
Henry Hillbrant DD 29   "   "
14 John Sumner DD 29   "   "

Edw. Edwards

Mr. Peter Heywood to Mrs. [Elizabeth] Heywood

Batavia, November 20th, 1791.

On September 1st we left the Island, and on the 16th arrived at Coupang, in the Island of Timor, having been on short Allowance 18 Days. We were put in Confinement in the Castle, and remained till October, and on the 5th went on board a Dutch Ship bound for Batavia. At Night weighed and set Sail, and after a very tedious and dangerous Passage, the Ship being twice near drove ashore, and so very leaky as scarce to be kept above Water with both Pumps constantly going, on the 30th anchored at Samorong, on the Isle of Java, where we unexpectedly found the Schooner I mentioned parting Company with.

On Monday the 7th anchored here at Batavia. I send this by the first Ship, which is to sail in about a Week, by one of the *Pandora*'s Men; we are to follow in a Week after and expect to be in England in seven Months. Though I have been eight Months in close Confinement in a hot Climate, I have kept my Health in a most surprising Manner, without the least Indisposition, and am still perfectly well in every Respect, in Mind as well as Body; but, without a Friend and only a Shirt and pair of Trousers to put on and carry me Home. Yet with all this, I have a contented Mind, entirely resigned to the Will of Providence, which Conduct alone enables me to soar above the Reach of Unhappiness. You will most probably hear of my Arrival in England (should it ever happen) before I can write to you, which I most earnestly long for, that I may explain things which I now cannot mention. Yet, I hope it will be sufficient to undeceive those who have been so ungenerous as to express, and others who have been so credulous as to believe, so undeserved a Character of me.

I can say no more, but remember me to my dearest Sisters, Brothers, etc., etc., etc., etc.,
and believe me still to be your most dutiful and ever obedient Son

Peter Heywood.

From The Journal of James Morrison, Boatswain's Mate of the Bounty

About 10 we were landed, and Conducted by a Guard to the Governors house, & from thence to the Castle where notwithstanding our Weak Condition we were put into Stocks and on the 19th the Yauls arrived & we were Joined by our fellow prisoners whose treatment had been better, but their fare the same—Immediately on our landing Provisions were procured which now began to move our bodys and we were forced to ease Nature where we lay, which we had not done during the Passage and some were now so bad as to require repeated Clysters, but the Surgeon of the Place who visited us could not enter the place till it had been washd by the Slaves. We had laid 6 Days in this situation when the Dutch Officer Commanding the Fort, being informd of our distress, came to visit us & taking Compassion on us, ordered Irons to be procured, and link'd us two & two; giving us liberty to walk about the Cell, and now a Guard of the Pandoras Men were placed before the Door in addition to the Dutch Soldiers.

As we were Yet Mostly Naked, we got some of the leaves of the Brab Tree, and set to work to make hats, which we sold to procure us Clothing; but evry article being dear we could purchace nothing here; and thread and Needles being very dear we made but little progress; however we made shift to supply ourselves with Tobacco and some little refreshments.

We found that there were prisoners in the Fort, Seven Men a Woman & two Children who had escaped in a Boat from Sidney (or Port Jackson, Botany Bay); they had passd some time on the Governer for Part of the Crew of the Ship Neptune which they reported to have been cast away, but not being able to keep within Bounds, they were discovered to be Cheats, and Confined in the Castle till they should pay the Debt they had Contracted.

October, 1791. We remain'd here till the 5th of October when we were removed on board the Rembang, ye Dutch Ship then in the Road—and Mr. Larkan, being the Officer on this duty, coming to the Prison with a Guard with Cords for the Purpose pinnioned us with his own hands, setting his foot against our backs, and bracing our arms together as almost to haul our arms out of their socketts; we were tyed two & two by the Elbows, & having our Irons knockd off were Conducted to the Beach and put on board a long Boat to proceed to the Ship but before we reachd her some of us had fainted owing to the Circulation of the Blood being stopd by the lasshings—When we got on board we were put both legs in Irons, and our lasshings taken off.

The Botany Bay men were now brought on board by a party of Dutch Soldiers and put in Irons with us, in the Same Manner, and the Ship Weighd in the Evening for Batavia & Next day McIntosh Coleman & Norman were let out of Irons with liberty to walk the Deck. Our hands being now at liberty we expected now to find some little ease, & prepared to go to work on hatts having brought our stuff on board with us, but happiness is not to be always found where it is expected and is ever of a short duration.

The ship was very leaky and we were ordered out of Irons two at a time, for two hours in the fore noon, & two hours in the afternoon with Centinals over us to work the Pumps—this new liberty, as we thought it, we gladly embraced, but soon found our strength unequal to the Task—and I one day told Mr. Larkan that I was not able to stand to the pump at Spell & Spell (the ship requiring the pump continually at work) to which he replyd Tauntingly, 'You dam'd Villain, you have brought it on yourself and I'll make you stand it; if it was not for you we should not have been here nor have met with this trouble,' to which I replied 'trouble often comes unsought' and he then ordered me to be silent.

However this work was soon at an end for hard work at the pump, and the deck where we lay being Constantly wet, and having no Cloathing under, or over us, soon put us past labour; and we were then kept below, the pumps being now left to the Dutch Seamen and Malay Slaves.

This ship was badly found and Worse Managed and if Captain Edwards had not taken the Command and set his Men to work she would never have reached Batavia, having Split Most of Her Sails in passing the Streight of Bally and having none to bend in their stead very narrowly escaped going on shore.

However we reachd Samarang, a Dutch Settlement on the Island of Java, by the 30th of October where we came to an anchor, and here we found the Schooner, which had arrived at this Island 6 weeks before, with all her Crew, consisting of a Masters Mate, Midshipman, Quarter Master and Six men, one of which died since their Arrival. They were Joyfully received by their shipmates and the Schooner being brought out of Harbour accompanied us to Batavia where we anchord on the 7th of November.

November, 1791. We were now put on board an old Hulk in the Road with the Pandoras Officers and Men & here McIntosh, Coleman & Norman had the liberty of the Deck as before and here we received 10/- per Man for short allowance in the Boats, with which we purchased some few refreshments in addition to the Ships Allowance, being Still Victualled by the Purser of the Pandora. The Schooner being put up for Sale the Captain Purchased her, and sent her as a present to the Governor of Timor & devided the Mony amongst the Ships Company.

Nankin Cloth was here purchased and served to the Ships Company, and as we had now recovered our health we commenced taylors as well as hat makers, and by Working for the Ships Company got some Cloaths for ourselves which we stood in much Need of, but this was prohibited by Capt. Edwards as soon as he knew it. We remaind here till the 23rd of December during which time we were not permitted to come on Deck but twice, each for about half an hour at a Time to Wash ourselves, and here we enjoyd our Health, tho the Pandoras people fell sick and died apace.

With respect to the City of Batavia I can say nothing, not having had a view of it, but it makes no shew from the Road, the Church & some storehouses being the only Buildings that can be seen from the Shiping. It is situated at the Bottom of a deep Bay or Inlet and surrounded by low and to all appearance Swampy land which has no appearance of Cultivation—the small river by which its Canals are filld emptys itself into the Bay and teems with such filth that the Road where the large Ships lye is little better then a Stagnate Pool; during the Night the Dew falls very heavy and the Morning is generally darkened by a thick Stinking fog which continues till it is exhaled by the Heat of the Sun.

As the Sea Breeze seldom reaches the Road till afternoon and some times not during the Day the Weather is Close & Sultry and the land Wind coming off in the evenings brings with it a sickly disagreeable smell sufficient to breed Distempers among Europeans—to prevent being infected by this, we apply'd for liberty to smoke tobacco which being Granted, all our leisure time was thus employ'd but particularly in the Mornings & Evenings, which we found very beneficial and freed us from headachs &ca. which we supposed to be occasioned by the pestilential vapours.

Part Seven. Passage to Batavia and England

The Climate of Batavia is by no Means calculated for Europeans and together with the new Arrack (a most pernicious liquor) carries off Great numbers daily and such a havock had Death made within the last 6 Months that the Fleet now in the Road were forced to send to Holland for Hands to Navigate them and even now they were not half Mannd, tho the Crews of the outward bound ships were put on board as fast as they came to an Anchor. It was said that 2,500 Officers & Seamen had been carried off this season exclusive of the Inhabitants—The Chinese & Natives of the Island do all the Labour in loading & unloading the Ships as the Dutch seamen are mostly removed as soon as the ship is made fast. Provisions here are Neither cheap nor Good, the Beef being all small and lean and Rice is the only substitute for bread, at least all that can be the fare of the Ships Company. Cloathing of all kinds and especially the Manufactures of Europe is dear also, and in fact I could find Nothing Cheap but Arrack which is as bad as poison, but nevertheless it is plentifully used by the Dutch, and it Cost the Pandoras Officers some trouble to keep their Men from using it also.

20th November. The First Lieut., Mr. Larkan, saild in a Dutch ship for Europe with part of the ships Company and on the 23rd of December the remainder were devided Lieut. Corner & Hayward taking each a party and with them the Botany Bay men—and we were put on board the Vreedenbergh in which ship was Captain Edwards with twenty three officers & men and on the 24th she weighd and dropd down to a small Island in the entrance of the Bay Calld Onrest on which the Dock Yard is, and to this place they send their Convicts where they are employd, making Rope & Careening the Ships.

We weighd from this place on the 25th, tideing it out through the Straights, and it was this afternoon before We got any Provisions, having been Victualled no longer then the 22nd by the Purser of the Pandora, and when we got it it was served after the Dutch Method which was thus—two drams of Arrack per Day, equal to 1/3rd of a Pint—three Pounds of Flesh (Beef & Pork) one & a half of Fish—ditto of Sugar, ditto of Tamarinds, half a Pint of Gee half a Pint of Oil, & a pint of Vinager with Rice in lieu of Bread to serve each Man for a fortnight—the rice was little better then Grains, most of it having the husks on it, and the Oil & Tamarinds were fit for no use that we could put them to—Such was our food, and two Quarts of water a day gave us plenty to drink, but our lodgings were none of the Best, as we lay on rough logs of Timber, some of which lay Some inches above the rest and which our small portion of Cloathing would not bring to a level, the Deck also over us was very leaky, by which means we were continually wet, being alternately drenchd with Salt water, the Urine of the Hogs or the Rain which happend to fall.

We passd the Streight of Sunda on the 1st of January 1792 and met with Nothing Material during our passage to the Cape except burying two of the Pandoras Men & several of the Dutch Seamen—this and the Method of Issuing the Provisions was the only thing that occur'd worth Notice, and which as it Shews the true Charracter of Dutchmen deserves Notice, they made Ranson, or fortnights allowance, to serve us Sixteen Days and by the time we reachd the Cape they had gaind upon us nearly a fortnights allowance.

March 14th. This day we were let out of Irons two at a time to walk the Deck for two Hours each, but were Scarce able to stand on our feet we were got so weak by living or rather existing on Our Miserable allowance—this was the First and last Indulgence of the kind we had during the Passage, except one or two Who had been let out for a few hours in a day by the intercession of the Dutch Surgeon, and we now found the weather Sharp and Cutting.

15th. Made the Cape of Good Hope and on the 18th came to an anchor in Table Bay, where to our inexpressable Joy we found an English Man of war was riding which we were soon informd was His Majestys Ship Gorgon from Port Jackson, and on the 19th we were sent on Board her, where our treatment became less rigourous and 2/3rds Allowance of Provisions was now thought Feasting.

Shortly after arrived the other Ships with the rest of the Pandoras men. We learnt here that the First Lieut. of the Pandora had saild some time and having left one of his men behind he was sent on board this Ship by Captain Edwards. McIntosh, Coleman & Norman were here at liberty as before and the Rest of us only one leg in Irons, and evry Indulgence Given & Lieut. Gardner of this Ship, in the absence of Captain Parker, very humanely gave us a Sail to lay on which by us was thought a Luxury; and was indeed such as we had not enjoyd for 12 Months before.

And here being supplyd with Shirts & Trowsers we laid what trifle of Cash we had out in refreshments and began to get our health & strength very fast having the Benefit of the fresh air which for some time before we had been strangers to, being removed from between Decks to sit on the Fore Castle for 6 or 8 hours evry day.

On the 4th of April Captain Edwards came on board in order to take his passage in the Gorgon and on the 5th she Weighd for England and on the 10th we were ordered full allowance.

18th. Made the Island of St. Helena which we passd near enough to show our Collours and see two Ships in the Road who returned the Compliment by hoisting theirs.

22nd. Made Ascencion and anchord the same day—found riding here an American Schooner belonging to New Providence and having got on board 28 fine turtle Saild on the 24th—after Crossing the Line we spoke an American Brig bound to Bengal, and an English Brig the Prince William Henry, bound to the South Fishery.

19th of June. Anchord at Spithead. On the 21st we were removed to His Majestys Ship Hector where we were treated in a manner that renders the Humanity of her Captain and Officers much Honor and had Beds given us and evry Indu[l]gence that our Circumstances would admit of allowed.

On the 12th of September our tryal commenced on board His Majestys Ship Duke in Portsmouth Harbour...[51]

PART EIGHT

The Unforeseen Voyage of *Matavy*

Brief summaries of *Matavy*'s voyage after its crew lost sight of H.M.S. *Pandora* near the Samoan island of Tutuila appear in Captain Edwards' dispatch to the Admiralty and George Hamilton's *A Voyage Round the World in His Majesty's Frigate Pandora*. In *The Discoverers of the Fiji Islands* (1933) G. C. Henderson lamented the fact that Edwards and Hamilton were our only sources of information about *Matavy*'s three-month journey and that "From Hamilton's narrative we can well believe that the sufferings and privations of the unfortunate crew in their voyage across the South-west Pacific to Endeavour Straits must have been intense, and that the story of their adventures would make exceedingly interesting reading."[52] Henderson was not aware that in 1842, William

The first manuscript page of "The Journal of David Thomas Renouard," in which the *Pandora* midshipman narrates the *Matavy* crew's unexpected and eventful voyage. They were the first Europeans to make contact with the people of Fiji. Renouard barely survived the harrowing journey and two members of the small crew died soon afterward (courtesy State Library of New South Wales).

Henry Smyth published an edited copy of *Pandora* Midshipman David T. Renouard's journal of the *Matavy* voyage in "The Last of the Pandoras."[53] Rolf E. Du Rietz brought this and other forgotten articles to the attention of scholars in "The Voyage of H.M.S. *Pandora*, 1790–1792: Some Remarks upon Geoffrey Rawson's Book on the Subject."[54]

In 1961, a copy of Renouard's "exceedingly interesting" narrative made in 1864 was offered by London bookseller Eric M. Bonner, and purchased by the National Library of Australia (the original seems to be lost). Pacific historian H. E. Maude transcribed and printed it as "Renouard's Narrative" in *The Mariner's Mirror*, August 1964. Maude's analysis of Renouard's account convincingly demonstrates that *Matavy*'s crew had unknowingly reached the Fiji Islands during their voyage. They were the first Europeans to make landfall there and establish contact with the natives, who provided the crew with desperately needed water and food. Maude concludes that they must have been at Ono-i-Lau, part of Fiji's Southern Lau Group, although entries in Captain Edwards' log—which also came to light in the early 1960s—suggest that *Matavy*'s crew *may* have miscalculated the starting point of the voyage and reached Matuku or Kadavu, in a different Fijian subgroup.[55]

The Journal of David Thomas Renouard, Midshipman, H.M.S. *Pandora*

His Majesty's Ship Pandora was commissioned at Chatham on the 10th August 1790; for the express purpose of finding the mutineers belonging to His Majesty's late Ship *Bounty* and the command of her given to Captn Edwd Edwards; on board of which Ship I made my entrance into the Service in my 16th year. We sailed from Portsmouth on the 7th November following and nothing material happened out of the usual course of sea voyages till after we quitted Rio Janeiro from whence we sailed on the 8th January 1791; and having weathered some hard Gales with a tremendous sea off the Coast of Brazil made Cape Horn on the 2nd February following; for a considerable time we met with nothing but adverse winds (the winter season being far advanced) which compelled us to stand well to the southward to avoid the dangers of a lee shore. It was about a fortnight before we had completely doubled the Cape and were fairly launched into the great Pacific Ocean which gave us no small pleasure after having been long tossed about in the boisterous Seas of this inhospitable climate. But like true Sons of Neptune with a return of fine weather and favorable breezes we soon forgot our late cares and toils. After having passed the Tropic of Capricorn we fell in with the usual trade winds and met with no occurrence worthy of remark till our arrival at Otaheite on the 23rd March 1791. Here we found fourteen of the mutineers but it is unnec-

Part Eight. The Unforeseen Voyage of Matavy 145

essary to enter into any other detail respecting them further than serves to elucidate my own narrative. Two parties of the *Pandora*'s people were sent on shore under the command of Lieu^{ts} Corner and Hayward, to secure the mutineers which was ultimately effected. Our boats chased and after a few hours came up with a small vessel in which some of them were attempting to make their escape; and of which I shall endeavour to give a short description, as it was in her I underwent many hardships. The mutineers conceiving themselves insecure in a place so well known as Otaheite with much perseverance built this boat with the aid of the natives, out of such inefficient materials as the island produced, and with the tools saved out of the plunder of the *Bounty*'s stores. She was handsomely shaped of about 18 or 20 tons burden, decked and rigged with two large matt sprit sails. By the declaration of these people, it appeared that they meant to attempt a passage to the N.W. coast of America, and had actually put to sea for this purpose, but whether it was their real intention to risk so long a voyage is of little or no moment here. They found their little bark so crank and little sea worthy that they deemed it expedient to return to Otaheite. Captn Edwards resolved to commission her and gave orders that she should be repaired, supplied with canvas sails and such other necessaries as the service required; and having christened the *Matuavi Tender* [apparently an error for *Matavy*] after a bay so named at Otaheite he gave her in charge to a master's mate, (commander) midshipman and quartermaster and six seamen. It is almost needless to remark that in a voyage like ours, when we were about to explore new regions and unknown seas, very great advantages were likely to accrue from the assistance of a tender for from the length of our voyage it would not have been practicable for the ship to lie to, during the night (always of considerable duration within the tropics) and the dangers of making in the dark, a course, probably never before traversed, was in a great measure obviated, as the Tender always made sail ahead by night and had strict orders to keep a good look out and make signals on the first approach of danger. We sailed from hence on the 8th May following. The Midshipman who was on board the *Matuavi* being indisposed I obtained permission to supersede him, & as I went on board in haste I took little more than change of clothes, a circumstance which I had afterwards much cause to regret. It will be sufficient to observe that, after having passed and partially explored several Islands, we arrived off the cluster called Navigators, on the 18th June 1791; and hence may be dated the commencement of all our troubles. The natives of these islands (unfortunately for us) were among the most the most [sic] ferocious Tribe of Savages who inhabit the Southern Archipelago. On the 25th June the ship arrived off the island of Otootooeba and we were reconnoitering close in shore (as usual when any land was made) while she remained in the offing to the best of my recollection and judgement about 4 or 5 leagues. The natives came off in their canoes, but from the behaviour we forboded no good; they kept continually hovering about our boat and though they had plenty of hogs fruit &c in their canoes we could not persuade them to traffic with us, not withstanding our utmost endeavours were exerted to bring on a friendly intercourse, by offering such articles in exchange as we conceived (from past experience) calculated to suit their fancy. Owing to the little wind (being nearly calm) our situation became very critical; we dreaded an attack and the sequel will show our fears were too well founded; for shortly after the savages becoming more daring, surrounded us in such numbers that we could scarce keep off their canoes, which however we did for some time by means of our boarding pikes. Mr Oliver our commander now gave directions to have our arms in readiness in case of emergency, and at the same time laid the strongest injunctions on his men not to fire, without his express orders; for actuated by humanity no less than by a sense of duty, he resolved not to shed human blood unnecessarily. Every moment became more alarming, and at length one of the savages more bold than the rest, flourished his club in defiance and uttering a kind of war-whoop (the signal for general attack) reached over the boat's stern, and aimed a blow at our commander which fortunately fell short. Mr Oliver then fired three pistols successively which either flashed in the pan or missed fire; when seeing our perilous situation (as the savages did not retire being unacquainted with the effect of fire-arms) he permitted our crew to fire, and the savage who leveled the blow was killed by the discharge of one of our seven barrel pieces and several others were wounded: the consternation became general, the savages, on seeing their companions fall immediately jumped into the sea setting up a horrid yell; & swam on shore dragging their canoes after them. To add to our misfortune the day was far advanced and the ship was seen standing out to sea with a brisk wind; while we could make little way after her, being almost becalmed under the highland. Towards sunset we caught the sea breeze which increased to a fresh gale accompanied with hazy weather, and we set every stitch of sail our boat would carry after the Frigate [*Pandora*]. When night came on we lose [*sic*] sight, but continued to stand on the same course in which before it became dark the ship was seen steering. At midnight we discerned as we thought her lights ahead and consequently kept on the same tack till day-break, firing muskets at intervals & hanging out her lights. As soon as day appeared, to our astonishment & dismay, the ship was out of sight. I will not attempt to describe the horror of our situation, but leave the reader to judge of it. We had only two alternatives, the one to go about & stand in for the land in search of the ship, the other to proceed to our rendez-vous (Anamooka Friendly Isl^{ds}) a distance of near seven hundred miles. Not a moment was to be lost & our commandant determined on the latter. Our little store of provisions was nearly expended and to add to our distress we had not received a fresh supply, which was actually on the Pandora's quarter deck in readiness for us, the day we parted Company, and if we had again made for the Island and not had the good fortune to find the Ship, our ruin would have been inevitable; as our late hostilities with the savages, precluded all idea of succour from them and had we lost a day's run, we should have had still less chance of reaching the rendez-vous appointed in case of separation. On examination our Provisions consisted of about a dozen pieces of Salt Beef & Pork, 20 lbs of bread, 3 or 4 lbs of Butter, a small quantity of flour and wheat, a Barrel of Sour Krout, a keg of salt, and nearly a gallon of rum; but what was of infinately more consequence scarcely 3 quarts of water. The review of this scanty allowance did not alleviate our misery; but instead of giving way to despair we trusted for our deliverance, to that kind Providence which guides the mariner in safety through the trackless deep. On the 22nd the wind blowing favorably, we shaped our course to Anamooka, and our stock of water being so very slender, we by mutual agreement abstained from taking any this day. On the 23rd the wind still continued the same, and we distributed about a gill of water to each man. On the 24th the weather still

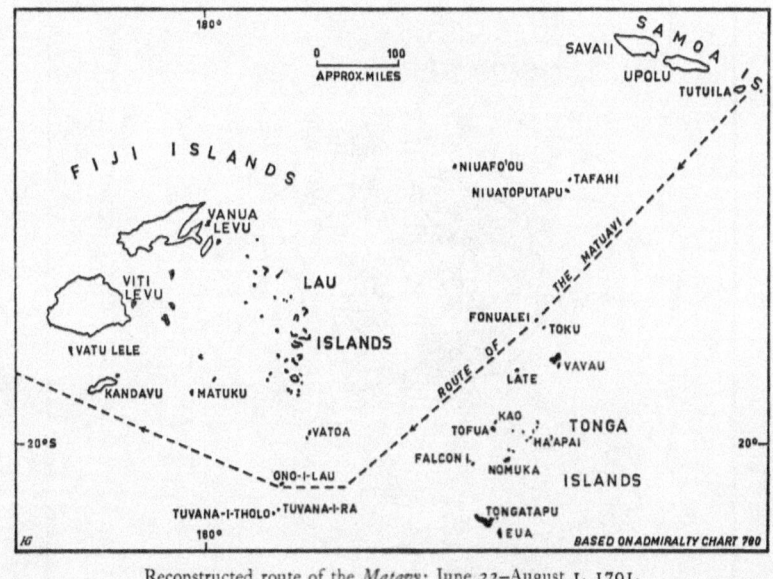

Reconstructed route of the *Matavy*; June 22–August 1, 1791.

The "Reconstructed route of the Matavy; June 22—August 1, 1791," a map created by British anthropologist H. E. Maude for his article, "The Voyage of the *Pandora*'s Tender," shows how *Matavy*'s crew reached the Fijian island group of Ono-I-Lau. The map is based on information provided by Midshipman David T. Renouard in his journal of the voyage. From H. E. Maude, "The Voyage of Pandora's Tender," *The Mariner's Mirror*, 50:3 (1964): 217-235 (reproduced by permission of the Society for Nautical Research).

continued favorable and the same allowance of water as on the preceeding day with a tablespoonful of rum was divided among us. With regard to eatables everyone was left to his own option, but our thirst became so intolerable that none of us had much inclination for them. For my own part I chose some biscuit well buttered to moisten my mouth. On the morning of the 25th we discovered a small island right ahead; our hopes & fears were now raised to the highest pitch for the Land appearing lofty made us conjecture that it probably contained water. We neared the island fast and about noon came to anchor in a small bay. A party immediately went on shore in a small canoe we had on board, (which answered the purpose of a skiff) in search of water; they soon returned crying out that they had found some, but could not procure it without the aid of cordage, as it was at the bottom of a deep hollow. We instantly bent some ropes together and went to the assistance of our comrades;

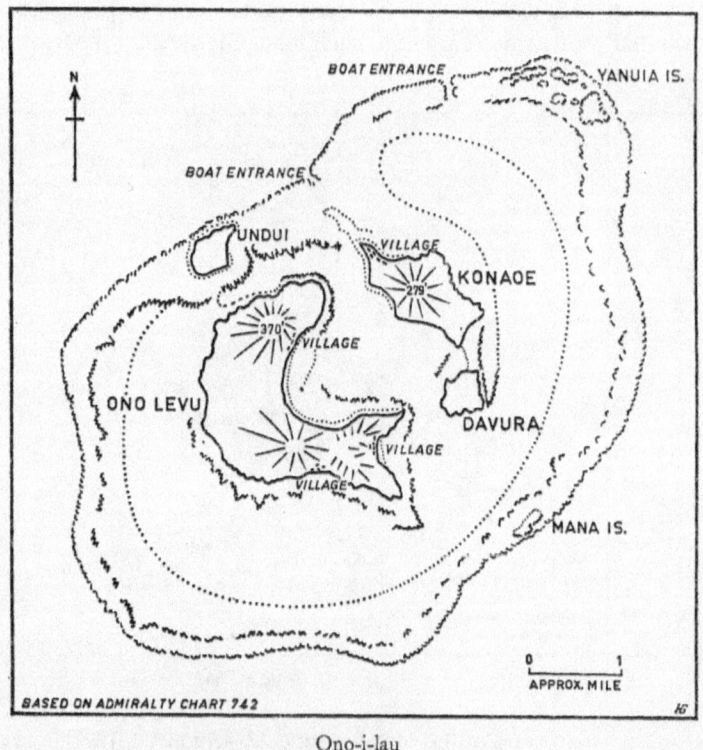

Ono-i-lau

The six islands of Fiji's Ono-i-lau group are depicted on this map in H. E. Maude's article, "The Voyage of the *Pandora*'s Tender." The *Matavy* sailed around this group for five weeks after it lost sight of H.M.S. *Pandora*. From H. E. Maude, "The Voyage of the Pandora's Tender," *The Mariner's Mirror*, 50:3 (1964): 217–235 (reproduced by permission of the Society for Nautical Research).

one of whom was let down but to our unspeakable disappointment, it was found to be salt, and we returned to the beach quite disheartened. The island bore evident marks of volcanic eruptions, the soil was parched up and mixed with ashes, and the hollow in its centre much resembled the crater of an extinguished Volcano; there was scarce any verdure to be seen. This inhospitable spot was uninhabited; but fires having been recently made in different parts; in [sic] may be presumed that it was occasionally visited by the natives of the neighbouring Isles on fishing excursions. We got under way not a little chagrined with our ill-success, and proceeded on our destination. Several islands were now plainly descried from our Deck, under our lee, about 6 or 7 leagues distant, but as they did not lie exactly in our route, to explore them would have been two [sic] hazardous an undertaking. Some sugar canes (which we had brought off from the desert Island) were now distributed in equal shares; they afforded at most, but a momentary relief, for our thirst became greater than before. Our small pittance of water was issued this day as usual, with two or three spoonfuls of rum to each; at different periods. On the whole of the 26th and 27th the wind continued favorable, but the clearness of the atmosphere gave us no hopes of rain. During these two days nothing remarkable occurred. Our suffering increased as our water diminished, & I am convinced that those only who have been in similar situations, can form any adequate idea of our distress. The truth of an old adage that 'necessity is the mother of invention' was verified in us for we had recourse to various contrivances to alleviate our misery. Some of our sailors drank sea-water in which sour crout had been steeped but it made them retch and vomit violently. We frequently dipped our faces in seawater which seemed to afford us a slight refreshment; and I had great difficulty in persuading our quartermaster to refrain from drinking it. His loss would have been irreparable, for he was not only an excellent seaman but also understood the business of a sailmaker, which was a matter of the utmost consequence as the sequel will shew. We took it in turn to boil water in a kettle (used for cooking our victuals) and by collecting the steam as it condensed in the lid, we procured in every two hours about a table-spoonful of fresh; which some mixed with their allowance of spirits, while others preferred it unmixed. This remedy was almost as bad as the disease; for those who procured it were exposed to the heat of the fire, in addition to that of the climate which was sufficiently oppressive. We had now run on the evening of the 27th between 600 & 700 miles by our log, & were according to our dead reckoning within a few leagues of our rendezvous; yet the much wished for haven was not in sight and our Commander deemed it would be prudent to lie to for fear of passing it in the night. Towards night as no land appeared (nor any birds, the usual sign of its vicinity) we began to despair all of us were much exhaused [sic], especially an old seaman who lay on his bed perfectly resigned to his fate; our last precious drop of water was expended and our rum nearly gone. On the first dawn of day we made sail with a moderate breeze in the same quarter. Our anxiety to see land was of course increasing every moment; but such was our depression of spirits and our want of bodily strength, that none attempted to keep a lookout at the masthead. As our last gill of water had been served out the day preceeding, this day an additional spoonful of rum was given to each man. I had, hitherto, (probably owing to my youth) supported my spirits better than my companions in misfortune, & about noon I mustered resolution enough to climb up to the Mast head (but not without considerable pain) and to my great Joy soon discovered land ahead in the form of two sugar loaves at the distance to the best of my judgment of about 6 or 7 leagues. I hailed the deck with the good news but so fearful were my shipmates of disappointment that they would not give credit to my assertions nor even for a while believe their own senses. However our wishes were soon gratified; the breeze freshened and our little bark drawing nearer, we plainly discerned three islands and about 4 P.M. altered our course and hauled up along the shore of the easternmost, bounded by a heavy surf in search of an opening, or Bay to run into. We remained for some time in the most tantalizing state for our eyes were feasted with abundance & several of the natives who attempted to come off to us had their canoes either upset or driven back by the violence of the surf. At length some canoes were seen standing out of a bay at a considerable distance ahead, and the sight of them coming along side filled with cocoanuts excited a sensation that I will not attempt to describe. The Savages were well disposed, (a favorable circumstance for in our reduced state we could have made but a very feeble resistance) and their canoes were soon lightened of their contents. It was now exactly a week since we had parted company, and I do sincerely believe that we could not have survived another day without nourishment. Having amply satiated our burning thirst with the milk of the nuts, we with grateful hearts returned thanks to the Almighty for our preservation. Our prospect now began somewhat to brighten and hope took place of despondency. When night came on we made a good offing to avoid being incommoded by the too numerous visits of our new friends; and indeed it would have been imprudent to have given them an insight into our weakness. This precaution having been taken we sat down to supper on some sweet potatoes, not a little thankful for such a delicious repast. We afterwards laid down to rest with a composure to which we had long been strangers; and got some sound sleep which greatly refreshed us. As soon as daylight appeared we cast our eyes around in search of our ship, alas! in vain: but though this occasioned uneasiness yet our orders being to remain Three weeks at our rendezvous we were not much alarmed as we expected she would shortly heave in sight; for we had not the least notion (at that time) that we had mistaken the island of Toofoa for that of Anamooka. Every person versed in nautical affairs will (I am convinced) readily allow the great difficulty and uncertainty of keeping a correct reckoning in a situation like ours; for our latitude was all we could depend on, and fortunately we had 2 quadrants on board, which gave us means of taking the sun meridian altitude, with tolerable accuracy; but we had no charts to refer to for information. We had many strong reasons for supposing these islands to have been our proper rendezvous; there were three principal ones which corresponded in many respects, with the description given by Captn Cook of Anamooka, Tongataboo, and Etood. The natives were amicable, and the islands abounded in hogs, yams, bread fruit and sugar canes; and in fact we were among the Friendly Isles, Toofoa being one of that group, & Anamooka was not a great many leagues to the westward of us: but our preservation would have been endangered if we had run far to leeward or westward for there was not any land in sight in that quarter, and we should not have been able to regain our former station off Tofooa; as our boat sailed very badly to leeward, & being within the track of the trade wind it of course invariably blew from the eastward. Having explained the ground which induced us to remain off Tofooa, I shall next proceed to a brief statement of the leading occurrences which took place during our stay. The late rencontre with the savages of Otootooeba put us on our guard and we adopted the following method of procuring subsistance; when the natives came off we only permitted a single canoe, or two at most to lie along side at a time, and stood out towards the sea with their canoe in tow, till a bargain was concluded; when they returned on shore, highly delighed [sic] with the articles given them in exchange for hogs, yams, bread fruit, plantains, &c. By repeating this manoeuvre as occasion required, our deck was speedily covered with provisions. On the second night after our arrival (30th June) there came on a violent storm of thunder, lightening, [sic] and rain, the latter a blessing we had often of late most ardently prayed for; all hands were now busily employed in catching the water by spreading the boat sails athawt [sic] her deck, in this manner was procured a quantity sufficient to fill several casks: thus the bounty of heaven amply supplied our wants. We were so plentifully supplied with provisions, that we every day enjoyed a wholesome meal of fresh meat with a profusion of tropical fruits: and we soon recovered our health & strength. The savages frequently made signs as if they wished us to come on shore, but we did not comply with their request; for to divide our small crew would have been too hazardous,—they were much adicted to theiving and one day gave us a specimen of their dexterity in that act, for while our attention was occupied in making some purchases, one of them had the audacity to steal away the cover of our harness cask being no doubt tempted by the iron about it, and actually bore off his prize in triumph, for he had with his companion, paddled away to some distance before we discovered our loss, a musket was fired at them, but it had not the desired effect, for it did not induce them to give it up. This little fracas happily did not break off our friendly connection. Having cruized about the islands, for 3 weeks in almost every direction, we began to despair of meeting with the Pandora, and (even on a supposition that we had mistaken our place of rendezvous) we did not dare, for reasons before assigned, to run further to the westward. We therefore began to consider about our means of making some European settlement, whence we might procure a passage to England. Our water for sea stock was laid in at a small island situated about 5 leagues from Toofoa, which we had before partially examined and found suited for our purpose; the natives not being very numerous. As we were obliged to keep close inshore while we were taking in our water, a business rendered very tedious by the natives who brought it off in very small quantities at a time, we put up a boarding net to prevent our being overpowered, or taken by surprise, in the event of an attack; nor were our precautions useless. Mr Oliver permitted four of our crew (who volunteered) to go on shore for water, but as the natives were much inclined to pilfer (a vice predominant in all the South Sea Islands) he ordered the cask which they took with them, to be covered with a piece of old hammock cloth that the savages might not be tempted to murder them for the sake of the iron hoops. Our sailors performed their errand and returned unmolested from their description, it appeared that the only water on the island, was supplied by a tank or resevoir, [sic] which filled itself during the rainy season. We had scarce completed our water before the savages meditated an attack, their canoes were collected on the beach opposite to us; and there being very little wind, favored their intentions (for as in light wind and calm their canoes had a great superiority over our boat, so in a fresh breeze & rough sea we had the advantage on our side) they advanced towards us in slow and regular order, frequently resting on their paddles as if deliberating on what they should do. Our canvas was all spread, yet we made little way: they were now about a quarter of a mile astern, and we could plainly discern that they had warlike weapons; and that some of them were preparing to shoot their arrows: on this we fired two musket balls among them, & they desisted from any further attempt. We again resumed our old station off Toofoa and procured a great quantity of yams, which being carefully dried were stowed away for sea use, & as we had given up all hopes of joining our Ship, every method was now tried to better the condition of our boat, & prepare for a voyage of more than 3000 miles. The nearest European Settlement was Port Jackson, but Mr Oliver resolved at all events to push for some of the Dutch settlements in India in preference to the former place; fearful of being blown off by the strong winds which (as he had been informed) prevail on the Eastern coast of New Holland. In our situation if a spirit of discontent or insubordination had manifested itself among our sailors, our case would have been desperate indeed, as it was by our united efforts only, that we could ever reasonably expect to sur-

Part Eight. The Unforeseen Voyage of Matavy

mount the difficulties we had to combat; but fortunately their conduct was highly praiseworthy. As we had experienced great inconvenience and even some degree of danger from the clumsiness of our large sprit sails, we altered them, and rigged our little bark, after the manner of a schooner which answered infinately better. Having taken in a sufficient proportion of yams to last on an average near 3 months, besides a number of Hogs and provender for them, with sundry other necessaries; we took leave of our copper colored friends, & set sail from the Friendly Islands on the 1st August 1791.

We now shaped our course to Northwestward for Endeavour Straits; fell in with several islands in our track and passed a cluster called the New Hebrides, but anxious to make the best of our way did not explore them. The quantity of provisions we had taken on board for our sea stock naturally much increased our Boat's draught of water, and at times, she labored a good deal, so that we had almost constant recourse to the hand pump, in order to keep her hold free, & prevent our yams from being spoiled; indeed our very existence, in a great measure depended on the preservation of our yams, as it was on them we chiefly relied for subsistence; and whenever the weather would permit of it, they were brought on deck and laid in the sun to dry. It

The *Matavy*'s crew beats over a dangerous reef between New Holland and New Guinea in 1791. This watercolor, dated 1827, is attributed to George Tobin, a skilled artist who also served on William Bligh's second breadfruit voyage (courtesy Australian National Maritime Museum collection).

was a most fortunate circumstance that (except some hard squalls) we met with no bad weather; for a heavy gale had sprung up after we left the Friendly Isles, & had our Boat which was very doubtful outlived the storm, all our live stock must either have perished, or have been washed overboard. It was about this period that I began to feel the effects of the privations I had undergone being attacked with fever and loss of appetite, which at intervals rendered me delirious.

Nothing more occurred worthy of particular observation, till we got into the latitude of the Straits, when we altered our course to due west, in order to gain the entrance; & by steering West the setting of the current was also to a certain extent ascertained. For some length of time, we continued in this track, in daily expectation of making Land; when one evening, about the latter end of the month, we discovered breakers right ahead, and found ourselves embayed by an extensive reef, stretching nearly North and South, as far as the eye could reach; but no land was in sight. We immediately hauled our wind and carried a press of sail, in hopes of clearing the weathermost or Northern point. The breeze freshened with the setting sun, the waves increased, and our position became dreadful. Our Boat, owing to the swell, & strong current setting in, was going fast to seaward on the rocks, on which the surf ran prodigiously high. Our destruction seemed unavoidable; when in this moment of peril, that power, by which we had hitherto been so signally protected, rescued us from a watery grave; for the wind veering near a point in our favour we cleared the weathermost part of the reef, & found ourselves in smooth water, when we brought up for the night. So dangerous & intricate is the navigation of these straits, that we were buffeting about a whole week, before we had completely cleared them. Our passage was impeded by numerous shoals, sandy keys, and small islands, under shelter of which we generally brought up during the night. These places abounded in turtles & birds eggs, which afforded us many comfortable meals,—some of the islands also produced, a species of fruit much resembling the damsen plum, both in appearance and flavour, and we found no bad effect from eating them. After having sought in vain for an opening to the westward, we were at last compelled to run all hazards, and push our boat over a shoal, endeavouring to find out a channel, by the color of the sea, in working our way thro' which, she struck more than once, but as we had fortunately light winds and smooth water, not with sufficient force to do any material damage. We could not discern the coast of New Holland, but had a very extensive view of the southern part of New Guinea. It was no small consolation after meeting so many obstacles, to find ourselves again in the main ocean. The wind continued to blow steadily from the Eastward, and in about a fortnight we made land, having run on an average nearly 100 miles p[er] day, since quitting the straights. The land we had made was the island of Timor, but found ourselves too far to the

Part Eight. *The Unforeseen Voyage of* Matavy 155

Southward to make for the Dutch settlement of Coupang. For some time we continued standing along the shore when to our great joy we fell in with a Dutch merchant vessel whose captain treated us with a humanity honorable to his feelings; He supplied several of our wants and shewed us his charts of the neighbouring islands; which enabled us to ascertain our situation with more precision, & the direction in which we ought to shape our course, to make some European settlement. We passed in sight along the southern part of the Islands of Flores, Cambova & Lomboc; & hauled up thro' the Straits of Balli; then stretched over the northern shore of the island of Java, and stood along the coast, till we came to a Dutch settlement called Cherebay; where we came to an anchor.

Mr Oliver immediately waited on the Governor to acquaint with our misfortunes, and to implore the protection & assistance due to British subjects in distress. The fate of the Bounty had been communicated to the different Dutch settlements in India; in consequence of which the Governor suspected the truth of our story; & our Commander being a non commissioned officer could not produce any warrant under the seal of office, to substanciate the validity of his assertions. The appearance of our vessel built entirely of Otaheitan wood, with other concurring circumstances, served to strengthen him in the opinion that we were in reality part of the Pirates who had seized on the Bounty. We were detained here for a month, but notwithstanding the Dutchmen's precaution were treated with great kindness. One of our poor fellows died here in the hospital; being far advanced in life, he fell an easy prey to the disease of the climate.[56] Mr Oliver & myself had a guard to attend us, who understood English, but we received the most polite and hospitable treatment from the Governor, and indeed none of us were kept in close confinement being permitted to ramble about the Town in the daytime. Our commander frequently pressed the Governor to let us depart, and at length orders were issued, that we should be forwarded to Batavia, in Proas (small coasting vessels) & we had the mortification to see our faithful little bark manned by a set of Dutch boors. These fellows were quite at a loss how to manage her, and their skill in manoeuvring her, very much resembled that, which may be often seen displayed by cockneys in a sailing boat on the Thames. We sailed hence, about the 22nd of Octr on four Proas with our Boat in company, and coasting along the shore with light and variable winds arrived at the Dutch settlement of Saramang on the 29th following. At this place I was conveyed to the hospital in a wretched state, for having quitted Cherebay I was attacked by fever and flux, and had been for 3 days without medical aid, and with no other nourishment than boild rice & unwholesome water. The very day after our arrival the Rembang Dutch Indiaman, put in here, having on board the remainder of the unfortunate Pandora's crew: thus a providential meeting took place no less joyful than unexpected. The pleasure that my late companions, in distress, must have felt, in again joining their old friends & shipmates, cannot be adequately expressed; but it was a happiness in which I could not participate, being at the time given over by the physicians. My worthy Captain (an old friend of my father's) came to pay me a visit in the hospital, and take a last farewell; however to the great astonishment of my friends, and in contradiction to the opinion of the Docters, my disorder at its crisis took a favorable turn. The wary Dutchmen at length convinced that we were no imposters, gave us up with the Tender to Captain Edwards; and I had now the satisfaction of being attended by my own surgeon, to whose kind assiduity I was much indebted; being carefully removed on board the Rembang. We remained at Saramang only a few days, and arrived at Batavia on the 7th November 1791. At this port I was again removed to the hospital in a state of convalescence. This Climate is so prejudicial to Europeans, that I was soon joined by several of my shipmates among whom was the unfortunate Mr Oliver.[57] Our feelings were much shocked at the horrid scenes we witnessed in this receptacle of human misery. We were surrounded by poor wretches whose pallid faces and emaciated bodies to plainly indicated their approaching dissolution; & our ears were frequently assailed by the agonizing and expiring groans of sad victims to the pestilential air of Batavia. Captn Edwards with his officers and men were distributed on board 4 homeward bound Dutch Indiamen, in which ship we set sail on the 25th Decr 1791 rejoiced at leaving a port which had proved fatal to so many of our crew; & not a little happy in the prospect of again revisiting our native Country. During our passage the Mynheers, treated us with much harshness, an ungrateful return for our assistance in navigating home, several of their richly laden ships. We experienced some heavy gales with a mountainous sea, off Madagascar, and after a tedious voyage of 3 months, arrived at the Cape of Good Hope on the 19 March 1792. His Majesty's Ship Gorgon, commanded by Captn Parker, was lying here, & it was with no small pleasure that we hailed the British flag. By favor of Captn Gorgon [sic] I was permitted to take my passage home in the Gorgon, & arrived in England in the month of June following. The officers & crew of the Pandora, did not reach Holland till the end of August; from whence they were conveyed to their own country in an English ship of War. On the 10th Septr 1792, they were tried by a court-martial for the loss of the ship and honorably acquitted.

Original copied by Alfred Purshouse Driver September 7th 1864.
The above copy was made from the original Narrative, written by the late David Thomas Renouard.

Appendix 1

Verses on the Loss of his Majesty's Ships, Bounty And Pandora, the former by Mutany the Latter by Accident upon the Coast of New holland near Endeavour Straits. A bad Catastrophe to the Latter On the 29th of August 1791.

The Mitchell Library, State Library of New South Wales, holds a large collection of manuscripts and papers related to H.M.S. *Bounty* and H.M.S. *Pandora*, much of it presented by William Bligh's grandson, William Russell Bligh. The collection includes a four-page copy of "Verses on the Loss of His Majesty's Ships Bounty and Pandora." As poetry, this work is undistinguished and holds slight interest for literary scholars, but it is noteworthy from a historical perspective.

The anonymous poet—probably an officer, as a high degree of literacy was not prevalent among British sailors at the time—succinctly narrates, in 256 lines, the *Bounty* Mutiny and *Pandora* Voyage up to the survivors' arrival in Batavia. Its primary interest lies in the poet's characterization of Captain Edward Edwards as a brave, resourceful, and compassionate commander. Like Edwards and Ship's Surgeon George Hamilton, the author refrained from describing Pandora's Box or the prisoners' acute suffering. The poem may very well have been composed to curry favor with Edwards. Or, the writer may simply have written it to express his gratitude for surviving the shipwreck.[58] Regardless of the author's intent, it remains a unique and surprisingly comprehensive account of these historic voyages.

> Seamen All Attention Lend
> to these few Lines that here are Pen'd,
> the Bounty's Loss I'll here Relate
> And the Good Ship Pandora's fate
>
> Say muse, What Dire affects are found
> When civil Discord, doth Abound

Appendix 1

by Spells the hands the Pumps oppl'd
When from their Limbs the Sweat run down
to Ease the Ship Was Ordered then
Engines of War Ov'r Board Was thrown
they Work with Pain And Equal Swetch
At Either Pump they Pant for breath
Striving in Vain for to Repell
the many Leaks through a wounded Side
All Night they Work the Pumps amain
the Leak Upon them fast did Gain
At three they heard a Dreadfull sound
the Water O're the Lurleys found
With Greif Our Captain Was Oppres'd
When he heard of this Distress
Most Gallantly he Did behave
And Studies how his men to Save
he called for his Officers
And Privately with them Confer'd
And Cato like he then Advis'd
To find some means to Save our Lives
Each Hatchway bailing all the Night
Wee keep't her Up Untill Daylight
by hard Fatigue Our men were Spent
the Ship heel'd Over And Down She went
An Equal Chance Our Captain Gave
to All Alike their Lives to Save
the Whole Stay'd by the Sinking Ship
Untill the Water Wash'd them off
With Peircing cries the Air Resound
of floating men a while many Drown'd
Ninety three Were Sav'd by Boats
And thirty five poor Souls were lost
On a Small Island All of Sand
Scarce two hundred yards Around
two Days we Staid to rest Our men
And then Prepar'd for Sea Again
the nearest Land or friendly Shore
It was An Island Call'd Timor
Four Hundred Leagues from this to rule
In Open Boats With many men

All the provision that Wee saved
it Was two hundred wt of Bread
forty Gallons of Water And
And One Barricoe of Wine
To Small Allowance then we Came
the Captain Officers And men
Each Day Was Serv'd to All Around
of Bread One tenth Part of a Pound
One Gill of Water to It Joyn'd
beside We had A Glass of Wine
Scarcely Enough Life to Sustain
Brave Edwards far'd like his men
To Divide the Crew for Each Boat
This Duty Larkin Went About
the Captain Chused the Pinnace
twenty three Men With him join'd
Brave Conner Went in the Long boat
With thirty men 'it was his Lot
too Six Oar'd Yauls had forty four
Including Larking And Passmore
then Our Small Squadron hoisted Sail
Attended With A Pleasant Gale
When Sixteen Days the Seas run O'er
Then We made the Isle Timor
Our Stock of Water being Gone
Wee went On Shore to look for Some
from this we found A Great Releif
the most of Us being Very Weak
Wee Launch'd Again with Intent
to Stear for the Duch Settlement
two Days We Run Along the Land
the third Arriv'd At Coupang
Wee went Ashore In A Weak State
the Ditch Proved Compassionate
And Let Us Lodging for Our Men
And Soon We Did Revive Again
Our Captain With Paternal Care
for All Our wants he Did prepare
With the best food this Land Affords
Dayly Unto us All Were Serv'd
When we Arrived hear We found
two Vessels for Batavia bound

The third leaf of a four-page manuscript, "Verses on the Loss of His Majesty's Bounty and Pandora," an anonymous poem that recounts the *Bounty* Mutiny and major incidents of H.M.S. *Pandora*'s voyage. This leaf recounts the efforts to save *Pandora* and events following the wreck. The unknown poet praises Captain Edward Edwards: "Bless'd be Capt[n] Edwards name/May All like him be just And true/the Darling of his Whole Ship's Crew" (courtesy State Library of New South Wales).

Appendix 1

And So it was in the Bounty
Wich Rag'd, at Last to Mutany

Our Master's mate did head A Gang
by Name Was Called Christian
the Simple Men he Did mislead,
And tempted them to do the Deed

When this was Done, their hearts was vex'd
And Greatly Was their Souls Perplex'd
Christian knew not Where to find
A Refuge for his troubled Mind.

He Sail'd Away his Skill to try
to Save themselves from Infamy
And Still Remains in Climes Unknown,
their Injur'd Country for to Shun.

Our Senitors doth Strictly try
Against those Who Our Laws Defy
to know Why this Rash Deed Was done
they Sent A Ship to Seek for them.

Our king being Vex'd to hear his Loss
Were Sore Abus'd to know the Cause
he Chus'd A Brave Veteran
Cap^{tn} Edwards, Was the man.

Whose Long try'd service Doth protest
the humane heart within his Breast
One So Good And just As You
Confes'd the father of his Crew

The Pandora of twenty Guns
And one hundred and fifty men
Was fitted Out for the South Seas
And there to Cruze for the Bounty.

Brave Officers Did her Command
Mann'd With A true and Loyal Band
for Otahite She Did Steer.
there found Some men As will Appear.

T'was in november Seventh Day
When from Spithead Wee Sail'd Away
Our first Course was for Santacruz
to take in Wine for the Ship's Use.

That Duty done we hoisted Sail
for Cape horn With a Pleasant Gale
Wich having doubled, And caught the trade
then Othahite Soon Was made.

Our Sails When furl'd the Ship we Moor'd
five Europians Came On board.

the Bounty's Men they Prov'd to be
of Which Wee Were All Glad to See.

Wee mann'd Our Boats And Sent Away
In Quest of Others Where they Lay
Which Soon Returned With nine more
The whole that there Remain'd on Shore.

Damp'd Was joy When we did hear
the Bounty Gone And knew not where
Christian Did not Care to Stay
he With Eight more did Sail Away.

Full nineteen months had Pas'd O'r
Since they departed from the Shore
With Native Girls its their intent
to find some place for Settlement.

To Seek the Ship we did Prepare
With hopes to find her Somewhere here
And Searching All those Islands round
but no Account of her was found.

We bore Away for Other Lands
And Soon made Isles call'd parmason [Palmerston]
There by hard fortune we were Cross't
Our Boat, And five young men Were lost.

What Greif Brave Edwards mind invade
When first the mournfull news he heard
My Unskill'd pen Cannot Relate
his Manly Sorrow for their fate.

The freindly Isles And many More
We Sail'd About from Shore to Shore
When finding All Our hopes was baulk'd
Wee then Suppos'd the Ship was lost.

From thence we sail'd for the Fegees,
With hopes to find the fugitives
As A hard Gale All Night Did last
Our tender With Nine men were mis'd.

this Second Loss we did Regrett
Our Captain Secretly Did frett.
The Worst Disaster doth Await
the Gallant Ship Decree'd by fate.

For Endeavour Straits We did Stear
With hope to find A Passage there
Where Reefs of Rocks, In Ambush lye
Our hop'd for Passage to Defy

this hardest task Our Seamen Join'd
And With Good will they All Combin'd

Appendix 1

Each to his Post All Ready Stand
Attentive to their Chiefs Command.

With A Sound Ship and Gallant Crew
No toil or Peril Can Subdue
Wile hem'd, We Were with Rocks al round
A Boat Was Sent Away to Sound.

this task to Connor [Lt. Corner] was Consign'd
third in Command of Genrous mind
Night Comming On we then hung Out
A Signal to Call Back the Boat.

Brave Edwards then with freindly Care
for men and boat began to fear
Night Signals then we did Apply
false fires With guns Alternately

the boat Return'd. When Sad to tell
the Dread mishap that us befell
both wind and tide Against us Strove
The Ship Upon A Reef Was Drove.

High Roll'd the Surf the Billows roar
no help was nigh or freindly Shore
One Barren Wind Alone Remain'd,
Our Distant hopes for to Sustain.

Our Captain Calm And truly brave
With Chearing Voice his Orders gave
the Petty Officers At hand
to Pass the word they did Attend

Next in Command Larkin by name
from Ireland doth his birthright Claim
With Conner Hayward And Passmore
Brave Officers As E're Left Shore

Divide the Crew was larkings [Lt. Larkan's] Care
for many Duty's here And there
to hoist out boats A Gang Appears
While Passmore Shouts their hearts to Cheer.

To Each Mast Head the topmen Run
to Gallant yards for to Send Down
Which having Done they Strike the masts
lastly Secure the Rigging fast.

Loud Roar'd the Sea ov'r the Rocks
her Batter'd Hull Endured the Shocks
And most tremendous was the Sight
With All the Horrors of the Night

Near four hours she thumping Lay
When the Rudder was throe'd away

And many Other Wounds beside
She Beat of [sic] with A flowing tide

Then A Large Reef wee did discern
And Scarce A Cable Length A Stern
the second Danger for to Shun
then Boath the Bowers we let Run

Our Anchors Gone the way Repell
The Carpenter did Sound the Well,
but his Report was Dread to hear
Nine feet Along His Line Appeard

to Work the Pumps most part was sent
Others to Bail with Buckets went
then fate Ordain'd to Blast Our hopes
two of the Pumps were Quickly Choak'd.

The Gallant Crew not dreading fate
their Cheif Example Immitate
With manly Words Each Other Cheer
And Scorn the wretch that Shrinks with fear.

by Spells the[y] hauled the Pumps round
When from their Limbs the Sweat run down
to Save the Ship Was Ordered then
Engines of War O'er Board Was thrown

they Work with Pain And Equal Stretch
At Either Pump they Pant for breath
Striving in Vain for to Repell
the many Leaks through wounds distil

All Night they work the Pumps a man
the Leaks Upon them fast did Gain
At three they heard A Dreadfull sound
The water Or'e the horlop [orlop] found

With Greif Our Captain Was Oppress'd
When he heard of this Disstres
Most Gallantly he Did beheave
And Studied how his men to Save

he Calles for his Officers
And Privately With them Conferr'd.
And Cato like he then Advis'd
to find Some means to Save our lives

Each Hatchway bailing all the Night
Wee kep't her Up Untill Daylight
by hard fatigue Our men were Spent
the Ship heel'd O'er and Down She went

An Equel Chance Our Captain gave
to All Alike their Lives to Save

Appendix 1

the Whole Stay'd by the Sinking Ship
Untill the Water Wash'd them off

With Peirceing cries the Air Resound
of floating men while many Drown'd
Ninety Nine Were Sav'd by Boats
And thirty five Poor Souls were lost

On A Small Island All of Sand
Scarce two hundred Yards Alround
two Days we Staid to Rest Our men
And then Prepar'd for Sea again

the nearest Land or freindly Shore
It was An Island Call'd Timor
four Hundred leagues from this to reach
In Open Boats With many men

All the provison that Wee Saved
it was two hundred w't of Bread
forty Gallons of Water found
And One Barrico of Wine.

To Small Allowance then we Came
the Captain Officers And men
Each Day Was Serv'd to All Around
of Bread One tenth Part of A Pound

One gill of Water to It join'd
beside We had A Glass of Wine
Scarcely Enough Life to Sustain
Brave Edwards fared like his men

To Divide the Crew for Each Boat
This Duty Larking Went About
the Captain Chused the Pinnace
twenty three Men With him plac'd

Brave Conner Went in the Long boat
With thirty men it Was his Lot
too Six Ore'd Yawls had forty four
Including Larking And Passmore

then Our Small Squadron hoisted Sail
Attended With A Pleasent Gale
When Sixteen Days the Seas run O'er
Then We made the Isle Timor

Our Stock of Water being Gone
Wee went On Shore to look for Some
from this we found A Great Releif
the most of us being Very Weak

Wee Launch'd Again with Intent
to Stear for the Dutch Settlement

Appendix 1

two Days We Run Along the Land
the third Arriv'd at Coupang

Wee went Ashore In A Weak State
the Dutch Proved Compassionate
And Let Us Lodging for Our Men
And Soon We Did Revive Again

Our Captain With Paternell Care
for All Our wants he Did prepare
With the best food this land Affords
Dayly Unto us we All Were Serv'd

When we Arrived hear We found
two Vessels for Batavia bound
full fourteen Days we here did Stay
And then Embark'd in One Straightway

We Sailed With A light Land breeze
Once Again to Cross the Seas
And Soon Arriv'd At Semeran [Semarang]
In the Duch Ship Called Rembang

Surprising joy to Us Alround
Our Long lost tender here we found
Our Master's mate Did her Command
Thoms Oliver Was Calld by name

We Waigh'd Again And put to Sea
Our tender then in company
And for the main of java Stood
And Anchor'd in Batavia Road,

Now to Conclude And End the theme,
Bless'd be Cap[tn] Edwards name
May All like him be just And true
the Darling of his Whole Ship's Crew.

Appendix 2

Statement by Captn Edwards as to the Loss of Ship Pandora

In his dispatch to the Admiralty, Captain Edwards' report of how H.M.S. *Pandora* sank is quite brief, especially when compared to the vivid descriptions by George Hamilton, James Morrison and Peter Heywood. Edwards knew that on his return to England he would face a court-martial for the loss of *Pandora*—just as William Bligh did for losing the *Bounty*, albeit for very different reasons—and accordingly prepared a far more detailed, formal statement that he submitted to the Admiralty prior to the court-martial.

In 1965, George Mackaness published a copy of the statement (which is missing a number of words due to paper damage) in the *Journal of the Royal Australian Historical Society*, stating, "The document is now printed for the first time."[59] Mackaness, who obtained the manuscript from one of Edwards' descendants, was unaware that William Henry Smyth, who had access to Edwards' personal papers, published the statement in 1843.[60]

The manuscript that Mackaness used, which is in Edwards' own handwriting, is clearly an earlier draft. A copy of the document that Edwards actually submitted to the Admiralty may be the one in "Personal Papers of Admiral E. Edwards, Commanding the Pandora, Concerning the Mutiny on the Bounty and the Voyage of the Pandora." This was probably transcribed by a professional copyist from Edwards' draft(s). The "Personal Papers" were in the possession of the Edwards family until a descendant presented them to the Admiralty Library, where they were overlooked until 1965.

The statement presented here is based on Smyth's published version, which reveals an editor's hand at work changing punctuation, eliminating superscripts, capital letters, etc. I have deleted most of these changes, based on a comparison with the copy in the "Personal Papers."

Statement by Captn Edwards

After finishing the search for His Majesty's Armed Vessel the Bounty in the South Sea I was proceeding towards England by Endeavour Straits agreeable to my

The first page of "Statement by Captain Edwards as to the loss of Ship *Pandora*," which Captain Edward Edwards submitted to the Admiralty before his court-martial for losing the ship. This copy is included in Edwards' "Personal Papers" (Courtesy National Library of Australia).

Appendix 2

Orders and as I supposed Captain Cook was the only person that had gone that way in a Ship I had recourse to the account given in his voyage for information on the subject and as I perceiv'd by it that he encounter'd great difficulties and dangers in getting through the Reef (that extends along the Coast of New South Wales) to the Southward and also in passing between the Islands, Keys and Shoals within it in his Passage from thence to the Straits Mouth which determined me not to follow his Track, at least until I had search'd for a safer or more commodious opening or clear passage to the Northward and I was the more readily induced to pursue the search that way as it was warranted by the Opinion of so able a navigator as Captn Cook (see his Voyage Hawkesworth Coll[ection] Vol 3 p 197 & 215) and with that view I hauled in to make the Land when we were by our account a little to the Westward of that part of New Guinea named by Monsr Bougainvil [sic] le Louisiade and saw two Capes. The Easternmost I named Cape Rodney and the Westernmost Cape Hood in passing the latter it was perceived that the Land inclined to the Northward to the Westward of that Cape and in that situation there is probably a passage through the Land usually called by us New Guinea or at least a very deep Bay and I desisted from pursuing the Coast of New Guinea and steered to the Westward in the Latitude of Endeavour Straits with intention to fall into the Northward of and to make an Island distinguished by Mr. Bligh by the name of Mountainous Island with a very high round Hill, until ½ past 9 of the Morning of 25th Augt 1791 when Breakers were seen from the Masthead bearing from WNW to W by S and we hauled up to the SW in order to pass to the Southward and to Windward of them a few Nights previous to making the Capes Rodney and Hood. Until this time it had been our usual custom to lye to during the Night and to sound frequently and this precaution was taken because Monsr Bougainville had represented this part of the ocean to be particularly dangerous and because after we had passed to the Westward of his Track it was also supposed to be entirely unknown. Before Noon another Reef was seen to the Southward and we passed to the Westward of it, it obtained the name of Stony Reef Isle & the Breakers first seen were named look out Shoal. At Noon we were in Lat. 9° 50' S° and Long. about 215° 27' W. Before two o'clock we bore away more to the Westward and soon afterwards saw a small high Island to the Westward of us. At 2 saw a Reef bearing about S W to S. We afterwards steered a little to the Northward of West to keep clear of the last mentioned Reef or Shoal and with intention to pass to the Northward of the small Island then in sight. (This and some small Isles near it were named Murray's Isles). We continued that course 'till about ½ past 5 when we perceived that our passage was obstructed that way by a Reef that extended from the Island to the NW and we hauled our Wind to the Southward and stood off and on during the Night. In the Morning we steered to the Westward with intention to pass to the Southward of Murray's Isles but our Passage was also obstructed on that side by a Reef that joined to the Isles and we pursued our way with caution in the direction of the Reef to the Southward in search of a Channel but none was found that promised safety for a Ship until 28th Augt in the morning when an opening was perceived in the Reef which we flatter'd ourselves would answer our purpose. A little before Noon Lieut. Corner was sent in a Yawl with directions to examine one of the Channels (for there appeared to be two) and then if the weather would permit to return on Board as soon as possible: at Noon we were in Lat 11° 23' 40" S° Longitude TK 216° 15' 22" W and a Sandy Key on the

Outside of the Reef near the Opening S° 75° W dist[ant] 3 or 4 miles. In the afternoon the Weather was moderate and the Sea was smooth. Between 4 and 5 in the afternoon (although I cannot be very exact as to times) a signal was made from the Boat to inform us that the Channel through the Reef was sufficient for the Ship. But I wished to have every information relative to it before I attempted to run through, and I also thought the day too far advanced at that time to risque so hazardous an enterprize and to expose the Ship to uncertain danger within the Reef in the dark. And in consequence of these considerations a Signal was made soon after for the Boat to return on board and some time after that the signal was repeated for the same purpose. At first I little doubted of her getting on board before night and although she did not make the progress towards the Ship I expected, she was on the outside of the Reef before dark and I expected and flatter'd myself that she would have increased her distance from it in her approach towards the Ship. A Tender which had been fitted out at Otaheite for the purpose of covering and attending on Boats in the search for the Bounty, etc., and which upon this occasion would have been of particular use unfortunately was separated from us some time previous to this, and I was apprehensive she was lost. I had also lost another Boat & Boat's crew, and these disastrous events greatly increased my anxiety for the safety of a third and as I had given positive orders to Lieut. Corner if possible to come on Board with the Boat and perceiving that she was on the outside of the Reef endeavouring to put those orders into execution I thought it my Duty to use my utmost exertions to endeavour to take them up. After dark, false fires were burnt and Musquets fired from the Ship answered by the Boat by firing Musquets reciprocally to point out the place of each other's situation. The flashes of the Musquets fired in the Boat were distinctly seen by us, and she was reasonably [and] anxiously expected on board every minute both on account of the safety of the Boat and the people in her, and for the assistance and information we expected from the knowledge they had acquired of the Channel through the Reef. All hands were kept upon Deck, the Deep sea Lead frequently hove but had no bottom at 110 fath^{ms} until about 20 minutes after seven when we got soundings in 50 fathoms water. The Boat at the same time was seen close under the stern some time previous to this the ship had been lying to with the Main and Fore Yards kept nearly square to prevent the ship from forereaching. Upon getting soundings the Topsails were filled but before the Tacks were hauled on board & other sail made & trimm'd the ship struck upon a Reef. We had a ¼ less 2 fath^{ms} on the Larboard side and 3 fath^{ms} Water on the Starboard side. The Sails were braced about different ways to endeavour to get her off but to no purpose; they were then clew'd up and afterwards furled. The TG Y^{ds} got down and the TG Mast struck. Boats were hoisted out with a view to carry out an Anchor but before that could be effected the Ship struck so violently on the Reef that the Carpenter reported that she made 18 inch^s water in 5 minutes, and in 5 minutes after there was 4 feet of water in the Hold. Finding the Leak to increase so fast it was thought necessary to turn the Hands to the Pumps and to bail at the different Hatchways, but she still continued to gain upon us so fast that in a little more than an hour and half after she struck there was 8½ feet of water in the Hold. At about 10 perceived that the ship had beat over the Reef and we had 10 fath. water, we let go the Small Bower Anchor and veered away a Cable and let go the Best Bower Anchor in 15½ fath^{ms} water under foot to steady the Ship. Some of our Guns were thrown over board and the Water gained upon us only in a small degree and we flatter'd ourselves that by the assistance of a thrumm'd Top sail which we were preparing and intended to haul under the Ship's Bottom we might be able to lessen the Leak and to free her of water but these flattering hopes did not continue long. For as she settled in the water the Leak increased again and in so great a degree that there was reason to apprehend she would sink before day light. During the night two of the Pumps were unfortunately for some time rendered useless. One of them however was repaired and we continued bailing and Pumping the remainder of the night and every effort that was thought of was made to preserve the Ship and to keep her afloat. Daylight fortunately appeared and gave us an opportunity to see our situation and the surrounding danger & it was evident that the Ship had been carried to the Northward by a Tide or Current. The officers whom I had consulted on the subject of our situation gave it as their opinion that nothing more could be done for the preservation of the Ship. It then became necessary to endeavour to provide and to find means for the preservation of the people. Our four Boats which consisted of one Launch one eight oar'd Pinnace and two six oared Yawls with careful hands in them were kept a stern of the Ship. A small quantity of Bread, Water and other necessary articles were put into them. Two Canoes which we had on board were lash'd together and put into the Water. Rafts were made and all floating things upon deck were unlash'd. At about ½ past 6 o'clock in the Morning of the 29th of August the Hold was full and water was between decks and it also washed in at the upper Deck Ports, and there were strong indications that the Ship was on the very point of sinking and we began to leap over board and take to the Boats and before every body could get out of her she actually sunk. The Boats continued a stern of the Ship in the direction of the drift of the Tide from her and took up the people that had hold of rafts and other floating things that had been cast loose for the purpose of supporting them in the water. The double canoe that was able to support a considerable number of people broke a drift with only one Man and was bulged upon a Reef, and afforded us no assistance when she was so much wanted on this trying and melancholy occasion. Two of the Boats were Loaded with Men and sent to a small Sandy Island (or rather Key) about 3 or 4 miles from the Wreck and I remained near the Ship for sometime with the other two Boats and pick'd up all the people that could be seen and then followed the two first Boats to the Key and after Landing the People and Clearing the Boats; Boats were immediately dispatched again to look about the Wreck and the adjoining Reefs for people y^t were missing but they returned without having found a single person. On mustering it appeared that 89 of the Ship's Company and 10 of the Mutineers that had been Prisoners on board were saved and 31 of the Ship's Company and 4 Mutineers were lost with the Ship. The Boats were hauled up in order to be fitted [out] for our intended Voyage to Timor, and we were two days employ'd in this business. In the mean time Boats were sent to the Wreck to endeavour to procure something from thence. They got a little of the Top Gallant Rigging, the Head of a Top Gall^t Mast which would serve for a spare Mast for a Boat and part of the Chain of the Lightning Conductor which was converted into Nails and these I believe were the only useful articles procured from the Wreck after she sunk. The Boats were all raised by surrounding them with a Breadth of Canvass nailed to the Boats sides below the row ports and supported upwards by uprights secured to the sides & Washboards; it broke off the Sea and contributed greatly to the preservation of the Boats and the people that were in them. We put ourselves, without distinction of Person, to a very scanty allowance of water and provision from the time of our Landing on the Key, and the Boats being finish'd on the 31st of August they were launch'd and at ½ past 10 o'clock in the Morning, we all embarked to the number of ninety nine in the four Boats and steered to the N W by W and W N W towards Endeavour Straits. On the 1st of September in the Morning saw Land which we supposed was part of New South Wales. Two of the Boats hauled in for it and got a small supply of Water; a very small, supply was also got by one of the Boats at Mountainous Island from the Natives but they gave us certain proof of their Hostile intentions which prevented our Landing in that part of the Island. However we landed at different parts of this and also at an other Island near it without being able to procure any; we then stood for the Prince of Wales's Islands where we got into a sound form'd by those Islands and called by us Sandwich's Sound. Water was procured here on an Island on the S.E. part of the Sound which we called Lafory's Island. Canvas Bags were made and other expedients used yet we had not Vessels and means sufficient to contain a Gallon of Water for each person in the Boats, and with this small quantity we left the Sound on the 2nd of September and stood through Endeavour Straits for the Island of Timor and all fortunately arrived safe at Coupang in that Island between the 17th and 19th of September 1791. I might have been much more prolix but I conceived that it would be only intruding on the time of the Court without throwing any light upon or that would be useful to elucidate the subject before them: and I therefore humbly beg leave to submit this short narrative to the consideration of the Court and if they find what I have asserted in it to be true I flatter myself they will think it a sufficient vindication of my Conduct and exculpate me from censure.

Appendix 3

Pandora Aftermath

Court Martial Sentence on the Captain and Survivors of H.M.S. Pandora

On September 10, 1792, just two days before the opening of the *Bounty* court-martial, Captain Edward Edwards, his officers and crew were honorably acquitted for the loss of H.M.S. *Pandora*.

Edwards had a long record of service when he was given command of the *Pandora*, receiving his lieutenant's commission in 1759. Although he remained in the employ of the Royal Navy, the *Pandora* was his last command. Edwards died on April 13, 1815.

Although little is known of George Hamilton's personal background, the naval records for him prior to his assignment to H.M.S. *Pandora* are fairly extensive. Beginning in 1777, he served on a number of ships and then was on half-pay from 1786 until 1790, when he began his service as Ship's Surgeon on *Pandora*. In December 1792, he was appointed to H.M.S. *Lowestoft*, where he lost his left arm during a battle with the French in 1794. He was discharged and retired, passing away a couple of years later.[61]

The *Pandora* was David Thomas Renouard's first ship, and although he would have a long career in the Royal Navy, a speech impediment prevented him from becoming a naval officer. After his service on *Pandora* and *Matavy*, he joined the *Orpheus*, where he served admirably, but realized that he would enjoy no further advancement. He secured a position as a clerk in the Royal Navy's Victualling Office and remained there until his retirement in 1834.[62]

Court Martial Sentence on the H.M.S. Bounty Mutineers

The court-martial of the ten *Bounty* prisoners who survived the wreck of H.M.S. *Pandora* was well documented, and the proceedings are readily available for readers interested in the evidences and defenses presented.[63] The stakes were high, as the penalty for mutiny was hanging by the yardarm on a Royal Navy ship. A prisoner could be acquitted and released; found guilty and sentenced to death; or found guilty and recommended to the King's Mercy. The strict law of the Royal Navy considered someone who remained neutral during a mutiny equally guilty with an active mutineer.

The cases of Peter Heywood and James Morrison were particularly interesting to the spectators. Heywood was young (the *Bounty* was his first ship), his family had relatives in the Royal Navy, and his behavior during the mutiny was unclear. He had not played an active part in taking the ship, but Bligh (who was not present at the court-martial) had directly accused him of being a mutineer. The fact that he had been friendly with Fletcher Christian as well as a fellow Manxman did not help his case, at least in Bligh's view.

Heywood had the advantage of being attended by a highly skilled attorney, but the articulate and literate James Morrison, whose case was similar to Heywood's, deftly handled his own defense. One of the spectators stated that he "...stood his own counsel, questioned all the evidences, and in a manner so arranged and pertinent, that the spectators waited with impatience for his turn to call on them, and listened with attention and delight during the discussion."[64]

The Court found Peter Heywood, James Morrison, Thomas Ellison, Thomas Burkitt, John Millward and William Muspratt guilty, sentencing them to death. The Court also "...in Consideration of various Circumstances, did humbly and most earnestly recommend the said Peter Heywood and James Morrison to His Majesty's Royal Mercy—and the Court further agreed That the Charges had not been proved against the said Charles Norman, Joseph Coleman, Thomas McIntosh and Michael Byrn, and did adjudge them and each of them to be acquitted."[65]

After the judgment was read, William Muspratt's attorney petitioned the Court: "I have not the most distant Idea of arraigning the Justice of the Court, but I have to lament that the Practice and usage of a Court Martial, should be so different from the Practice of all Criminal Courts of Justice on Shore, as that, by the one I have been debarred calling Witnesses whose Evidence I have Reason to believe, would have tended to have proved my Innocence, whereas by the other I should have been permitted to call those very Witnesses on my behalf. This Difference, my Lord, is dreadful to the Subject and fatal to me."[66] This petition was successful, and Muspratt received a Royal Pardon on February 11, 1793.

Heywood and Morrison received their pardons and were set free on October 26, 1792. Ellison, Burkitt, and Millward were executed on board H.M.S. *Brunswick* three days later.

Heywood spent some time recuperating with his family before re-entering the Royal Navy on May 17, 1793. Sadly, his devoted sister Nessy died less than a year after his release. He had learned to speak Tahitian fluently, and compiled a vocabulary of the language (now lost, except for a brief excerpt published in 1797)[67] that was intended to be an appendix to James Morrison's *Journal*. The London Missionary Society made good use of the vocabulary and Morrison's manuscript *Journal* during its first missionary voyage to the South Seas.[68]

Heywood joined H.M.S. *Bellerophon*, which was commanded by his uncle, Commodore Thomas Pasley. After serving on a number of ships, he was promoted to Post Captain on April 5, 1803. After more than 29 years of honorable and distinguished service—he became a highly skilled hydrographer, with a distinct talent

Appendix 3

for accurately mapping waters to ensure safe navigation—Heywood retired in 1816, married, and spent his remaining years in London with his wife, Frances, and stepdaughter, Diana. He died on February 10, 1831.

After receiving a Royal Pardon, Morrison completed his *Journal*, which provides the fullest first-hand account of what happened on the *Bounty* after Bligh was set adrift, as well as closely-observed descriptions of Tahitian life before the missionaries arrived. It was not published during his lifetime, but Morrison's keen observations of Tahitian customs, like Heywood's Tahitian vocabulary, were used by the London Missionary Society and continue to be a fruitful source of information for researchers.

When he re-joined the Royal Navy, Morrison saw a considerable amount of action in the Mediterranean. His last position was Master Gunner on H.M.S. *Blenheim*, under the command of Rear-Admiral Thomas Troubridge. In February 1807, the *Blenheim* sank with all hands during a gale off Rodriguez Island in the Indian Ocean.

Glossary

Acoucheur—Midwife

Aft—At, near or toward the stern (back) of a ship

Alto relievo—Crafted in relief

Anchylosed—A stiffened back

Antiscrobutics—Antiscorbutic, a substance, such as Vitamin C, that prevents scurvy

Ballast—Weight placed at the bottom of a vessel to provide stability

Bark—A sailing vessel with three masts

Barricois—Kegs

Bittern—A solution of salts that remains after seawater crystallizes

Blocks—A pulley with one or more grooves

Boom—A long pole used to extend the bottom of a particular sail

Bow—The front (forward) part of a ship

Bower anchor—The anchor at the bow of a ship

Bowsprit—A spar that extends forward from the prow of a ship

Bread—Ship's biscuit

Breaker—A small keg

Brecco—Apparently a container of some kind for water. May be related to the New Testament Greek Βρεχο, transliterated brecho, "to moisten, wet, water"

Brutum fulmen—Literally, a "meaningless thunderbolt," an empty threat

Bunburry—Bunbury, a village in Cheshire, England

Cable—A strong, thick rope used to hoist and lower the anchor of a ship; the term also is used as a nautical measurement of distance: one cable length equals one tenth of a nautical mile, 100 fathoms, or about 200 yards

Cag—Keg

Careening—Mooring a vessel in shallow water for repair

Glossary

Carronade—a light cannon

Cartouch—A gun cartridge

Cartridge paper—Wadded paper for holding a musket ball and gunpowder charge

Clew'd up—To raise the lower corners of a square sail

Clyster—An old term for enema

Coaming—A low vertical lip or raised section around the edge of a cockpit, hatch, etc., to prevent water from running below the deck

Cooper—A craftsperson who makes and repairs barrels

Coup de soleil—Sunburn

Couping—Selling or bartering

Crank—A sailboat that is easily swamped or capsized

Crossing the Line—A ceremony performed when a ship's crew or passengers cross the earth's equator for the first time; in the Royal Navy, the ritual frequently included dunking in the water

Cutter—A small boat with one mast

Debarassoit—Relieved of or removed

Degage—Offhand, cavalier

Disembogue—To flow forth

Dismaloes—Depression, misery

Driver boom—The boom used to extend the bottom of a driver sail

Driver yard—The yard of a driver sail

(Eighteen) 18-pounder—A ship's long gun capable of discharging an 18-pound shot

False fire—A flame used for signaling

Fathom—A unit of measurement relating to the depth of water or to a length of cable; one fathom equals six feet

Feegee—Fiji

Floor—The lowest timber of a wooden ship's frame

Fodder or fother—Drawing a sail under a ship to stop a leak

Fore—Something positioned at or close to the bow of a ship; often used as a prefix such as "forescuttle" and "foretopsail yard"

Fore Castle—Forecastle, a compartment with berths for seamen, forward from the mast

Forereach—A forward movement into the wind

Gangway—A narrow portable platform used as a passage by persons entering or leaving a vessel moored alongside a pier

Glossary

Garniture—Decoration or adornment

Gill—A quarter of a pint

Grape Shot—A type of iron ordnance shot from a ship's cannon

Grapnel, Grapple—A small anchor or an iron hook used to fasten to a boat

Gravesend—A town in Kent, England located near the river Thames

Grog—A mixture of rum and water given to sailors in a daily ration

Hæva—Heiva, a Tahitian festival

Harness Cask—A tub of salt meat lashed to a ship's deck

Hatchway—An opening in the deck that provides access to the space below, or a deck opening provided with a watertight cover

Heave—To stop a ship and hold it in position, particularly in stormy seas

Heel—Leaning due to the wind

Hold—The area of a ship below the decks

Hollands Geneva—Dutch gin

Hove to—A ship that has stopped before the wind

Ipse dixit—An unproven assertion or statement

Jack—A small ship's flag

Jill—A word derived from gill

Jolly-boat—A small ship's boat

Junk—Salt beef or pork

Keel—The backbone of a vessel, running along the center line on the bottom of the hull

Kellick—Killick, a small anchor usually made with a rock or stone in a wooden frame

Kelson—A piece of timber placed in the middle of the ship that binds the floor timbers to the ship's keel

Key—A small, low island

Knee—A wooden support brace

Larboard—An old term for the left side of a ship; the name eventually was changed to "port"

Launch—A small boat used to transport people to and from a larger vessel

League—About two to four nautical miles

Lee—The side of a ship against the wind

Lee shore—A shoreline that lies downward of a ship's position

Leeward—From or toward the side of a vessel against the wind

Letch—Craving

Merendas—Afternoon entertainments

Missive—An object held or thrown

Molds—A thin length of wood used to pattern a ship's timber

Moor—To attach a boat to a mooring, dock, post, anchor, etc.

Morai—Marae, sacred spaces where religious rituals were conducted

Mynheers—Dutchmen

Nankin—A pale, yellowish cloth

Nautical mile—1.151 statute miles or 1.852 kilometers

Oakum—Tarred hemp for caulking the seams of a ship

Orlop—A ship's lowest deck

Otium dignitat—Leisure time

Paroquets—Parakeets

Paterreros—Variant spelling of "pedrero," a piece of ordnance for firing salutes

Pinnace—A small, two-masted sailing vessel that sometimes includes oars

Poop—A superstructure installed on a raised afterdeck

Portable Soup or Broth—An early type of dehydrated food that kept well for an extended period of time; it had a jelly-like consistency and was believed to help prevent scurvy

La pucelage—The practice of cutting a woman's hymen with a sharp object

Rencontre—Encounter, combat

Ribband—A thin strip of wood holding molds in place during ship construction

Rupture—Hostility or war

Sally—Break out or leap forth

Scite—Setting

Scupper—An opening in a deck, cockpit, toe-rail or gunwale to allow water to run off the deck and drain back into the sea

Scuttle—A small deck opening or lid of an opening

Senitor—Probably a misspelling of "senator," a statesman or official

Sheet—A line that adjusts or controls a sail

Shoal—Shallow

Skiff—A small, light sailing craft

Spar—The round, wooden pole that supports a sailing ship's rigging

Sprit—A light spar that crosses diagonally across a four-sided fore-and-aft sail to support the peak

Starboard—In the direction of the right side of the ship when facing forward

Stem—The front part of a ship

Stern—The back part of a ship

Streak—A line of planking that runs from the bow of a ship to the stern, alongside the hull

Sugar loaves—Cone-shaped hills

Supercargo—An on-board representative or employee of a ship's owner

Tack—The lower forward corner of a triangular sail; the direction that a boat is sailing with respect to the wind

Tender—A small boat used to carry out tasks outside a larger ship

TG or Top gallant—The mast or sail above the mainmast and mainsail

TG Rigging—Topgallant rigging

TGY—Top gallant yard

Thrummed or thrumbing—Sewing rope fibers onto canvas to fashion a thick mat

Thwart—A seat in a small boat

Time-keeper—A marine chronometer

TK—Abbreviation for Time-keeper

Touchstone—A stone once used to test for gold

Trade Wind—The steady winds that occur in a belt around 30° North and 30° South of the earth's equator

Unreeve—Remove a line from a block

Utile dulce—"Sweet profit"

Washboards—A plank fastened above a gunwale to keep out water

Weather—The direction from which the wind blows, as in "weather side" of a sailing vessel

Yard—A spar from which a square sail is hung

Yaul (Yawl)—A sailboat equipped with two masts; the shorter mizzenmast is placed aft of the rudderpost

Notes

1. James Cook named this area "Endeavour Straits," and this term was used throughout the 1790s to designate the entire passage between Australia and New Guinea. Torres Strait itself lies between Cape York and Prince of Wales' Island.
2. The following articles discuss the voyage of *Resolution/Matavy*: [Smyth] 1842, pp. 1–13 [cf. p. 282]; Langdon August 1961, pp. 29–33; Maude August 1964, pp. 217–235; David 1977, pp. 207–213; Reid 1978, pp. 241–244; and Rogers 1983, pp. 452–455.
3. Hamilton, 1998, p. 15.
4. A brief segment in the 1935 MGM film *Mutiny on the Bounty* inaccurately presented Bligh as *Pandora*'s Captain and Edward Edwards as Lieutenant of the ship.
5. Brownlow 1996, and Turner, 1998, discuss David Lean's and Robert Bolt's attempt to make the *Bounty/Pandora* films.
6. Bonner Smith 1936, 221.
7. Heywood 2013, p. 67.
8. Anon. *The London Chronicle* Vol. 71, No. 5648, Tuesday, October 30, to Thursday, November 1, 1792, p. 417.
9. [Barrow] 1831, p. 172.
10. [Smyth] 1843, p. 411.
11. *Ibid.* p. 412.
12. Wahlroos 2001, p. 150.
13. [Smyth] 1843, p. 414.
14. Salmond 2011, pp. 309–10.
15. Mackaness 1951, p. 201.
16. Morrison, *Memorandum*, p. 51.
17. [Smyth] 1843, p. 420.
18. *Ibid.*
19. Danielsson 1963, p. 185.
20. Morrison 1935, p. 133.
21. Sharp 1969, pp. 163–65.
22. [Barrow] 1831, p. 149.
23. "Captain Edwards' Reports to the Lords Commissioners of the Admiralty from November 1790 to July 1792," p. 32.
24. "At a Court Martial assembled on board His Majesty's Ship Hector in Portsmouth Harbour on the 10th day of September 1792," p. 14. Two manuscript copies of the court-martial sentence are present in "Personal Papers of Admiral E. Edwards, Commanding the Pandora, Concerning the Mutiny on the Bounty and the Voyage of the Pandora."
25. Rutter 1931, pp. 43–4.
26. Wahlroos 2001, p. 165.
27. The island of Tofua was about 30 nautical miles from *Bounty* at the time of the mutiny.
28. The *Seaman's Daily Assistant* was a standard work on practical navigation.
29. John Brown of the brig *Mercury* remained on Tahiti when his ship sailed on September 2, 1789. Brown had slashed another sailor's face with a razor.
30. Edwards "Captain Edwards' Reports," p. 29.
31. Hamilton 1793, pp. 120–121.
32. A seamark that guides mariners toward the navigable channel of the Lymington River.
33. Louis-Antoine de Bouganville (1729–1811), a French navigator and explorer.
34. Edwards apparently is mistaken here. In *The Bounty: The True Story of the Mutiny on the Bounty*, p. 13, Caroline Alexander states that the *Bounty* anchored in Tubuai, about 350 miles from Tahiti, on May 24, nearly one month following the mutiny.
35. Tapa cloth, made from paper mulberry tree bark.
36. Fort Venus, where a transit of Venus was observed in 1769 during Captain James Cook's expedition to Tahiti.

Notes

37. Sir Joseph Banks, President of the Royal Society, set the *Bounty*'s breadfruit mission into motion and recommended that William Bligh serve as Commander of the ship.
38. Kava, or *Piper methysticum*, an intoxicating plant.
39. Symptoms of venereal disease.
40. Paraphrased from James Thomson's "The Four Seasons, and Other Poems," 1735: "...for loveliness/Needs not the foreign aid of ornament/But is, when unadorn'd, adorn'd the most/Thoughtless of beauty, she was beauty's self..."
41. Quartermaster John Norton, one of Bligh's companions in the *Bounty*'s launch, was murdered by natives at this site in Tofua.
42. John Byron, a British Naval officer, explorer and a grandfather of the poet, Lord Byron.
43. William Bligh stated that Joseph Coleman, Charles Norman, and Thomas McIntosh were held on the *Bounty* against their will during the mutiny, so Captain Edwards thought it safe to release them from Pandora's Box when he needed extra hands to work the ship's pumps.
44. Roti Island in Indonesia.
45. Prisoner James Morrison, who conducted Divine Services on Sundays during his stay on Tahiti.
46. The Dutch East India Company.
47. Great Britain began establishing a penal colony at Botany Bay, near Port Jackson in New South Wales (Australia) in 1787. The story of the escaped convicts who were posing as shipwreck survivors in Coupang when the *Pandora* wreck survivors arrived, has been the subject of many non-fiction books, novels, plays and films.
48. See Part Eight for a full account of *Matavy*'s voyage.
49. Batavia, current day Jakarta, was a dangerous destination. Its marshy areas were breeding grounds for mosquitos, resulting in deadly malaria epidemics.
50. Robert Gordon, Commander of the Garrison at the Cape of Good Hope.
51. See Appendix 3 for an account of the *Bounty* court-martial judgments.
52. Henderson 1933, p. 247.
53. [Smyth] 1842, pp. 1–13 [cf. p. 282].
54. Du Rietz 1962 pp. [1963: 2–4].
55. A transcription of *Pandora*'s logbook was published in *Memoirs of the Queensland Museum/Culture*, Volume 9, Chapter 4, 77–116.
56. [Smyth] 1842, p. 10. Smyth's transcript of Renouard's account identifies the seaman as "William Parker," but he is identified as Able Seaman Thomas Barker in Gesner 2016, p. 65, using *Pandora*'s musters and pay book as sources.
57. Master's Mate Oliver, who was in command of *Matavy*, died a few days after leaving Batavia.
58. Salmond 2011, p. 309.
59. Mackaness 1965, pp. 200–204.
60. [Smyth] 1843, pp. 411–420.
61. Hamilton 1998, pp. 23–26.
62. [Smyth] 1842, p. 3.
63. Stephen Barney's *Minutes of the Proceedings of the Court-Martial Held at Portsmouth, August* (misprint for September) *12, 1792 on Ten Persons Charged with Mutiny on Board His Majesty's Ship the* Bounty, which covers the evidence for the prosecution, was reprinted in *A Book of the 'Bounty'* 1938, 1981, and in *The* Bounty *Mutiny* (2001). The evidence for the defense was published in Rutter 1931, 1989.
64. Alexander 2003, p. 261.
65. Rutter 1931, p. 199.
66. *Ibid.*
67. [Haweis] 1797, pp. 23–25.
68. [Haweis] 1799, pp. 13–14. The impact of Peter Heywood's Tahitian vocabulary and James Morrison's *Journal* on the first missionaries to the South Seas is discussed in Du Rietz 1986 (Banksia 3).

Bibliography

Primary Sources

Anon. "A Copy of Verses on the Loss of his Majesty's Ships, Bounty and Pandora, the former by Mutiny the Latter by Accident upon the Coast of New holland near Endeavour Straits. A bad Catastrophe to the Latter On the 29th of August 1791." Mitchell Library, State Library of New South Wales, Sydney. Safe 1/44 (Copies at CY Safe 1/44 and CY 178).

Edwards, Edward. "Captain Edwards' Reports to the Lords Commissioners of the Admiralty from November 1790 to July 1792." Kew: The National Archives, ADM 1/1765/79. The first page of Edwards' dispatch is stamped "134." The second and subsequent pages are hand-numbered in the upper left hand corner or lower right hand corner of each page, pp. 2–32. Citations are to these numbers.

_____. "Statement by Captn Edwards as to the Loss of Ship Pandora." This unnumbered manuscript is in "Personal Papers of Admiral E. Edwards, Commanding the Pandora, Concerning the Mutiny on the Bounty and the Voyage of the Pandora." Microform provided by the National Library of Australia, Canberra, Interlibrary Loans/Document Delivery. Call Number MFM G 1888. The originals are in the Admiralty Library, Portsmouth: MSS 180, "The Papers of Edward Edwards." There are 396 leaves in this collection and three pages of front matter. For accounts of the discovery of these papers, see Robert Langdon, "New Light on the 'Bounty' Mutiny" and H. E. Maude, "The Edwards Papers."

"Edwards' Sailing Orders," in Bonner Smith, D., "Some Remarks about the Mutiny of the Bounty." *The Mariner's Mirror* 22 [April 1936]: 200–237.

Hamilton, George. *A Voyage Round the World in His Majesty's Frigate Pandora*. Berwick: W. Phorson, B. Law & Son, London, 1793.

Heywood, Nessy. "Correspondence of Miss Nessy Heywood during 1790–92, relating to the imprisonment, as a mutineer on the *Bounty*, conviction and pardon of her brother Peter." The Newberry Library, Chicago. Call # Case MS E5_H5078_86 and Case MS E5_H5078_87.

Heywood, Peter, and Nessy Heywood. *Innocent on the Bounty*. Edited by Donald A. Maxton, and Rolf E. Du Rietz. Jefferson, NC: McFarland, 2013.

Maude, H. E. "The Voyage of the *Pandora's* Tender," *The Mariner's Mirror* 50, no. 3 [August 1964]: pp. 217–235.

Morrison, James. "James Morrison—Journal on HMS Bounty and at Tahiti, 9 Sept. 1787–1791, written in 1792." http://acms.sl.nsw.gov.au/_transcript/2015/D33357/a1221.html. The original manuscript is in the Mitchell Library, State Library of New South Wales, Sydney. Safe 1/42 (Microfilms CY 265 and CY 515).

_____. *The Journal of James Morrison, Boatswain's Mate of the Bounty, Describing the Mutiny & Subsequent Misfortunes of the Mutineers, Together With an Account of the Island of Tahiti*. Introduction by Owen Rutter. London: The Golden Cockerel Press, 1935. Limited to 325 copies. All citations are from this edition.

_____. "Memorandum and particulars respecting the Bounty and her crew." Mitchell Library, State Library of New South Wales, Sydney, Safe 1/33 (Microfilm CY 265).

183

Renouard, David Thomas. "Voyage of the Pandora's Tender, 1791." Microform provided by the National Library of Australia, Canberra, Interlibrary Loans/Document Delivery. Microfilm: CY 515 frames 794–824 (*D 377). The original manuscript is held at the Mitchell Library, State Library of New South Wales, Sydney.

———. "Renouard's Narrative," in Maude, H. E., "The Voyage of the *Pandora*'s Tender." *The Mariner's Mirror* 50 [August 1964]: 217–235.

Secondary Sources

Alexander, Caroline. *The Bounty: The True Story of the Mutiny on the Bounty*. New York: Viking Penguin, 2003.

Anon. *The London Chronicle*, Vol. 72, No. 5648 [Tuesday, October 30, to Thursday, November 1, 1792]: 417.

———. "'Pandora' Yields Up Secrets." *Pacific Islands Monthly* 55 [February 1984]: 51.

[Barrow, Sir John]. *The Eventful History of the Mutiny and Piratical Seizure of H.M.S. Bounty: Its Cause and Consequences*. London: J. Murray, 1831. First American edition published as *A Description of Pitcairn Island and its Inhabitants: With an Authentic Account of the Mutiny of the Ship Bounty*, by J & J Harper, New York, 1832. Harper's Family Library, No. XXXI.

Bligh, William, and Edward Christian. *The Bounty Mutiny*. Introduction by R.D. Madison. New York: Penguin Books, 2001.

Bonner, Eric M. Catalogue "Camel," 1960.

Brownlow, Kevin. *David Lean, A Biography*. New York: St. Martin's Press, 1996.

Danielsson, Bengt. *What Happened on the Bounty*. Translated from the Swedish by Alan Tapsell. London: George Allen & Unwin Ltd., 1962. Second (revised) edition published in 1963. The second edition also was published by Rand McNally and Company, Chicago, New York and San Francisco, 1963.

Darby, Madge. "Losses in the Pandora." *The UK Log*, no. 22 [July 2001]: 10–12.

David, Andrew C. F. "Broughton's Schooner and the *Bounty* Mutineers." *The Mariner's Mirror* 63 [August 1977]: 207–213. A fair amount of research has been devoted to the ultimate fate of *Matavy*. A rare article by Samuel Greatheed titled "Authentic History of the Mutineers of the Bounty," published in *The Sailor's Magazine and Naval Miscellany* mistakenly states that the schooner was purchased by Captain William Broughton for use as a tender for H.M.S. *Providence*—and that it saved his entire crew of 112 after *Providence* was lost on a reef between Taiwan and Okinawa. Sir John Barrow, William Henry Smyth, and other writers repeated the error. Andrew C.F. David presents a full account of how this error persisted through the years. Also see Alan Reid, "Broughton's Schooner."

Dening, Greg. *Mr. Bligh's Bad Language: Passion, Power and Theatre on the Bounty*. Cambridge: Cambridge University Press, 1992.

Du Rietz, Rolf E. *The case of Peter Heywood and George Stewart of the Bounty. A reply to Caroline Alexander*. Banksia, 8. Uppsala: Dahlia Books, 2010.

———. *Peter Heywood's Tahitian vocabulary and the narratives by James Morrison: Some notes on their origin and history*. Banksia, 3. Uppsala: Dahlia Books, 1986.

———. "The Voyage of H.M.S. *Pandora*, 1790–1792: Some Remarks upon Geoffrey Rawson's Book on the Subject." *Ethnos* 28 [1963: 2–4]: 210–218. Reprint: Lund: Hakan Ohlsson, 1965. This article presents Rolf du Rietz's discovery of several articles of vital importance to research on the *Bounty* and *Pandora*: William Henry Smyth's publications in *The United Service Journal* and Samuel Greatheed's essay in *The Sailor's Magazine and Naval Miscellany*. Du Rietz includes a bibliography that provides detailed information about these resources.

Edwards, Captain Edward, and George Hamilton. *Voyage of H.M.S. Pandora, Despatched to Arrest the Mutineers of the Bounty in the South Seas, 1790–91*. Introduction and notes by Basil Thomson. London: Francis Edwards, 1915.

Gesner, Peter. "Pandora." *The UK Log* 24 [July 2002]: 23–25.

———. *Pandora: An Archaeological Perspective*. South Brisbane: Queensland Museum, 1991. Reprinted and updated, 2000.

———. "*Pandora*'s People and Some Subsequent Careers." *Memoirs of the Queensland Museum/Culture*, Chapter 3. Brisbane: Queensland Museum, 2016. https://www.qm.qld.gov.au/About+Us/Publications/Memoirs+of+the+

Queensland+Museum/891+MQM-C+Vol+9#.XUs0FYVX9i8

_____. "Situation report: HMS Pandora." *Bulletin of the Australian Institute of Maritime Archaeology* Vol. 14, Issue 2 [1990]: 41–46.

[Greatheed, Samuel] (Nausistratus). "Authentic History of the Mutineers of the Bounty." *The Sailor's Magazine and Naval Miscellany* (London), 1 [October 1820]: 402–406; 1 [December 1820]: 449–456; 2 [January 1821]: 1–8.

Hamilton, George. *A Voyage Round the World in His Majesty's Frigate Pandora.* 200th Anniversary Commemorative Edition. Adelaide: Williams Torrens Publishers Pty. Ltd., 1990. Edited and with an Introduction by Geoffrey Kenihan. Limited to 250 copies.

_____. *A Voyage Round the World in His Majesty's Frigate Pandora.* Sydney: Hordern House Rare Books Pty. Ltd., for the Australian National Maritime Museum, 1998. Foreword by Alex Allan, Introduction by Peter Gesner. This edition of Hamilton's book includes photographs of artifacts recovered from the wreck of H.M.S. *Pandora*, which was discovered in 1977 off the eastern coast of Australia. A continuing series of excavations by the Queensland Museum has yielded a treasure trove of objects, including a cannon, the ship's stove, Captain Edwards' dinner service, and George Hamilton's pocket watch and medical equipment. For a full account of the expeditions and their findings to date, see Peter Gesner's *Pandora: An Archaeological Perspective.* Also see *Memoirs of the Queensland Museum* at https://www.qm.qld.gov.au/ and the Queensland Museum website, which features a wealth of information and images associated with *Pandora*: https://www.qm.qld.gov.au/Site+Tools/Search?query=pandora&site-search-submit=-.XQluYoVX9i8

[Haweis, Thomas] Ed. "Curious tradition, Among the Inhabitants of Otaheite." *Evangelical Magazine* 5 [January 1797]: 23–25.

_____. *A Missionary Voyage to the Southern Pacific Ocean, Performed in the Years 1796, 1797, 1798, in the Ship Duff, Commanded by Captain James Wilson.* London: T. Chapman, 1799. Reprinted with additional biographical and bibliographical data, Frederick A. Praeger, Publishers, New York, 1968. The lengthy Appendix to this volume, with its detailed descriptions of Tahiti, is based on James Morrison's manuscript *Journal*, which remained unpublished until 1935.

Henderson, G.C. *The Discoverers of the Fiji Islands: Tasman, Cook, Bligh, Wilson, Bellinghausen.* London: John Murray, 1933.

Henderson, Graeme. "The loss of HMS *Pandora* in 1791." [Chapter 5]: 67–80 in *Swallowed by the Sea: the Story of Australia's Shipwrecks.* Canberra: National Library of Australia, 2016.

_____, David Lyon, and Ian MacLeod. "H.M.S. Pandora: Lost and Found." *Archaeology* 36 [January/February 1983]: 28–35.

H.M.S. Pandora: In Pursuit of the Bounty. David Flatman Productions, Pty Ltd., Sydney, Australia, 1986. (Film).

Lady Belcher (Diana Jolliffe). *The Mutineers of the Bounty and their Descendants in Pitcairn and Norfolk Islands.* London: John Murray, 1870. First American edition published by Harper & Brothers, Publishers, New York, 1871. Diana Jolliffe was Peter Heywood's stepdaughter.

Langdon, Robert. "Ancient Cornish Inn Is Link With The Bounty." *Pacific Islands Monthly*, Magazine Section [April 1961]: 75–76.

_____. "The Bell Mystery Solved." *Pacific Islands Monthly* 31, no. 11 [June 1961]: 131.

_____. "Court Story Over Alleged Wreck." *Pacific Islands Monthly* 32, no. 3 [October 1961]: 133.

_____. "Have These Men a Place in Fiji History?" *Pacific Islands Monthly* 32, no. 1 [August 1961]: 29–33.

_____. "Lost 'Pandora' Logbook Turns Up in U.K. After 170 Years." *Pacific Islands Monthly* 36, no. 4 [April 1965]: 33 & 35.

_____. "Old Wreck Could Be Another Chapter In The Bounty Story." *Pacific Islands Monthly* 31, No. 6 [January 1961]: 37 & 39.

_____. "Whose Bell Is It?" *Pacific Islands Monthly* 31 no. 10 [May 1961]: 19 & 142.

Lee, Ida. *Captain Bligh's Second Voyage to the South Sea.* London: Longmans, Green & Co., 1920.

Mackaness, George. "The Court-Martial of Captain Edward Edwards, R.N. of H.M.S. Pandora, wrecked on the north-eastern Australian Coast when returning home after searching the Pacific for the *Bounty*," *Journal of the Royal Australian Historical Society* 51, Pt. 3 [September 1965]: 200–204.

_____. Ed., *A Book of the 'Bounty'.* London:

J. M. Dent & Sons Ltd., 1938. Everyman's Library. Reissued with a new Introduction by Gavin Kennedy, London: J. M. Dent & Sons Ltd., 1981.

———. *The Life of Vice-Admiral William Bligh, R.N., F.R.S.* New and revised edition. London: Angus & Robertson, 1951.

Marden, Luis. "In Bounty's Wake: Finding the Wreck of H.M.S. Pandora." *National Geographic Magazine*, October 1985: 423–450.

Marshall, James Stirrat, and Carrie Marshall, Eds. *Pacific Voyages: Selections from Scots Magazine, 1771–1808*. Portland, Oregon: Binfords & Mort, 1960: 55–63.

Marshall, John. "Peter Heywood, Esq." *Royal Naval Biography* vol. 2, part 2 [1825]: 747–797.

———. *Royal Naval Biography of Peter Heywood (Mutiny on the Bounty)*. New York: George R. Gorman, 1936. Reprint.

Maude, H. E. "The Edwards Papers." *The Journal of Pacific History* 1. [1966]: 184–185.

———. *Of Islands and Men: Studies in Pacific History*. London: Oxford University Press, 1968.

———. Review of *Pandora's Last Voyage* by Geoffrey Rawson. *The Journal of the Polynesian Society* 73, no. 2. [June 1964]: 240–241.

Maxton, Donald A. *The Mutiny on H.M.S. Bounty; A Guide to Nonfiction, Fiction, Poetry, Films, Articles, and Music.* Foreword by Sven Wahlroos. Jefferson, NC: McFarland, 2008.

———. "The Odyssey of *Resolution/Matavy*." *The UK Log* [July 2010]: 9–11.

———. "Peter Heywood's Tahitian Vocabulary and James Morrison's Journal." *The UK Log* [January 2008]: 9–11.

McKay, John. *The Armed Transport Bounty*. Revised edition. London: Conway Maritime Press, 2001.

McKay, John, and Ron Coleman. *The 24-Gun Frigate Pandora 1779*. Cedarburg, WI: Phoenix Publications, 1992.

Morrison, James. *After the Bounty: A Sailor's Account of the Mutiny and Life in the South Seas*. Edited and annotated by Donald A. Maxton. Foreword by Glynn Christian. Washington, D.C.: Potomac Books, 2009.

———. *Mutiny and Aftermath: James Morrison's Account of the Mutiny on the* Bounty *and the Island of Tahiti*. Edited by Vanessa Smith and Nicholas Thomas. Honolulu: University of Hawaii Press, 2013.

Murray, John. "H.M.S. Pandora: On the Trail of the Bounty." *Sea Frontiers* 35, no. 6. [Nov.—Dec. 1989]: 328–335.

Nordhoff, Charles, and James Norman Hall. *Mutiny on the Bounty*. Boston: Little, Brown & Company, 1932.

"Pandora's Secrets." *Journeys to the Bottom of the Sea Series*, BBC Two, Series 1, Episode 3, 2000. (Film).

Rawson, Geoffrey. *Pandora's Last Voyage*. London: Longmans, Green & Co., 1963. First American edition published by Harcourt, Brace & World, New York, 1964.

Reid, Alan. "Broughton's Schooner." *The Mariner's Mirror* 64 [August 1978]: 241–244.

Rogers, G. A. "Sojourn of the *Pandora's* Tender at Ono-I-Lau, Fiji." *The Mariner's Mirror* 69 [November 1983]: 452–455.

Rutter, Owen, Ed. *The Court-Martial of the "Bounty" Mutineers*. Edinburgh and London: William Hodge & Company, 1931. Introduction and notes by Owen Rutter. Reprinted by the Notable Trials Library, Birmingham, AL, 1989.

Salmond, Anne. *Bligh: William Bligh in the South Seas*. (Berkeley, Los Angeles and London: University of California Press, 2011.

Sharp, Andrew. *The Discovery of the Pacific Islands*. Oxford: Oxford University Press, 1960.

[Smyth, W. H.] "The Bounty Again!" *The United Service Journal* 3 [1831]: 305–314.

———. "The Last of the Pandoras." *The United Service Journal* 3 [1842]: 1–13 [cf. p. 282]. An editorial note on p. 282 identifies another *Pandora* survivor: George Reynolds, 1766-1851.

———. "The Pandora Again!" *The United Service Journal* 1 [1843]: 411–20.

———. "Sketch of the career of the late Capt. Peter Heywood, R.N." *The United Service Journal* 1: 468–487 (1831).

Tagart, Edward. *A Memoir of the Late Captain Peter Heywood, R. N., With Extracts from his Diaries and Correspondence*. London: Effingham Wilson, 1832.

Turner, Adrian. *Robert Bolt: Scenes from Two Lives*. London: Hutchinson, 1998.

Wahlroos, Sven. *Mutiny and Romance in the South Seas; A Companion to the Bounty Adventure*. Topsfield: Salem House Publishers, 1989; Lincoln, Nebraska: iUniverse.com, Inc., 2001. Citations are to the iUniverse edition.

Index

Numbers in **_bold italics_** indicate pages with illustrations

Admiralty, Lords Commissioners of the 1, 4-5, 7-9, 25, 29, 71, 132, **_133_**, 143, 165, **_166_**; issue Edwards' sailing orders 25, **_26_**
Allen, William 135
Alredy, Queen (concubine) 45
Anamooka/Annamooka 58, 71-73, 75-76, 85-86, 88-90, 99, 129, 131, 146-147, 150-151; as rendezvous point 72, 85, 125, 146, 151; thieving by natives 72
Ascencion 128, 130, 142

Balthazar, King 122
Banks, Sir Joseph 58; and *Bounty*'s mission 182*n*37
Bantan 127
Barrow, Sir John 4, 7
Batavia 3, 5-6, 13-14, 18, 25, 29, 48, 105, 124-127, 130-136, 138-141, 155-157; Hamilton's account of 121-122; Morrison's description of 140-141
Belcher, Diana **_106_**
HMS *Bellerophon* 172
Betham (Richard) 49
HMS *Blenheim* 173
Bligh, Lt. William 1-5, 7, 11, 13, 15-17, 25-27, 42-44, 48-49, 53, 58, 67, 72, 74-76, 79, 86, 91, 108-109, 114, 117, **_134_**, 153, 157, 165, 167, 172-173; open-boat voyage of 4, 27; second breadfruit voyage of 1, **_153_**
Bligh, William Russell 11, 157
Bolabola 40, 64, 78-79
Bolt, Robert 3
Bonner, Eric M. 144
Bougainville, Monsieur 72, 75, 85, 87, 93, 98, 167
Bowling, Mr. (Edward) 104, 111
breadfruit 21-22, 27, 42-43, 59-60, 65, 88, 151, 153; as cheap food source 1, 59; used for ship's caulking 22; used for ship's timber 19, 21
Brown, John 40-41, 46
Brown, William 44, 46
Bryant, Charlotte 135
Bryant, Emanuel 135
Bryant, Mary (Broad) 135

Bryant, Mary (child of William and Mary Bryant) 135
Bryant, William (child of William and Mary Bryant) 135
Burkitt, Thomas 18, 21, 42, 51, 53, 103, 118, 135, 138; execution of 172
Butcher, John 135
Byrn, Michael 18, 21, 23, 44, 50, 53, 103, 118, 138, **_138_**; acquittal of 172; illness in Pandora's Box 55

Cape Hood 27, 30, 37, 128, 144, 159
Cape Horn 30, 37, 128, 159; Edwards' sailing orders 27; Renouard's account of 144
Cape of Good Hope 7, 28, 130, 132, **_134_**, 137, 142, 156; Hamilton's account of 127
Cape Rodney 77, 93, 130, 137, 167
Cape St. Juan 37
Carteret, Captain 76, 91
Carysfort Island 30, 39, 128, 137
Cathcart, Lord 127
cava (kava) 62, 182*n*38
Chatham's Island 129, 137; Edwards' account of 84-85; Hamilton's account of 71
Cherebay 155
Cherry's Island 77, 129, 137
chiefs 18, 27, 40, 42, 45-47, 56-58, 60, 62, 65-66, 74-75, 78, 84-86, 88-90, 116, 161; *see also* names of chiefs
children of mutineers on Tahiti 5, 47, 53, **_59_**
Christian, Fletcher 7-8, 15-17, 27, 40, 43-44, 64-65, 67, 70, 79, 131, 159-160, 172; attempt to colonize Tubuai 13; and *Bounty* mutiny 1, 3; leaves Tahiti 3, 13; settles on Pitcairn Island 3-4, 7
Christian's Island 114
Churchill, Charles 18-19, 21, 40, 44, 57
cloth 53, 58, 140, 152; manufacture of in South Seas 61; as present 24, 55
Coleman, Joseph 40, 44-45, 53, 55, 58, 102, 104, 118, 135, 138-140, 142; acquittal of 172; building *Resolution* 21-23
convicts and deserters from Port Jackson 131-132, 134-135, 139

187

Index

Cook, Capt. James 40, 43-46, 56-58, 63-64, 66, 72, 77, 79, 82, 84, 87, 94, 109, 112, 151, 167
Corner, Lt. Robert/Cornor 25, 40-42, 45-46, 52, 68-70, 78, 80-83, 86, 89, 95, 102, 105, 111, 113, 118, 130, 132, 136, 141, 161, 167-168; and capture of *Bounty* mutineers 42, 145; propagates plants 37, 58, 73; shoots natives at Annamooka 74
Cornwallis's Land 114
Coupang (Kupang) 25, 27, 80, 107, 109-110, 120-122, 130-131, 138, 155, 164, 170; Hamilton's account of 116-118
courts-martial 1, 4-5, 7-8, 10, 13, 16, 156, 165-166; of Bligh 172; of Burkitt 172; of Byrn 172; of Cole 172; of Edwards 171; of Ellison 172; of Heywood 172; of McIntosh 172; of Millward 172; of Morrison 172; of Muspratt 172; of Norman 172
Cox, James 40, 131, 135
Cunningham, Joseph 111, 135-136

Dadleberg, Captain 122
Dalrymple, Admiral 31
Danielsson, Bengt 6
Divine Services 18, 182*n*45
Dodds, Quartermaster James 66
Driver, Alfred Purshouse 11, 156
Ducie's Island 8, 30, 39, 128, 137
Duff 35; *see also* Heywood, Peter, creates Tahitian/English vocabulary; Morrison James, *Journal*
Duke of Clarence's Island 70, 84, 92, 129, 137
Duke of York's Island 70, 79-80, 82-84, 92, 129
Du Rietz, Rolf E. 144
Dutch East India Company 131-132, 134-136

Edea, Queen 45, 63, 65
Edwards, Edward 1, 3-9, 25, *26*, 28-30, *32*, 35, 40, 46-48, 52, 58, 64-65, 71, 74, 78, *80*, *94*, 96, 102-105, 107-108, *109*, 110, 118-120, 122, 125, 130, *133-134*, 135-138, 140-145, 156-157, *158*, 159-161, 163-165, *166*; acquittal 171; arrives at Coupang 110; dispatch to Admiralty and letters 143, 165-170; loses sight of *Pandora* 50, 143, *148*; navigational skills 5; "Personal Papers" 4, 9, 165, *166*, 181*n*24; statement as to loss of *Pandora* 165-170; treatment of *Bounty* prisoners 5-7, 120
Ellison, Thomas 6, 18, 21, 23, 42, 44, 51-52, 55, 118, 120, 135, 138; execution of 172
Endeavour/Endeavor Straits 5, 8, 28, 30, 64, 77, 94, 108, 110, 112-113, 125, 131, 143, 153, 157, 160, 165, 167, 170; *see also* Torres Strait
Etood 151
The Eventful History of the Mutiny and Piratical Seizure of H.M.S. Bounty: Its Cause and Consequences (Barrow) 4

Fallafagee Islands 72, 85, 89
Fattahfahé, Chief 86, 88-89

Fenow, King 71, 84
Fiji (Feegee) 3, 59, 72, 143-144, *147*, 148; *see also* Ono-I-Lau
Friendly Islands 27-28, 58, 72, 75, 84-88, 91-92, 105, 146, 151, 153-154

Gesner, Peter 3
Good, James 134
Gordon, Col. Robert 127
HMS *Gorgon* 7, 132, 134-136, 142, 156
Grenville's Island 76, 91, 129, 137

Hæva 56, 62
Hahpy Islands/Happy 85-86
Hall, James Norman 1
Hamilton, George 3, 9-10, 25, 30, *31-32*, *100*, 110, *127*, 130, 136, 143, 157, 165, 171; naval career 171; observations on sailors' diet 34-36, 38
Hammond's Island 114
Hawkesworth, John 82, 167
Hawkesburys Island 109, 114
Hayward, Lt. Thomas 16, 18, 37, 40-42, 44-48, 50-53, 58, 67-68, 70, 72-74, 79-80, 82-83, 85, 110, 130, 132, 136, 141; and capture of *Bounty* mutineers 145; and Peter Heywood 40, 44, 53, 118
Heywood, Mrs. Elizabeth 14, 48, 105, 138
Heywood, Nessy 4, 10, *14*, 48, 106, 172
Heywood, Peter *2*, 3-4, 9-10, 13-14, 25, 48, *49*, 104-106, 135, 138, 165, 172-173; behavior during *Bounty* mutiny *2*, 14-17; considered mutineer by Bligh 13, 172; creates Tahitian/English vocabulary 172; receives Royal Pardon 172; and Thomas Hayward 40, 44, 53, 118
Hillbrant, Henry 6, 18, 20-21, 42, 44, 51, 79, 82, 138; building *Resolution* 21-23; drowning of 6, 103-104
Hodges, Joseph 8, 103
Honroost (Dutch Arsenal) 127
Hoornwey (Dutch East India ship) 132, 135-136
Hornweg (Dutch East India ship) 136
Horssen (Dutch East India ship) 132, 136
Howe, Lord 31
Howe's Islands 75, 78-79, 88, 129, 137

Island of Flores 124, 155

The Journal of James Morrison, Boatswain's Mate of the Bounty 5, 8, 10, 13, 18, 50, *54*, *59*, 102, 118, 139, 172-172

Kadavu 144
Kangajunk 124
King, Sir Richard 31
kings 41, 45, 47, 55-57, 60-62, 65-67, 71-74, 78, 122-123, 159, 172; *see also* names of kings

Lafory's Island/Laforey's 109, 113, 170
Larkan, Lt. John 6-7, 55, 110, 118, 130-132, 136, 139, 141, 161

Index

The Lawbreakers 3
Lean, David 3
Le Font, Monsieur 35
Lilley, Nathaniel 135
Little Anamooka 72, 85
London Missionary Society 172-173
The Long Arm 3
Look-out Shoals 78, 94, 137, 167
Lord Hoods Island 30, 39, 128, 137
HMS *Lowestoft* 171

Mackaness, George 165
The Mariner's Mirror 9, 144, **147-148**
Martin, Isaac 44
Martin, James 135
Matavy (Resolution) 9-10, 13, **80**, **127**, 143-145, **147-148**, 171; blessing of, by Tahitian priests 23; commissioned by Edwards 145; construction of 18-24; disappearance of 85; found at Samarang 124; launching of 24; logbook 11; *Matavy* voyage as described by Hamilton 30-39; *Matavy* voyage as described by Renouard 145-156; naming of 24; as *Pandora's* tender 3, 64
Matavy Bay/other spellings 3, 13, 18, 27, 30, 39-40, 44, 47, 50-51, **54**, 129
Matte, Chief 18-19
Matuara, King 57, 66
Matuku 144
Maude, H.E. 10, 144, **147-148**
McIntosh, Thomas 18-22, 51, 53, 55, 102, 118, 120, 135, 138-140, 142; acquittal 172; building *Resolution* 21-23
McKoy, William 44
Memorandum and Particulars Respecting the Bounty and Her Crew 10
Men Against the Sea (novel) 1
Mills, John/Jno. 44
Millward, John 18, 42, 44, 51, 53, 118, 135, 138; building *Resolution* 22-23; execution of 172
Mitre Island 77, 92, 129, 137
Morrison, James 3, 5-10, 13, 18, 25, 42, 44, 50, **54**, **59**, 100, 118, 135, 138-139, 165, 172-173; building *Resolution* 21-23; drowns on *Blenheim* 173; and *Journal* 8, 10, 13, 18-24, 50-55, **59**, 102-105, 118-120, 139-142, 172-173; receives Royal Pardon 172
Morton, William 135
Moulter, William 8, 103
Mountainous Island 108-109, 112, 114, 167, 170
Murderer's Cove 72, 74; *see also* Tofoa/Toofoa
Murray's Islands/Isles 78, 95, 130, 167
Muspratt, William 42, 44, 51, 53, 103-104, 118, 135, 138; receives Royal Pardon 172
Mutiny on the Bounty (films) 1
Mutiny on the Bounty (novel) 1
Mynheer Company 123
Mynheer Fry, Lieutenant-Governor 118
Mynheer Vanion, Governor 118, 122, 124

HMS *Narcissus* 5
Navigator's Isles 72, 75, 84-87, 92, 145
New Guinea 28, 77, 94, 125, **153**, 154, 167
New Hebrides 153
New South Wales 10-11, 108, 110-111, 114, 122, 157, 167, 170; established as penal colony 182n47; *see also* Port Jackson
New Years Harbor 28, 30, 37
Nordhoff, Charles 1
Norman, Charles 18-19, 42, 44, 51-52, 55, 102, 118, 135, 138-140, 142; acquittal of 172; building *Resolution* 20-22

Oattooah 85-86, 131
Oedidy/Oediddee, Chief 45-46, 57, 64, 66-67, 78-79
Oliver, Mr. (Thomas) 66, 74, 125, 146, 152, 155-156, 164
Omai 66, 79
Ono-I-Lau 144, **147-148**
Oripai, Chief 42, 47, 55, 65
Orpheus 171
Otaheite 27-28, 30, 37, 40, 42-45, 55, 57, 60-61, 64, 66-67, 70-74, 79, 129, 131, 135, 138, 144-145, 168; *see also* Tahiti
The Otoo 40-43, 45, 47, 57, 65-66
Otootooeba 145, 151
Ottoo, Peggy 57
Otutuelah 71, 75, 129
Overstraaten, Governor 125, 131

Palmerston's Islands 28, 68-69, 80, 129, 135, 160
Pandora's Box 3, 5-6, 8, 25, **49**, 53, **54**, **59**, **97**, 103, 157
Papara 21, 40-42, 45, 52
Parker's Islands (Island Isles) 114
Pasley, Thomas Commodore 4, 49, 172
Passmore, George 64, 111, 130, 136, 161, 163; rescues ship's cat **100**, 101
Pitcairn Island **2**, 3-4, 7-8, **100**, **106**
Pitcairn's Island (novel) 1
Pitt's Island 77, 93, 129, 137
Plum Island/Plumb 109, 112
Poeno, Chief 18-20, 23-24, 51
Point Venus 23, 42, 44-45, 56
Port Jackson 10, 131-132, 134-135, 139, 142, 152; escapees from 131-132, 134-135, 139
Prince of Wales's Islands 109, 112, 114, 170
Proby's Island 76, 90, 129, 137

Queens 41, 45, 55, 60-61, 63, 65; *see also* names of queens
Quintall, Matthew 44

Rembang (Dutch East India ship) 6, 13, 122, 124, 131, 139, 155-156, 164
Renouard, Midshipman David Thomas 3, 9-11, 66, **143**, 144, **147**, 156, 171; fever and convalescence 54; *Matavy* journal **143**, 144-156

Index

Resolution 3, 13, 24; *see also Matavy*
Rickards, Mr. (Thomas) 52, 68, 110
Rio de Janiero 10, 25, 28-29, 35, 65, 128, 144
Rodriguez Island 173
Rutter, Owen 8

St. Helena Island 128, 130, 142
Samarang/Samorong 124, 127, 131, 138, 140
Sandwich's Sound 109, 113-114, 170
Santa Cruz 25, *32*, 33, 76, 91, 128
Scott, James 135
HMS *Shark* 29, 22
Simms, John 135
Sival, Midshipman John (Sevill) 52, 68, 135
Skinner, Richard 6, 40, 44-45, 53, 103-104, 135, 138; drowning of 104
Smith, Alexander 44
Smyth, William Henry 4-6, 144, 165; *see also* Du Rietz, Rolf E.
Society Islands 27, 67, 80
Spithead 27-28, 33, 142, 159
Staten Island 28, 30, 37, 128
Stewart, George 6, 40, 44, 47, 135, 138
Stony-reef Island 78, 167
Straits of Alice 124
Straits of Balli 155
Straits of Magellan 37, 128
Straits of Sunda 28, 127, 130, 135, 141
Sumatra 127
Sumner, John 6, 18, 21, 42, 44, 51, 53, 104, 135, 138; drowning of 6, 104

Tahiti 1, 3, 7-8, 10, 13, 18, 25, *54*, *59*, *65*, 172-173; Tahitian wives and friends of *Bounty* mutineers 5, 47, 53, 55 *59*
Tamatrah 45
Tatafee 73-75
Tatahu 67
Teneriff 27, 29, *32*, 33, 128
Thompson, Matthew 18, 40, 44, 57
Thomson, Basil 9
Timor 1, 6, 13, 27, *80*, 97, *109*, 110, 117-120, 124, 134-135, 138, 140, 154, 163, 169-170
Tobin, George *153*
Tofoa/other spellings 27, 74, 86, 89 90, 125, 150-152

Tommare 50-52
Tongataboo 75-76, 84, 86-88, 129, 151; *see also* Fattahfahé, Chief
Toobouai/other spellings 13, 17, 42-44, 81
Torres Strait 3, 7, 96; *see also* Endeavour/Endeavor Straits
Troubridge, Rear-Adm. Thomas 173
Tutuila 3, 143
Tumaluah 75; *see also* Navigator's Isles

Ulietia 28, 64, 66, 78, 129
Ulk 124
United Service Journal 4, 9; *see also* Smyth, William Henry

venereal disease 62, 66, 182n39
"Verses on the Loss of his Majesty's Ships, Bounty and Pandora" 157-164
Vlydt (Dutch East India ship) 1
Vreedenberg (Dutch East India ship) 131-132, 136, 141
Voyage of H.M.S. "Pandora" Despatched to Arrest the Mutineers of the "Bounty" in the South Seas, 1790–91 9-10, *65*; *see also* Thomson, Basil
Voyage Round the World in His Majesty's Frigate Pandora 10, 25, 30, *31*, 44, 55, 64, 98, 110, 121, 143; *see also* Hamilton, George

Wahlroos, Sven 5
Wallis's Island 76, 91, 129
Wanjon, Gov. Timotheus *109*, 130-131, 134-135
Wasdel, William 135
Wells's Shoals 77, 93, 130, 137
West Indies 1, 27, 33, 38, 73
Whytootackee 7, 28, 43-44, 66-67, 79, 129
Williams, John 44
Wolf's Bay 113
Wreck Island 118, 130

York Island 57, 66
Young, Edward 44

Zwan/Swan (Dutch East India ship) 132, 136

www.ingramcontent.com/pod-product-compliance
Lightning Source LLC
Chambersburg PA
CBHW032046300426
44117CB00009B/1203